How to
INCORPORATE
and Start a Business
in FLORIDA

ALSO AVAILABLE FROM THIS SERIES BY J.W. DICKS, ESQ.:

How to Incorporate and Start a Business in Alabama
How to Incorporate and Start a Business in Arizona
How to Incorporate and Start a Business in California
How to Incorporate and Start a Business in Colorado
How to Incorporate and Start a Business in Connecticut
How to Incorporate and Start a Business in Florida
How to Incorporate and Start a Business in Georgia
How to Incorporate and Start a Business in Illinois
How to Incorporate and Start a Business in Indiana
How to Incorporate and Start a Business in Kentucky
How to Incorporate and Start a Business in Maryland
How to Incorporate and Start a Business in Massachusetts
How to Incorporate and Start a Business in Michigan
How to Incorporate and Start a Business in Minnesota
How to Incorporate and Start a Business in Mississippi
How to Incorporate and Start a Business in Missouri
How to Incorporate and Start a Business in Nevada
How to Incorporate and Start a Business in New Jersey
How to Incorporate and Start a Business in New York
How to Incorporate and Start a Business in North Carolina
How to Incorporate and Start a Business in Ohio
How to Incorporate and Start a Business in Oregon
How to Incorporate and Start a Business in Pennsylvania
How to Incorporate and Start a Business in South Carolina
How to Incorporate and Start a Business in Tennessee
How to Incorporate and Start a Business in Texas
How to Incorporate and Start a Business in Virginia
How to Incorporate and Start a Business in Washington State
How to Incorporate and Start a Business in Wisconsin

The Small Business Legal Kit
The Small Business Legal Kit & Disk

How to INCORPORATE and Start a Business in FLORIDA

J.W. Dicks, Esq.

Adams Media Corporation
Holbrook, Massachusetts

To J.R. Dicks, David Edmunds, and Charles C. Smith, Sr.,
three fathers who showed their sons the good and bad of entrepreneurship.

Copyright ©1997, Adams Media Corporation. All rights reserved.
This book, or parts thereof, may not be reproduced in any form
without permission from the publisher; exceptions are made for
brief excerpts used in published reviews.

Small portions of this book have been reproduced from government documents.

Published by Adams Media Corporation
260 Center Street, Holbrook, MA 02343

ISBN: 1-55850-587-3

Printed in the United States of America.

J I H G F E D C B

Library of Congress Cataloging-in-Publication Data
Dicks, J.W. (Jack William)
How to incorporate and start a business in Florida / by J.W. Dicks.
   p.   cm.
ISBN 1-55850-587-3
1. Corporation law—Florida—Popular works.
2. Incorporation—Florida—Popular works. I. Title.
KFF213.Z9D53   1997
346.759'06622—dc21   97-11177
                             CIP

This publication is designed to provide accurate and authoritative information with regard to the subject matter covered. It is sold with the understanding that the publisher is not engaged in rendering legal, accounting, or other professional advice. If legal advice or other expert assistance is required, the services of a competent professional person should be sought.
      — From a *Declaration of Principles* jointly adopted by a Committee of the
American Bar Association and a Committee of Publishers and Associations

This book is available at quantity discounts for bulk purchases.
For information, call 1-800-872-5627.

Visit our exciting small business website: www.businesstown.com

Contents

Acknowledgments		ix
Introduction	Incorporating—Are You Ready for This?	xi
Chapter 1	**Selecting the Best Operating Entity**	1
	Sole Proprietorships	1
	Partnerships	3
	The Corporation	8
	The Sub Chapter S Corporation	12
	Limited Liability Companies	13
	Limited Liability Partnerships	15
Chapter 2	**Five Steps to Incorporating Your Business**	17
	Step 1: Choosing the Name	17
	Step 2: Preparing Your Articles of Incorporation	19
	Step 3: Write Your Bylaws	28
	Step 4: Holding the Organizational Meeting	32
	Step 5: Issuance of the Stock	33
Chapter 3	**Raising Capital for Your Business**	35
	Selling Stock in Your Company	36
	Selling Notes, Bonds, and Convertibles	37
	Forming Corporate Partnerships	37
	Finding Venture Capital	38

	Creative Financing... 40
	Securities Laws 41
	How to Borrow Money for Your Corporation 47
	Venture Capitalists... 55
	The Importance of Formal Financial Planning.............. 62
	Checklist of Financing Sources for Your Business 64

Chapter 4 **Dealing with the Law and Lawyers........................ 65**
How to Find a Good Lawyer................................... 65
How to Pay a Lawyer 68
How to Handle a Legal Dispute 69
Alternatives to Lawsuits.. 69
Going to Court 72

Chapter 5 **How to Prepare Your Own Business Contracts and Leases.... 75**
The Basics of a Contract 75
How to Develop a Contract Strategy........................ 76
Negotiating Your Lease 77
Cautions and Caveats 80

Chapter 6 **How to Hire Your Best Employees 85**
Planning for Employees.. 85
Hiring and Employee 88
Working with New Employees 94

Chapter 7 **Mastering Employment Laws 97**
The Fair Labor Standards Act 97
Child Labor Laws 99
Discrimination.. 100
Age Discrimination and Employment Act 101
Americans with Disabilities Act 102
The Occupational Safety and Health Act................... 103

	Workers' Compensation Law 104	
	The Employee Polygraph Protection Act of 1988 105	
	The Electronic Communications Privacy Act of 1986 105	
	The Family and Medical Leave Act 106	
Chapter 8	**Buying an Existing Business** 107	
	Where Do You Find Good Businesses for Sale? 108	
	Pricing the Business 109	
	Drafting the Purchase Agreement 123	
	Financing the Purchase 124	
	Making and Evaluating Offers. 126	
	Closing the Transaction 127	
Chapter 9	**Providing Credit for Your Customers** 131	
	Credit Law 132	
Chapter 10	**Protecting Your Business with Insurance**. 141	
	Where Do You Find a Good Agent? 141	
	What Type of Coverage Should You Get? 142	
	How Much Coverage Should You Get?. 142	
	Types of Policies. 143	
	Business Insurance Checklist 147	
Chapter 11	**Copyrights, Trademarks, Patents, and Licenses**. 149	
	Copyrights. 150	
	Trademarks 151	
	Patents. 154	
	Licenses. 155	
Chapter 12	**Your Business and Taxes** 163	
	Estimated Tax Returns. 163	
	Dividend Reporting Forms 164	
	Employment Taxes 164	

	Taxpayer Identification Number	166
	Recordkeeping Requirements	166
	Accounting Periods and Methods	168
	Travel, Entertainment, and Gift Expenses	170
	Local Transportation Expenses	178
	Car Expenses	180
	Recordkeeping	183
	Summary	186
Chapter 13	Maximizing Corporate and Executive Benefits	195
	Salary	196
	Free Insurance	197
	Loans	198
	Paid Vacations	198
	Day Care	199
	Educational Benefits	199
	Deferred Compensation	200
	Travel and Entertainment	200
	Automobiles	200
	Business Publications and Subscriptions	201
	Stock Options	201
	Retirement Plans	202
	Selling Your Company's Stock	202
	Sample Forms	205
Chapter 14	The Entrepreneur's Black Book of Resources	211
Chapter 15	Florida State Compliance	223
Index		279

Acknowledgments

Every book is created by more than just the author. To those many people who have shared ideas and passed them on to me, my thanks.

To Charles Smith who works with me to test and develop many of the ideas described in this book.

To Debi McDade for always working two or more jobs.

To Shielah Constable for mastering the art of manuscript editing.

To the Small Business Administration for providing some free booklets and information available to everyone. I have obtained excellent information from them for this book, particularly in the chapters on buying a business and raising capital. I encourage everyone to utilize their materials and seminars.

To Pam Liflander of Adams Media Corporation who offered me the challenge of writing a book covering the laws of 50 states.

To Bob Adams who continues to offer me new opportunities with his growing publishing firm.

To the Internal Revenue Service. I never thought I would thank them for anything, but their books and pamphlets comprise much of the tax section.

And finally to the entrepreneurs who read and use this book. You are the men and women in the arena, building the economy, providing jobs and helping the country to grow.

INTRODUCTION

INCORPORATING— ARE YOU READY FOR THIS?

If you are reading this book, you have already made the decision to go into business. Consequently, I will not bore you with the many advantages and disadvantages of starting your own business. Suffice it to say that there will be trade-offs. As I frequently tell my children, you can do anything you want to in life, you just can't do everything. This truism certainly applies to your business career. Considering the time, money, and effort that it takes to start and operate a new business, there will be trade-offs in other areas of your life. Sooner or later, you will have to face the inevitable question of whether having your own business is worth these trade-offs.

Having posed the most difficult question that a new business owner must face, I will now tell you that I, too, have faced this question and have answered it positively. There are trade-offs in starting a business from scratch, but it is an exhilarating and entertaining, if not sometimes frustrating, ride.

The purpose of this book is twofold. The first is to help you focus on the decision of whether to incorporate and the best way to accomplish it. In the beginning, I think it is important for me to disclose to you that I am definitely biased in my conviction that in business today it is almost a necessity that you be incorporated. Although the reasons for my bias should become evident as we progress, it is mainly based on the belief that our society has become overly litigious. Those who enter into business must face the fact that sooner or later someone will sue them or their business for something. If you do not have a corporate structure, you will expose yourself and possibly your entire family's assets to the plaintiff in the suit. The corporation is the single most important tool to protect you personally from liability.

The second objective of this book is to convey to you the legalities of creating an actual business operation. Operating a business is a highly regulated proposition. You have to understand a little about business law to learn to spot potential problems. You may not actually handle the problem yourself, but by understanding some of the legal implications, you will be able to use your understanding of your own business operation to give your attorney better leverage in dealing with the legal problem. More often than not, I have discovered that legal problems usually are solved by business decisions because most legal problems involve money and money is ultimately an economic business decision. The law usually is nothing more than a tool to bolster your business position.

In the upcoming chapters, I walk you through the entire business process. Chapter 1 discusses the various business entities available to you as an entrepreneur and looks at the advantages and disadvantages of each. I have already warned you about my bias for incorporating a small business, but it is important for you to understand the other business options available to you, as sometimes both money and time prevent you from incorporating. Making this decision should be based on facts and understanding of the potential liabilities you are setting yourself up for, not just on accident or chance.

Moreover, your corporation will likely use each of these entities as it grows. For example, joint ventures, general partnerships, and limited partnerships are frequently formed by businesses who have common goals and objectives in developing a particular product or service. A general partnership with another corporation would expose your present corporation to liability, but it may nevertheless be the rational thing to do, especially with joint ventures, which often are set up for a specific purpose or time. So it is important that you read carefully about and understand each business entity instead of simply skipping to the discussion on corporations, even though they are the main focus of this book.

Throughout, you will see that I have highlighted items designated as a Profit Strategy. These strategies are key ideas and concepts that are especially important for you to master. Each of them comes from personal experience, and I have labeled them as profit strategies for a reason: they will make you money.

Chapter 2 discusses the five steps to incorporating your business. Although these are not the only things necessary to incorporate your business, they are the five essential things that must be done by any corporation. In Step 2 I have broken down the articles of incorporation and described each essential element. This is important for you when you get to the final chapter of this book, which is the State Corporate Kit. In that chapter you will actually get the form used by your state for filing the articles of incorporation. By comparing that form to Step 2 in Chapter 2, you can easily fill out the form, understanding any nuances that most lawyers charge a great deal to their clients for. Also of particular importance in this chapter is the creation of your corporate by-laws. In Chapter 15 I have included a set of by-laws that you can actually use for your corporation, but the information in Chapter 2 will help you decide whether to change any of the by-law provisions to fit the special needs of your new corporation.

Chapter 3 is a primer on raising capital for your company. As you go, I hope you will take advantage of my personal experience in this area. My law practice specializes in securities and business and is involved in helping small businesses develop their company and raise money. As you will quickly see, financing strategies for raising capital are numerous and varied, and you will likely use all of the strategies at one time or another in your business career.

In addition to working on the legal side of raising capital, I have started a number of businesses over my career, which all needed money. Money is an essential element of every business operation. Throughout the chapter, I share with you my personal ideas and words of caution.

Chapter 4 delves into an area of business that many people would like to skip over: dealing with the law and lawyers. If you're going to go into business, you must learn to deal with both. One problem with being in business today stems from the fact that we are a very litigious society. This is not a social commentary, but a fact. The entrepreneur has two alternatives. The first is to take a passive role to conflicts that will come up in your business. The second is that you can be prepared, stand up for your rights, and fight those who will try to take away any gains that you make. Between the two, there is very little middle ground.

In Chapter 4 I will show you how not only to find a lawyer, but also to use his or her services. Many people feel that finding a lawyer is creating a new problem rather than finding a cure for the old one, but their feelings are simply based on their inability to find an attorney they can work with. There are good attorneys, and there are bad attorneys, just like there are good and bad professionals in any area of specialty. If you take the same care in selecting a lawyer that you would in selecting your brain surgeon, you will be happy with the results. If you select just any lawyer, you may make a painful mistake.

Chapter 5 teaches you how to prepare your own business contracts and leases. I do not necessarily recommend that you do your own legal work. I do, however, encourage everyone to understand the legal ramifications of what you are doing. Throughout your business career, there will be times where you will actually need to draw up your own contracts. These occasions usually arise in the heat of a deal where breaking away to find a lawyer to draft a contract might not only be difficult, but also ultimately spoil the deal. As you go through this chapter, one of the things that I hope will become apparent is that the structure side of writing a contract or lease is not as difficult to master as the business side. The business side is important because your business contracts will ultimately determine the profitability of your company: almost all of your major expenses, such as the lease on your property, equipment, and inventory, are controlled by contractual arrangements. If you add to that the fact that your employees also should have contracts, you can quickly see that contract mistakes could put your business under. I don't, and I hope you don't, expect that you will master the art of contract law in one chapter, but I do hope that it will open your eyes to its importance.

Chapters 6 and 7 discuss how to hire your best employees and employee law. I mentioned the importance of having employees under contract. There was little need for such careful arrangements between employers and employees in the past, but employment contracts are becoming increasingly important, even in small businesses. Increased legal regulations between employers and their employees and the possibility of large monetary awards for individual employees or groups of employees make understanding regulations and compliance a necessity. Such new laws as the Americans with Disabilities Act and the expansion on the civil rights laws to include new classes of people have empowered workers and created increased conflict between employers and employees. Because of this growing conflict, even small business owners have to be extremely cautious about the way in which they hire new employees and let them go. In this chapter we discuss the various laws and regulations that you as an employer should be careful about. If someone in your business is in charge of employees, make sure that he or she reads this chapter.

Chapter 8 is all about buying a business. If you are buying a business, you are probably doing it because you want to shorten the start-up time for a business or because you want to buy a franchise. Unfortunately, buying a business does not ensure that you will be short-cutting anything. There are a lot of rewards, but also a lot of problems and potential pitfalls, to buying a business. In Chapter 8, I attempt to focus on these potential problems and show you how to overcome them. A lot of success comes out of caution. If you go into a business transaction where you are blinded by a desire to purchase a business, you can rest assured that you will ultimately lose out. There are times where businesspeople reach a stage where they simply are tired of operating their business and are willing to accept a reasonable profit to pass it to someone else, but these instances are extremely rare. Most successful businesspeople recognize the time and cost of what they have created and are interested in selling only if they get that value. Truth be told, most business sellers seek more than what their business is actually worth, and it is only through careful counseling and negotiating that the buyer will be able to bring realism into the picture. This chapter contains more technical information than some of the others, but I hope that it will bring into perspective the type of knowledge and information you need before buying a business.

This is the age of the consumer. The consumer controls what happens in most businesses. If you aren't paying attention to your customer and the people who consume your product, your business will be left behind by those companies who are catering directly to the individual needs of their customers. All of these consumers are now credit oriented. You simply cannot run a business today that does not offer credit to customers. Chapter 9, Providing Credit for Your Customers, expains what you have to do to offer credit to your customers and the laws that govern extending credit. Make sure that you read this chapter before you start your business: you will discover there are a lot of things that you need to do first to be able to offer credit to your customers. You will quickly see that it isn't as easy as it looks, and a lot of people are closed out of the credit game. Financing is a necessity, and it is important for you to find out how you are going to use credit before you even open your doors.

When I do financial seminars, I frequently tell people that making money and keeping it are two different things. Similarly, in business, starting your operation and protecting what you have are two different things. I mentioned that entrepreneurs have to deal with lawyers. They also have to deal with insurance companies. Make them your friend. Not all insurance is alike. You have to make sure that what you're laying your money out for is the kind of insurance that you need and the coverage that you want. It is a complicated game with a stacked deck in favor of the insurance companies. I personally don't think the insurance game is fair, but who says business has to be fair? What you need to understand is that business has risks and for a price, those risks can be passed on to other people. However, insurance companies know their game very well and are extremely careful to minimize the risks that they accept. You have to understand how to read insurance policies or know a very good insurance agent who you feel is able not only to read the policies, but also to advise you about alternatives. Operating without insurance is a mistake, but operating without the right insurance can be equally disastrous. Chapter 10 is devoted to helping you understand and select the best insurance plan for your business.

The modern-day gold rush is on, and it doesn't have to do with precious metals. Instead, the modern era of mining has to do with copyrights, trademarks, patents, and licenses. Billion-dollar financial empires are being created today through license rights of famous designers such as

Ralph Lauren and superstar athletes such as Michael Jordan. Below the billion mark also are millions and hundreds of thousands available to lesser knowns who are able to take advantage of the laws of intellectual property. In Chapter 11, Copyrights, Trademarks, Patents, and Licenses, I give an overview of what is important in this area and how to spot an opportunity for making additional profits in your business. It is not necessarily an easy business to break into, but if you do, the rewards can be great and create an income stream for a long time.

Making money and paying taxes go together. If you go into business, you're going into it with the intention of making money, and if you make money, you will have to pay taxes. Chapter 12 focuses on the difference between what you make and what you keep. Contrary to what a lot of people think, there still are many loopholes available in tax laws. If you are the type of individual who thinks that loopholes are wrong, please let me persuade you otherwise. Loopholes are created in the law as exceptions. The exceptions have been specifically written into the law to motivate the tax payer to choose a particular method of operation over another. If you follow these preferred methods of operations, tax laws will reward you; if you don't follow them, tax laws will penalize you. These rewards and penalties can amount to a great deal of money, so the chapter tells you how to get additional information. The laws on taxes are constantly changing, and the entrepreneur needs to stay on top of them. This chapter will help you get started.

If you have gotten this far in the book, you will now be rewarded in Chapter 13 by learning some of the perks available to you as a corporate owner and the strategies you should use to take advantage of them. As mentioned, the tax laws are designed to motivate you to operate in a certain fashion. The laws also give corporate benefits for you and your employees. However, to maximize these benefits, you must structure your operation in a certain fashion. This chapter is devoted to pointing these techniques out to you.

The Entrepreneur's Black Book of Resources is one of my favorite chapters. I am firmly convinced that the contents of this chapter alone are worth more than the cost of the book. These resources have not simply been thrown into this chapter idly, but have been hand-picked as recommendations to new entrepreneurs. I would encourage you not only to go through this chapter carefully, but also to make sure that you review it on other occasions. You may not need some of the information now, but it will become more valuable to you as your business grows.

The final chapter of this book is your state's corporate kit. First you will find all the forms and information that you need from your particular state to incorporate, such as the actual articles of Incorporation for your state, an explanation of the costs for filing, and the name and address of the Division of Corporations where the articles need to be sent. Second, I have added your state's specific laws about corporations. I give you not only an overview of the state's specific laws, but also the names, addresses, and telephone numbers you need to obtain additional information. Finally, I have included complete documents to make up an entire corporate kit. With these documents and your filed articles of incorporation, you can start and operate your business. The only thing left for you to do is to act.

One final question you may have at this point is: When do I incorporate? My simple answer is *as soon as possible*. If after reading this material you conclude, as I believe you will, that a corporation is the best entity from which to operate you business, then you will want to take advantage of all of its protections as soon as possible, whether or not your business is currently profitable.

Best wishes for a successful business!

CHAPTER ONE

SELECTING THE BEST OPERATING ENTITY

Let's start your new business by selecting your operating entity. As you will quickly see, there are advantages and disadvantages to each selection, so choose carefully and not just because one is easier.

Sole Proprietorships

Sole proprietorships are formed everyday throughout this country. A person gets a business idea, and overnight they can be in business. Sole proprietorships are the simplest method of operation because they require almost nothing to start the business. If you operate out of a city or county municipality, you will likely need to get an occupational license and potentially other permits to operate. If you are a member of a profession that is licensed by the state, you will need to get a state license no matter what business entity you choose. But with those exceptions, once you hang out your sign, you are virtually in business.

Although the process of starting a sole proprietorship is easy, it doesn't mean you shouldn't lear n more about operating a small business. You will also need to check with your local city or county municipality to see if they have any special local license requirements for operating your business and make sure you also comply with trade-name registration and zoning laws.

With the simplicity of the sole proprietorship goes the disadvantage that you expose yourself to the greatest liability. As a sole proprietor, everything that goes on in the business is treated as though you were doing it personally. Consequently, if there is an accident involved in the operation of the business, your personal assets are involved. Someone unhappy with the operation of your business can sue you individually, not just your business. Not only are the money and assets of your business at risk when you operate as a sole proprietor, but so are all of the assets that you own, even if they have nothing to do with the business. In addition, depending on the nature of a lawsuit and/or the involvement that your spouse may or may not have in the business, spouses' assets may also be targeted in a lawsuit. Fortunately, most states have adopted various laws that allow you to insulate some of your assets in an action against creditors. However, to exercise that right, you may have to declare bankruptcy and subject all of the assets that are not excludable under the law to creditors' claims. This process offers some protection, but the cure may be almost as bad as the problem.

PROFIT STRATEGY:

Operating any business will open up many new deductions not available to employees. Make sure you understand these and incorporate them into your daily life for big money savings.

The advantage to operating as a sole proprietor is the simplicity. You are not bogged down with many of the detailed recordkeeping requirements, filing fees, and other administrative costs that formal entities such as corporations require. All of the earnings that come into the business are treated as though they are individual earnings, subject to your own taxable income. In addition to the income aspect of this operation, you are able to take business deductions against not only your business income, but also any income derived from other sources because all your income and losses are lumped together.

One of the advantages of operating your business as a sole proprietorship is that you benefit from a variety of tax deductions that can shelter your total income. Expenses such as meals, travel, entertainment, and automobile all become deductible if they relate to business (see Chapter 12 for a complete discussion, including limitations on deductions). In addition, it is easy to shift income to other members of your family, such as a child, by hiring them to do various work for the business. This technique shifts income to a family member that is in a potentially lower tax bracket than you and results in a tax savings.

One of the disadvantages of operating as a sole proprietor is that you are unable to take advantages of some of the tax benefits that you would be able to use in a corporation, such as full health insurance deductions, life insurance benefits, and medical expense reimbursements. These types of benefits are allowed only in a corporate structure, and neither individuals nor partnerships qualify for passing them along to their owners.

One area of good news for sole proprietors is that retirement benefits have been generally equalized between individual sole proprietors and corporate plans. Sole proprietors can open not only individual retirement accounts (IRAs), but SEP (Self-Employed Pension) plans, as well as the more complicated Keogh plans. These plans allow more generous contributions similar to those used by corporations for their employees. (See Chapter 12 for details.)

Traditionally, one of the main reasons new businesses operated as sole proprietorships and avoided a corporate structure was the cost of forming and operating the corporation. Lawyers did a good job of keeping the task of corporate formation an almost mystical secret. I hope that this book will help demystify the task of forming and operating a corporation and explain how to incorporate without a great deal of expense.

> **Sole Proprietorship Example**
>
> *Sue Barton likes to paint and make crafts. She wants to see whether she can turn a hobby into money by selling her work at local craft fairs. Because she isn't sure about her business, she decides not to go into the trouble of incorporating. She does know that having a formal business can save you money in taxes, so she opens up a separate checking account under the name of S.B. Crafts. The name is a fictitious name, so Sue will have to register the name. She also will need to get a sales tax ID number to report her sales. Other than that, Sue's in business.*

Partnerships

We discuss two major types of partnerships in this chapter. The first is the general partnership, and the second is the limited partnership. The general partnership is the least complicated of the two and the easiest to form.

General Partnerships

A general partnership is formed when two or more individuals decide that they want to work together in some type of business arrangement. If it is of a continuing relationship, it is referred to as a general partnership, and if the venture is for either a short term or a limited purpose, it generally is referred to as a joint venture.

Partnerships may be formed either orally or in writing. Unless you are looking for trouble down the road, there is no question that you should put the terms of your partnership in writing. Oral communication between individuals is difficult at best. When you throw in money as well as the fact that time will pass between when the agreement is made and the money divided, the opportunity for confusion is increased.

A lot of partnership agreements are not written because people mistakenly believe that they have to be written in some special form. In reality, there is no specific form necessary to form a partnership, although using precise language is better for everybody. Nevertheless, if partners do nothing more than sit down and write on a piece of paper what their rights and responsibilities in the partnership are, they will be better off in the long run. There simply are too many questions that need to be answered in a business partnership relationship. How much are the partners going to contribute? Who is going to work? How much time is each person required to contribute to receive pay for his or her work? How will the income be divided? If money is needed to start the partnership, will the contributing partner be paid any interest on that money? Who owns the customer list if the partnership dissolves? What are the assets of the partnership? Who is to get the assets if the partnership dissolves? What are the procedures for dissolving the partnership? Each of these questions is an example of the types of issues that need to be explored in planning a partnership agreement. As you can tell, the more partners you have, the more difficult the answers become. If the questions are difficult to deal with now while everything is agreeable, you can imagine the problems that arise once you

> **PROFIT STRATEGY:**
> General partnerships are best in low-risk businesses such as consulting.

have people at odds. The solution to this dilemma is to put a partnership agreement in writing and make it as clear and as thorough as possible. If you have difficulty expressing yourself, use specific examples to illustrate what you mean. A judge once told me that if everyone used examples in their contracts, it would make it a whole lot easier for him to see exactly what the parties meant.

As discussed, the main disadvantage of operating as a sole proprietor is personal liability. A general partnership does not free you of that liability. In fact, in many ways, it increases your liability, because you are liable not only for your actions, but also for those of your partners if they fall within the scope of the business of the partnership. However, you will very likely find that what the plaintiff in a lawsuit believes is within the scope of the partnership and what you believe is within the scope of the partnership are two different things. The result is a lawsuit that you have to defend, and if you are defending a lawsuit, you are already spending time and money to benefit the only people who win in a lawsuit—the attorneys.

In a general partnership, creditors can go not only after the assets of the partnership, but also after the personal assets of the individual partners. Individuals supplying the greater part of the money or their balance sheet in return for someone else's labor should be particularly cautious: in a general partnership that person's entire assets become at risk for anything that goes on with the partnership. Consequently, you may end up risking not only the amount that you initially put into the partnership, but ultimately your entire asset base.

Like a sole proprietorship, a general partnership does not pay taxes, but all income and losses flow directly to the general partners on a pro rata basis. Each partner then reports his share of income and losses on his own individual tax return. To the extent that there are losses, these losses may be used to offset other income. Partnerships are, however, required to file what is known as an Informal Partnership Tax Return, Form 1065, which just provides information to both the federal government and the relevant state on the income of the partnership. The taxing entities are notified that the individuals who make up the partnership will be filing the income or loss on their own individual returns.

> **General Partnership Example**
>
> *Sue Barton's crafts sold well at the local fairs, and she met several other people who also had good products. Four of them got together and decided to form a partnership to sell their crafts over the Christmas holidays. They agreed that they would put in an equal amount of money and rent store space just for the month of December. Each person could sell his or her own products, but they would share all expenses equally. They also agreed to sell other people's crafts and split any profits on those equally. To make sure everyone understood and remembered what their agreement was, they decided to draw up a general partnership agreement to outline their understanding.*

Limited Partnerships

Limited partnerships offer several advantages over a general partnership, but they also have a very large disadvantage. The limited partnership is formed when two or more individuals form a business entity. At least one partner is named a general partner, and the other named a limited partner. The limited partner has limited liability and the general partner has general liability. The limited partners' liability is limited to the amount of their contribution, plus potentially the distributions (income) that they have received during the operation of the partnership. The general partner is liable for all of the debts of the partnership.

The result of this arrangement is that the limited partnership is an entity that can be used to shelter the liability of some of the partners. Although the general partner, as previously said, will have general liability, that, too, can be limited by making the general partner a corporation.

The disadvantages of operating a limited partnership are the complexity of putting one together and the cost of organization and operation. In addition, limited partnership interests are securities. Therefore, unlike a general partnership, a limited partnership must comply with state and federal securities laws. This requirement opens up a whole new level of cost to ensure that you are complying with those laws.

Forming a limited partnership is more complicated than forming a sole proprietorship or general partnership. Consequently, a limited partnership agreement is needed to set out the various responsibilities and liabilities of the partners, be they limited or general. These types of agreements can be obtained in sample form from various sources, but an attorney should be hired to review the structure and make sure it meets the requirements of the various government bodies that will regulate the entity.

In addition to a formal agreement, the limited partnership will also need to file a special certificate of partnership with the state. The certificate is similar to the articles of incorporation filed by corporations. In addition, like a corporation, the limited partnership will need to file fees with the home state that increase the cost of formation and operation. Finally, the limited partnership is treated as a separate tax-reporting entity. You need not only to file an information tax return, but also to complete and send to each limited partner a Form K-1 that reports to the limited partner their pro rata share of the operations of the business. A limited partnership usually necessitates hiring a professional to do the tax filings on behalf of the entity as well as the K-1 reports for the individuals. This cost makes a limited partnership one of the most expensive entities to operate.

The third major disadvantage is compliance with state and federal securities laws. As a limited partnership is a security under both federal and state laws, you must meet the requirements of the federal government and the state. In addition, should you operate in other states, you have to make sure that you also comply with the laws regarding the operation of a foreign entity in those states. Furthermore, if investors from another state become limited partners, then that state's securities laws also must be checked for compliance. Before these additional burdens totally eliminate limited partnerships from your mind, I would point out that there are adequate exceptions to the various securities laws that exempt smaller entities from some of the regulatory constraints I have mentioned. Every state has what are collectively referred to as limited offering exemptions. Federal law has its own exemptions, primarily known as Regulation D of the 1933 Act. However, you must have an attorney review these rules before you enter into a limited partnership arrangement because the penalties for being out of compliance should be avoided.

> **PROFIT STRATEGY:**
> Use a limited partnership to protect personal liability for limited partners, but maintain personal deductions and avoid double taxation.

> **Limited Partnership Example**
>
> *The building that Sue Barton and her copartners rent is owned by a limited partnership. The general partner of the limited partnership is Main Street Properties, Inc., a local real estate company. The limited partners are two individual investors that wanted to own real estate but did not want any personal liability if things went wrong. Main Street Properties, Inc., is a professional real estate company that put together investments. As the general partner of the limited partnership, the company, a corporation, is generally liable for any problems with the property. This is an acceptable risk for its owners. Because the company is a corporation, as shareholders, they are protected from personal liability.*

The Corporation

This section highlights the advantages of choosing a corporate entity to operate your business. When you form a corporation, you are, in fact, creating a new entity. The entity has a life of its own. It has its own name, mission of operation, and even social security number, which in the case of a corporation is referred to as its tax ID. Because you have formed a new entity and that entity is operating your business, it is that entity that is responsible for everything that goes on in your business, either good or bad. From this viewpoint, it is easy to see why a corporation insulates you as the founder from liability because the entity has a life of its own.

A corporation can be formed with one or more shareholders. Specific laws for your state regarding the number of shareholders, directors, and officers will be covered in the state section of this book. When a corporation is first formed, it is created by one or more incorporators. The incorporator may be a shareholder or simply someone who does the corporate formation, such as an attorney, and who later assigns his incorporator interest to the shareholders. The incorporator creates and files the registration statement of the corporation, which is referred to as the articles of incorporation. These articles of incorporation state the major points about the corporation, such as its name, where it is located, how many shares are in existence, and the purpose of its operation. For a sample of the articles of incorporation for your particular state, refer to Chapter 15. The articles of incorporation are the central foundation on which a corporation is formed. These articles must be filed in your state capitol with the corporate office that runs corporations.

Once the corporation is formed, the incorporators turn the corporation over to its shareholders and directors, who will own and run the company. They must remember to treat the organization as a separate entity. That means that the corporation must have regular operational meetings, timely filings with the state, and a corporate tax return filed instead of an individual return. Failure to treat the corporation as a separate entity may result in a creditor having an opportunity to "pierce the corporate veil" and reach the individual shareholder for any liability. This potential problem is frequently explained to new incorporators, but failure to follow rudimentary guidelines for operation is still a mistake frequently made by new corporations. If you are going to go to the trouble to form a corporation, make sure you take the time to do the little things that keep the corporation acting as a separate entity so that you will not be responsible for any problems that arise in the business.

PROFIT STRATEGY:

Family limited partnerships are good estate-planning and asset-protection devices. The general partner can have control over assets but no ownership. The actual ownership will be vested primarily with the limited partners. As with other limited partnerships, the limited partner will have protected liability, but the general partner will be at risk.

If the shareholders, officers, and directors of the corporation continue to operate the company on a regular basis in a manner that treats the corporation as a separate entity for both liability and tax purposes, then you can be comfortable that you are free from personal liability for acts of the business. The exception to this would be if you act outside the scope of your duty in the corporation and do something on your own that you are not authorized by the corporation to do. To ensure that this doesn't occur, the corporation should have regular meetings of its officers and directors who give guidance to the corporation. It is very important to keep records of these meetings and the authority given to various individuals in their capacity as officers and directors.

Because the corporation is an individual entity for liability purposes, it is also treated as an individual entity from a tax standpoint. Corporations file a separate income tax return on Form 1120-A or Form 1120 and will be taxed at different rates from individuals and based on the corporation's own taxable income (see Exhibit 12-1 on page 164 for corporate taxable income rates). In addition to its own income taxes, the corporation will be responsible for paying other taxes, including state income taxes, unemployment taxes, workers' compensation taxes, and state sales taxes. These various types of taxes are discussed in other parts of this book, especially Chapters 12 and 15.

One of the major disadvantages of operating a regular corporation is that the earnings of the company may be subject to double taxation. This occurs when the corporation has profits at the end of the year, pays taxes on those profits, and then makes distributions to the shareholders in the form of dividends. These dividends are then taxed to the shareholder once again as a dividend distribution. The result of this taxation process is that the income earned has been taxed twice, reducing the true benefit to the stockholders of the company.

For most small companies, the solution to this is to arrange that there are no profits in the corporation. This is done by paying out salaries to the shareholders assuming that they also are working as the owners of the company in a capacity that could receive a salary. If this is the case, and salaries decrease the taxable income to such a level that no taxes are due, the potential problem of double taxation is totally avoided. There is some risk in doing this as the Internal Revenue Service wants to make sure that salaries of individuals are not so structured that they really are attempts to avoid double taxation and are truly deserving salaries for the work performed by those individuals. If the IRS can show that the salaries are out of line for the duties performed, they will likely reinterpret the payments as being dividends to the officers and directors, and not salary. This problem can also arise if the income of the corporation grows substantially and the officers and directors as owners raise their salaries to such a level that they are outside the normal ranges for people doing the same type of work. In this case, the Internal Revenue Service would likely construe the salaries to

---

PROFIT STRATEGY:

To make sure that shareholders avoid personal liability, hold regular board of director meetings and shareholder meetings. Always keep minutes of each meeting in the corporate book.

be unreasonable and the amount over their determination of reasonableness would be treated as a dividend payment to the shareholders, resulting in double taxation.

Double taxation is an area of concern. You should address the issue with your CPA while discussing compensation of owners of the company and make it a point to consider as you weigh the use of other types of operating entities that do not subject you to double taxation.

However, a corporation offers a considerable amount of fringe benefits to the owners of the corporation. These can come in the form of retirement plans, medical plans, and various expenses that in other situations might be construed as an individual expense. An example of how these benefits can be used would be entertaining clients. Because the expense of entertaining is business related, the expense becomes a deductible business expense for the corporation. Entertaining the same individuals in a social setting would not allow for such a deduction. For more information about benefits available within a corporation, see Chapter 13.

> **PROFIT STRATEGY:**
> Set your business up as a corporation so that all of your medical expenses can be deductible under a corporate reimbursement plan.

In August 1993, a law was enacted that allows incentives for investing in small corporations. Investors who purchase qualified small-business stock and hold the stock for five years or more can deduct from their income up to 50% of any capital gains tax that would be due on the sale of the stock. This reduces the now-favorable capital gains tax rate of 28% to only 14% on the sale of any qualifying stock. This law would normally not be a major consideration for a single individual who formed a company, but it could be a significant incentive to outside investors who may become stockholders and help expand the business.

> **Corporation Example**
> *In our previous example, Main Street Properties, Inc., the general partner of the limited partnership is a corporation. The corporate structure was used because it allows the owners (shareholders) of the real estate company to protect themselves from personal liability while operating their business. They have the advantage of control because they own all of the shares in the company, but are personally insulated from liability if something goes wrong.*

The Sub Chapter S Corporation

The Sub Chapter S corporation is a specific type of corporation. It is created under the Internal Revenue Service code by filing Form 2553, Election by a Small Business Corporation. The result of filing this form is that a corporation is no longer treated as a special entity for tax purposes. Instead, all of the profits and losses will flow directly to the shareholders, as in a partnership. This unique structure allows you to have all of the tax advantages of a partnership *and* all of the liability protection of a corporation. For most small businesses, the Sub Chapter S is the entity of choice. Some states have variations on how they recognize Sub S Corporations, so make sure you check your state chapter.

Once you make a Sub Chapter S election either through your board of directors meeting or through unanimous vote on the part of the shareholders, your corporation should thereafter be operated just like any other corporation. From a practical matter, no one will know that your corporation is an S corporation or a regular corporation because taxation is the only difference. In order to be able to qualify for Sub Chapter S corporate treatment, a corporation must meet certain tests not required for regular corporations. An S corporation can have 75 shareholders, up from 35 required under the old rules. Shareholders can include trusts that have multiple income beneficiaries and certain charitable beneficiaries. Starting in 1998, pension plans will also become allowed for shareholders, although they will be taxed on their share of S corporation income. An S corporation is also able to own 80% or more of the stock in another company. Dividends produced could be disregarded under the passive income restriction on S corporations. If an S corporation owns 100% of a subsidiary that is itself eligible for S corporate status, then the S corporation can elect to treat the subsidiary as a division, and not as a separate taxpayer. In essence, an S corporation can now own separate businesses in separate corporations and limit each business's liability exposure to the separate businesses' own assets.

> **PROFIT STRATEGY:**
> Use your corporation to hire your children to do work and shift family dollars into a lower bracket. Have your child then fund a tax-deductible IRA with the income.

The S corporation election must be filed after unanimous consent of the shareholders on or before the 15th day of the third month of its taxable year to qualify for that year. Once the election is made, it is valid until the election is terminated or a change occurs that would have disqualified the corporation in the beginning, such as adding a seventy-sixth shareholder.

Because there are tremendous differences in tax treatment between a regular corporation and a Sub Chapter S corporation, great care must be made to ensure not only that you have filed the form required to receive the treatment from the federal government, but also that the form is returned to you and with the approval for Sub Chapter S treatment. Confusion in getting the right tax treatment established could result in unfavorable tax treatment for the shareholders of the company. In addition, switching between a regular corporation and an S corporation mid-year can cause serious tax complications, including the elimination of various losses that might be trapped in your regular corporation and never be used. A business owner is advised to consult a professional when dealing with the conversions between regular corporations and S corporations to ensure the best tax treatment for all entities involved.

There also are two major differences between benefits provided by an S corporation and a regular corporation. One is medical expense reimbursements. This valuable benefit is lost in an S corporation. The other difference is that there are greater restrictions on retirement plans. Both of these differences should be a consideration in selecting between corporate types.

> **Sub S Corporation Example**
>
> *Things were going well for Sue Barton and her partners, and they decided to open a store year round. However, when they went to sign a lease, the owner wanted everyone to sign personally and be responsible for the lease if the business went bad. To avoid personal liability, they decided to form a corporation. Because they wanted the income to be taxed equally to each of the partners, they elected Sub S status for their corporation. Now, they are personally protected from liability and the income is still not taxed at the corporate level.*

Limited Liability Companies

There are two relatively new entities now available for operating a business. The first one we will discuss is called a limited liability company (LLC). The second is the limited liability partnership (LLP).

The LLC is a creature of state law. It has been created as an answer to individuals who liked the partnership tax treatment but needed the liability protection of a corporation and were not able to qualify for Sub Chapter S classification.

The problem with LLCs at this time is that they are relatively new. Wyoming enacted the first legislation authorizing LLCs in 1977. Unfortunately, when you are the first, you generally get to be the test case. This was the situation for a Wyoming LLC when the IRS determined that the company would not qualify for partnership status because no one individual had personal liability. In a reversal of fortune, the IRS changed its mind and in 1988 decided that, as long as the LLC met other requirements for taxation as a partnership, they wouldn't disallow it simply because no one had personal liability. After that decision became clear, almost every state rushed to adopt legislation that authorized LLCs. As of this writing, only Hawaii, Massachusetts, and Vermont have not executed LLC legislation, and they are likely to do so soon.

The first question that normally arises regarding LLCs is why there is even a necessity for this type of company with the Sub Chapter S status that allows income to be passed to the individual shareholders. The reason LLCs came about is the shareholder requirements for Sub Chapter S corporations were sometimes difficult to meet. These requirements caused people to lobby their individual state legislators to create LLCs. However, most of these restrictions were changed, and LLCs may not flourish as much as was once expected.

The LLCs also became favored over limited partnerships because the limited partnerships still required at least one individual to be a general partner who maintains control of the partnership. This combination of problems for many individuals resulted in the need for a restructuring that favored individual shareholders.

Before the LLC becomes more popular, certain problems will need to be resolved. One problem is that there have not been enough court decisions that thor-

> **PROFIT STRATEGY:**
> Use an S corporation to avoid double taxation at both the corporate level and shareholder level.

oughly answer the questions of liability and taxation. Although this body of law is not necessary to operate under the LLC, it does provide some comfort in operation, and it is for this comfort that a corporate entity is formed in the first place. In addition, you should be cautioned to read carefully the requirements of the LLC because some states may actually offer less favorable treatment under certain circumstances. For example, in Florida LLCs provide individual tax treatment, but there is a special tax on income that a Sub S corporation does not have to pay. Depending on whether you feel your entity will have income or losses, the additional tax would have a direct effect on the type of entity that you would select under that circumstance.

What do all of these issues mean for you as a business owner? For now, I think that if you want your corporation to have partnership tax treatment, you should still use the Sub S corporation if you can meet the shareholder tests. If you can't, then you should consider the LLC if your corporate activity is expected to remain within the state in which you incorporated. If you anticipate that your corporation may operate outside the state, then you should consider LLC only after careful review by your corporate counsel of the rules in each state you intend to do business in.

> **Limited Liability Company Example**
>
> *Main Street Properties, Inc., was growing, too. It was developing another small shopping center a few blocks away. If Main Street Properties, Inc., owned that property under the same name as the first property, both properties would be subject to liability if something happened at one of them. To avoid this, Main Street Properties, Inc., formed a new wholly owned subsidiary company called Second Property, LLC. They formed an LLC because it allowed for ownership by a corporation and would also allow them to add additional shareholders who might be individuals. Because the company was an LLC, the profits and losses could be passed directly to the shareholders both as individuals and corporations.*

Limited Liability Partnerships

The final type of entity is the limited liability partnership (LLP). Like the LLC, the LLP also is a fairly new entity. The purpose of the LLP is to create an entity that offers both the advantages of a general partnership and the liability protection of a limited partnership. At this juncture, the problem with LLPs is that they are still too new for you to assess the results of possible litigation. Nevertheless, this entity is on the forefront of new law for small business owners and should be considered as an option for forming your business entity.

Note that, even though you avoid personal liability for the actions of your partners, you still have personal liability for your own negligence. To avoid that liability, you would need to form your own corporation that would then act as a general partner in this partnership.

> **Limited Liability Partnership Example**
>
> *Sue Barton's reputation as a successful businesswoman began to grow. Other artists began to contact her about doing craft shows together. Sue recognized the importance of having structured agreements, but had learned about avoiding personal liability. By using an LLP she could have the best of both worlds: a working partnership agreement without personal liability for the action of her partners. In addition, it was easier to establish and less expensive to establish than a limited partnership, which had to be registered with the state.*

CHAPTER TWO

FIVE STEPS TO INCORPORATING YOUR BUSINESS

Step 1: Choosing the Name

Choosing the name of your corporation can be a frustrating experience, but it also can be a lot of fun. The best way to enjoy the experience is to understand that the process you're going through is very similar to naming your first child. You want to think about all of the ramifications of the name, including the nicknames that your business may be called as it establishes itself, developing into what will hopefully be a major corporation. As far as your state corporation department is concerned, you can name your new corporation anything you want, as long as it has not been previously taken, is being used by another corporation in your state, or is trademarked by another company. If you later expand your company to other states, you may face new conflicts if you don't do a name check of all states when you first form your company, but rarely do start-up companies concern themselves with other states unless they know they will be expanding. If your new company is planning to go national and you are using a specific name that you also intend to trademark, then you should first do a national name check and then go through the process of trademarking the name once you have incorporated in your own state. (See Chapter 11 about trademarks.)

The right name for your business is important for many reasons. It will be the first thing that people see and learn about your corporation. In many ways the name will be part of the actual identity that your corporation takes on as it relates to the public. The right name also can create value to you and your other shareholders. A few years ago, my partner and our families formed a corporation to operate a family business in our local area. We literally spent months brainstorming to find exactly the right name that would appeal to all ages. Everyone had their chance at input, including our children, parents, and friends. Eventually, we selected one that everybody agreed to and for several years became the focal point of that small business. For numerous reasons, that business ultimately ceased operations, but not without years of fun associated with the name and enterprise. The interesting twist that came from the selection of the name was at the end of our business operation, we were offered a substantial sum of money for the rights to the name by a major company who had adopted that name and intended to use it for franchising nationally. As you can see, names are important, and potentially profitable in and of themselves.

The only requirement in a name for most states is that you have the word corporation, company, or abbreviations thereof, such as "Inc.," "Co.," or "Corp." as part of the name. This is the general rule, but to check any specific rules regarding your particular state, please refer to Chapter 15.

At some point, you will hear a reference being made to "fictitious names" in regard to corporate names. The term *fictitious name* is confusing. Most people believe that the creation of a name other than your own name as the corporation's name is fictitious. This may be true from a practical sense, but it is not, from a legal standpoint. Once you decide on a name and incorporate under that name, it is the legally designated name for your company. A fictitious name would be any name that your company did business under other than its incorporated name. For example, you incorporate a company under the Big Sky Adventures, Inc., to sell outdoors camping equipment. You made up that name after brainstorming with your family over a weekend of fun out in the big sky. Although the name was made up, because you incorporated under that name, it is the real name for your company. After operating that business for a couple of years, you decide to add a travel agency. Instead of forming a separate company, you decide to keep the travel agency in your Big Sky corporation, but you want to use a separate name so that people will think about travel. You decide on Wilderness Expeditions as the name to operate the travel business from. If you use the term Wilderness Expeditions as a name to promote your business, then that name is a fictitious name used for your company, Big Sky Adventures, Inc. To operate under the name Wilderness Expeditions and have business rights such as being authorized to sue under that name, you would need to file a fictitious names act recording. A fictitious names act recording is not a complicated process, but one that must be followed to have the benefits of using your fictitious name. Like most things with corporations, you simply need to remember to document what's going on to preserve the benefits. See Chapter 15 regarding specific fictitious names act filing requirements in your state.

> **PROFIT STRATEGY:**
>
> When selecting a corporate name, try to pick one that helps describe what you do. Although this isn't necessarily easy, it can help generate business when people hear your name. If there is any doubt in your mind, what does TOYS "R" US make you think of?

Step 2: Preparing Your Articles of Incorporation

The articles of incorporation are the main structure of your company, the equivalent of the birth certificate and informational filing that were done when you were born. The articles lay out the specific structure of your business and state what you intend to do and how you intend to operate.

The articles of incorporation for small businesses generally tend to be one or two pages in length and basically simple in nature. The articles of major corporations, on the other hand, tend to be numerous, lengthy, and very complicated, such as naming various classes of stock and preference rights of shareholders. If you are forming a small company with just a few shareholders, there is no reason to write overly complicated articles of incorporation. Like any other document for the corporation, they can be changed later if something develops or your corporation grows beyond the simple articles that you initially incorporated under. Generally, the requirements for changing the articles of incorporation are either a majority vote or a two-thirds vote of the existing shareholders. If you have a small group of shareholders, that type of voting is easy. If it proves difficult to do, then you probably need to change shareholders and start a new company before expanding your business, anyway. To help you understand the process of forming your articles of incorporation, I walk you through the articles that are relevant in most states.

Article 1: Name

Filling in the first blank in the articles should be rather easy. I would remind you that prior to the selection of the name, it is always a good idea to call the corporation department for your state and reserve the corporate name. There is nothing more frustrating than spending the time to select a name only to discover that between the time you selected it, checked with the Corporation Department to determine name availability, and actually filed for that name, someone else selected it and it is now being used. To safeguard your right to the name, you can reserve the name for a limited time with your state's Corporation Department.

Article 2: Principal Office

If you already know where your company will be operating, then this blank is easily completed. However, if you have not yet entered into a lease or purchased a facility, you can simply put your own residential address at this time. The state Corporation Department simply needs an official address that they can mail important documents to, which is why it is required in the articles. Make sure that you use an address that you feel will be viable for some time, because you don't want to miss any notifications from the Secretary of State regarding your corporation or any notices of either deficiencies or defaults.

Article 3: Shares

In this article, you will describe the types of shares that the company is authorized to issue and the number that it will have outstanding. The structure of corporate shares is probably the most important section of the articles. For a small business it need not be overly complicated. Yet, everyone dreams that ultimately this business will grow into the next Microsoft. In some ways, let me put your mind at rest in the beginning. If you grow to the size of a company that has an opportunity to become as big as Microsoft, you will make numerous changes in the articles of incorporation as you grow, and that means numerous changes in the structure of your shares. In addition, if you grow and develop into a larger company, you will have considerable resources to hire some of the best corporate lawyers to structure your shares in the most advantageous way.

In a small corporation, there is no great need for a large number of shares. Sometimes, the State Division of Corporations uses either the number of shares authorized or the stated per value of the shares to calculate your company's filing fee. Consequently, to save money you may want first to determine how your state calculates its fees and adjust your shares accordingly. For example, if you determine that once you reach 10,000 shares the price of forming the corporation goes up, then you would want to stay under that threshold amount.

As a general rule, initially 1,000 shares of corporate stock is a good number to have authorized in the corporation. There is no need to issue all of those shares to the shareholders, and, in fact, you would likely want to keep some in reserve in case you need to issue additional shares. For example, if two people are forming a corporation and you authorize 1,000 shares, instead of issuing 500 shares to each of the individuals, a good structure for a small business would be to issue 50 shares to each of the two shareholders for a total of 100 shares, leaving 900 shares in the corporation as treasury stock to be issued at a later date if needed. Using this structure, each of the shareholders has 50% of the issued stock in the corporation, so they are 50–50 owners in that corporation. If at a future date the existing shareholders need to add another investor to their group, they would only need to issue an additional 50 shares to that new investor, and then all three shareholders would have equal ownership in the corporation.

The next issue is how much each of the shareholders will pay for the corporate stock. Generally, you would sell the corporation's stock for a price that would bring into the corporation the amount of money that it needs to begin business, including something held back for reserves. For example, if a corporation wanted to raise $10,000 and was going to issue 100 shares to initial shareholders, then each share would be priced at $100. Each of the shareholders would pay $5,000 for his or her 50 shares, and the corporation would now have in its reserve $10,000 paid for the 100 issued shares.

The price paid by the initial shareholders has no correlation to what shares may be sold for in the future. Indeed, the shares may be sold for less, or they may be sold for more. Following our example, if the company added an additional investor who wanted to become an equal partner, they might very well charge more to that new investor simply because he came in at a later date. For example, the existing shareholders might decide that a new investor needs to put in $10,000 and in exchange receive a one-third interest in the company, even though $10,000 would have represented the exact same amount that the original investors put in for all of the company. To get one-third of the company, this new investor would be issued 50 shares in exchange for the $10,000, paying $200 for each share.

Pricing shares is an interesting science in and of itself. In most cases, people tend to price the shares at a lower amount simply because people like to get more shares for their money. There is no requirement as to what each share costs. The largest per-share price among U.S. public companies is $33,500, for the Berkshire Hathaway Company controlled by Warren Buffet, who is considered to be the most successful investor in the United States, and perhaps the world. Stocks priced under $10 per share are generally referred to as *penny stocks*. The low price tends to make not only investors, but also regulators nervous.

As there is no requirement as to what the price of the stock should be, I think it would be a prudent policy always to think about pricing your initial shares at least $10. The only other consideration is the number of shares to be issued so that investors feel like they have a large enough number. You may find that authorizing 10,000 shares is better than 1,000 because giving people more shares makes them feel as though they have more control of the company. That decision is up to you, your board of directors, and the amount of fees charged by your state.

In addition to setting the number of shares of a corporation, stock may be further divided up into classes of shares. This normally is not done for small corporations, but it can be a useful planning tool in family corporations. For example, one member of the family could have all of the class of stock that is considered voting stock, and other members of the family could be issued nonvoting stock. This arrangement would give the one individual all of the day-to-day control in the affairs of the company, while allowing other members in the family to receive income from the corporation.

Another type of share you may issue is *preferred stock*. *Preferred stock* simply gives the holder a right to preferred distributions in dividends over common stock holders. This type of stock is a good type to issue to people who are in essence passive investors with the corporation. If you had issued to these individuals debt instruments, such as promissory notes or bonds of the company, these instruments would carry current interest payment requirements. The preferred stock would require that these individual shareholders only be paid when there is money in the company to pay them. It would ensure that they get paid first, but only provided that there is money in the corporation to make the payment.

Preferred shares can be *cumulative* or *noncumulative.* If they are *cumulative*, it means that the stated amount will be paid for each year, even though it may not be paid in the present year. For example, let's say that your corporation issues a cumulative 10% preferred stock. In year 1 of operation, the company is unable to pay the 10% preference to the preferred stockholders. This means that the common stockholders also receive nothing. In year 2, the corporation now owes the preferred shareholders at least a 20% return before paying anything to common stockholders. If they were able to pay 5% to the preferred shareholders, then the 15% preference that they have not paid rolls into the third year, and now the preferred shareholders would be entitled to a 25% return of their money prior to any distributions to the common stockholders. This type of stock is attractive to passive investors because they have a preference and get paid before the organizers holding common stock get anything from the company,

> **PROFIT STRATEGY:**
> Use different classes of stocks to maintain control of the company even if you don't have a majority of shares.

giving the common stockholders an incentive to work harder to make sure that they ultimately get money themselves, after the preferred shareholders are paid.

In addition to classes of stock, the organizers of the company also must determine whether stocks shall be issued for *par* or *no-par value*. The original purpose for setting par value was to determine the amount that the corporation set as the minimum acceptable amount for its stock. This traditional setting of the price was used by states to establish a number on which to base the fees that they charge. However, most of these rules have been eliminated. Nevertheless, before making any final decision, make sure you read the state chapter of this book.

Article 4: Initial Registered Agent and Street Address

The registered agent is the individual that the state will contact in the case of any formal correspondence between the state and the corporation. Traditionally, the registered agent has been the attorney doing the corporate filings, but this is not required. For small corporations, the registered agent can simply be the individual the shareholders collectively agree should be the person to receive official correspondence and contact by any regulatory body.

Article 5: Incorporators

There must be one or more incorporators for every corporation. The incorporator may be either an individual or another corporation. The purpose of designating an incorporator is that the incorporator will actually sign the articles when they are submitted to the state for filing. The incorporator has no responsibility after filing the information with the state because the shareholders, directors, and officers take control of the company once it has been incorporated. Until the state accepts the corporation, however, the incorporators will be the people who deal with the state to handle any deficiencies in the filing of the articles.

Article 6: Purpose of the Corporation

Some states require that the corporation actually state its purpose for being in existence. Most business owners do not know when they incorporate what the ultimate potential is for their company. To prevent it from having to refile in the future, states allow a corporation to designate that its purpose is "any lawful business purpose authorized within the state." Even if you state the specific purpose of operation that you presently know about, it would be wise to add similar language in your articles that will allow for future expansion of your business. For example, if you stated that your business was to operate a travel company and later you decide to go into shoe manufacturing, you would have to change your articles of incorporation, unless you used the phrase "for any lawful business purpose" in your corporate articles.

Article 7: Duration

Many states require that a corporation designate the period that it intends to be in existence. There is no required length of time, and the organizers may select any duration. As most business owners don't know how long they will operate, the best thing to do is to designate a "perpetual existence." This allows a corporation to exist forever, as long as it continues to pay its required annual reporting fee with the state. However, even though you have selected the perpetual existence, it doesn't mean that you must go on forever. The corporation may be dissolved at any time if the board of directors elects to do so or by vote of the shareholders. In addition, corporations can be involuntarily dissolved by an action of the state, including the failure to pay the annual filing fees.

Article 8: Special Provisions

This article is not required to form a corporation, but is necessary if a corporation wants to designate special requirements in its initial articles of incorporation. Special provisions could include unusual voting requirements, specific dates for shareholders' and/or directors' meetings, different classes of stock, indemnification provisions for acts of officers or directors, and any other rule or regulation that the initial incorporators want to make potential stockholders aware of. Some of these provisions could certainly be listed in the bylaws of the company. However, the bylaws are not required to be officially filed, and shareholders could argue that they had not been given copies of the bylaws and so did not receive adequate notice. If the provisions are filed with the articles of incorporation, the fact that the articles are filed with the official records of the state is considered notice to any shareholder about the particular provision in those articles.

**Exhibit 2-1
Sample Articles of Incorporation**

ARTICLES OF INCORPORATION

The undersigned incorporators, for the purpose of forming a corporation under the state act, hereby adopt the following Articles of Incorporation.

Article 1: Name
The name of the corporation shall be: _____

Article 2: Principal Offices
The principal place of business and mailing address of this corporation shall be:
_____
_____

Article 3: Shares
The number of shares of stock that this corporation is authorized to have outstanding at any one time is: _____

Article 4: Initial Registered Agent and Street Address
The name and address of the initial registered agent are: _____
_____

Article 5: Incorporators
The name and address for the incorporators of these articles are: _____
_____
_____
_____
_____

Article 6: Purpose
The purpose of this corporation is: _____
_____
_____
_____
_____

Article 7: Duration
The period of time this corporation will be in existence is: _____
_____

Article 8: Special Provisions
The following special provisions apply to this corporation: _____
_____
_____
_____
_____
_____
_____
_____

The undersigned incorporators have executed these Articles on this ___ day of _____, ___.

_____
Incorporator

_____
Incorporator

Step 3: Write Your Bylaws

The bylaws of a corporation are the internal rules and regulations by which the corporation intends to operate. It is not necessary to file the bylaws with any regulatory body, and they are normally kept in the minute books of the corporation. Although the bylaws are not filed with a regulatory body, they are nevertheless important in that they govern the operations of the company. The bylaws can be generally altered, amended, or appealed by a majority vote of either the board of directors or the shareholders. A specific example of corporate bylaws for your state is included in Chapter 15.

Article 1: Offices

The opening article of the bylaws generally states the location of the main office and any additional offices where the company conducts business. Generally, the board of directors designates in the bylaws the specific office that is to be the registered office for shareholders or any member of the outside public to contact as the official place of business for the corporation.

Article 2: Shareholders

Shareholders of a corporation generally meet at least once a year. The bylaws designate the normal meeting time or method of determining the meeting time. In addition, special meetings may be called by the board of directors, and the bylaws will stipulate the method that the board of directors can use to determine whether additional meetings are to be held.

To ensure that the meetings are properly held, bylaws state that notice must be given to all of the shareholders for a shareholders' meeting and all of the members of the board of directors for a board meeting. Notice is required to ensure that everybody was properly notified of the meeting. If the procedures for proper notice are followed, a member who does not attend cannot overrule any decisions made at the meeting.

As meetings are held periodically and notice is required to be sent out advising the people of meetings, a method to determine who are shareholders or board members at a specific date for the purpose of any particular meeting needs to be set up. This method of determination is referred to as *fixing a record date*. Official shareholders and board of director members are fixed by that date.

The bylaws should state the minimum number of members needed to constitute a quorum for an official meeting. For example, if less than a majority (over 50% of the required number) of the members attend the meeting, the meeting may not be considered official and decisions reached at that time may be overturned.

Proxies give a person the right to vote on behalf of another person at a meeting. The bylaws will state how proxies are to be solicited and used at a meeting.

Sometimes both shareholders and directors take informal actions without meeting. The parameters for such actions should be defined in the bylaws. In addition, some states authorize meetings not to be held if all of the shareholders agree and sign a formal resolution instead of actually meeting.

Cumulative voting is an important issue normally set within the bylaws. Cumulative voting allows a shareholder to group all of his shares and vote for one candidate or issue. Without cumulative voting, a small shareholder has less rights than a larger shareholder. By allowing cumulative voting, the shareholder can bunch up his shares and have a better opportunity to elect at least one member of the board of directors for the company.

Article 3: Board of Directors

The business and affairs of a corporation are run by the board of directors, and the bylaws state the number, qualifications, and time that a board member will serve. The type and length of meetings that the board of directors is expected to hold should be described, as well as the number of people required to constitute a quorum at any particular meeting. The bylaws also should provide any provision for holding or taking action without a meeting as well as filling any vacancies should they come up between regular election periods. Frequently, the bylaws also state the compensation to be derived by board members as well as the authority of the board members to hire officers and directors and the compensation to be provided those individuals.

Article 4: Officers

Although the board of directors runs the company, it does not run the day-to-day operations. The daily tasks are run by officers who are elected by the board of directors. Generally, a company will have a president, one or more vice presidents, a secretary, and a treasurer. In the case of companies that have only one shareholder, state law will determine whether all of these offices may be held by one individual.

Officers normally are appointed for a stated period, although they may be elected for an undefined time and/or until they are removed from office. In any event, a method of removal should be included in the bylaws. Next, the bylaws describe the officers and directors that are to be selected. The specific duties of those individuals should be stated to allow for a division of responsibilities and to avoid confusion.

Article 5: Contracts

In this article, the bylaws state the methods by which the company will actually do business. Among these considerations are the formalities that need to be followed, including whether or not more than one signature is required to bind the corporation to any act. Without this kind of designation in the bylaws, a sole officer or director could be considered to have the power to act on behalf of the corporation and bind it to contracts and other expenditures.

The right and the methods for borrowing money also should be considered in this section of the bylaws. Whether checks are acceptable with only one signature or whether cosignatures should be required by one or more officers, should be defined. Similarly, the bylaws should indicate whether all the terms can be agreed to by any one officer or whether the loan must be specially approved in total by the board of directors.

Article 6: Certificates of Shares and Their Transfer

This article describes the stock certificates for the company, how they are designed, and who shall sign on behalf of the company. Frequently, both the president and secretary are named as authorized parties, and the seal of the corporation must be affixed to make the certificate valid. The seal is an official stamp created by the cor-

> **PROFIT STRATEGY:**
> The corporate bylaws set out the day-to-day plan for corporate operations. Make sure you understand them, and follow them to protect your corporate status.

poration that is pressed into the certificate to show final authorization.

The bylaws should describe the method of transferring stock between parties and the specific procedures through which stock should be sent to the company for cancellation and/or redeeming. Without a specific method, a corporation can find itself with outstanding stock held by more than one party, which would result in not only confusion as to who owns the stock but also potential liability and lawsuits.

Article 7: Fiscal Year

Corporations can adopt any calendar month as the beginning of their corporate year, but most simply adopt the calendar year beginning in January and ending on the 31st of December.

Article 8: Dividends

The bylaws authorize the board of directors to set corporate dividends and determine how they should be paid and to whom. This authority granted in the bylaws must be consistent with the specific shares authorized under the articles of incorporation that have been filed with the state.

Article 9: Corporate Seal

The board of directors should design a corporate seal, which normally is a metal press used to show the official designation of the corporation. This corporate seal will be used on all official documents and will be required by banks for any loans, as well as by various other institutions, on official documents.

Article 10: Waiver of Notice

This article describes the procedures for giving notice to individuals about either shareholder or board of directors meetings. These notices may, under certain circumstances, be waived, and the provisions for waiving them should be spelled out in the bylaws.

Article 11: Amendments

In general, bylaws are broader than the articles of incorporation and more concerned with the actual operation of the company. Therefore, they should provide for amendments on a more liberal basis. This means that, as the corporation grows, it may want to become more restrictive and have not only more formal meetings, but also more formal notice requirements. The amendment procedures should allow for frequent amendments, but also describe the number of shareholders needed to make those changes. In most cases, a majority vote is necessary to amend the bylaws.

Step 4: Holding the Organizational Meeting

The first meeting of the shareholders of the company is considered the company's organizational meeting. At that meeting, the shareholders should pass a resolution adopting the articles of incorporation that were filed by the incorporators, and they also should adopt the bylaws created by either the incorporators or one or more of the shareholders. Once the bylaws are adopted, they will immediately be put to use in the election of a board of directors that should take place at this same organizational meeting. Once the board of directors is elected, the shareholders can then vote on any additional business they may have or turn over the operation of the corporation to the board of directors who will handle the affairs of the corporation. If there is no other business, the meeting is adjourned.

The first meeting of the board of directors should be held immediately afterward, and that is considered the organizational meeting for the board. During this meeting, the board should elect the chairperson, as well as the secretary who is responsible for keeping the records of shareholders' and directors' meetings in the future.

In a small corporation that has only one board member, it may seem at times silly to hold meetings and actually keep official records. That is precisely where corporations fall into potential problems: it is the meetings that ultimately show proof that the individual is operating as a corporation and not as a sole proprietorship. Consequently, the structure of these meetings is extremely important, and formal records must be kept as minutes of the meeting and placed in the official record book of the corporation. *I cannot overemphasize that failure to do so can have disastrous results and void all of the benefits of forming the corporation in the first place.*

During the first meeting of the board of directors, officers for the corporation should be selected. In small companies, the president also may be the secretary, and in fact, all of the officers of the company. In any event, the offices should be specifically named and an individual designated beside the title, even if that individual is the same person for all offices. Again, the reason for this formality is to prove that due process was followed and that the individual has been designated by the corporation to do the specific functions as stated in the bylaws.

When selecting officers, the specific salaries that the officers are to receive should be defined. The minutes should reflect the consideration that has gone into making a determination in setting the value of the compensation for the officer. This recording of the process may become important if the officer's salary is ever challenged by the IRS as being unjust for the amount of work being done by that officer, because the IRS prefers some of the income generated by small companies to be passed down to the shareholders as dividends instead of seeing officers and directors take all of the income. This documentation can then play an important role in helping the company and shareholders avoid the potential double taxation of the income generated.

Step 5: Issuance of the Stock

The final step in our incorporation act is to make sure that the stock of the company is actually issued to the individuals who have purchased it. *Again, I cannot overemphasize the necessity for actually filling out the stock certificates in exchange for checks written directly to the corporation and for depositing those checks in a separate corporate account.* If separate checks are not written, then a creditor could argue that there was no consideration paid for the stock and that the transaction was invalid. If organizers were not valid shareholders, they would likely be considered as operating under a general partnership, and everyone would be exposed to potential liability.

The stock can be authorized to be issued at the organizational meeting of the incorporators prior to the shareholders' meeting and prior to the first board of directors' meeting. The stock certificate should be of the type that is described in the bylaws. These certificates can be purchased at most stationery stores.

The corporate stock certificates should be treated like money. Lost or stolen certificates have to be verified for accuracy, and confusion in court can arise when certificates are not properly issued and/or properly canceled. Stock certificates can be issued directly to the purchaser, or the original can be kept on file with the corporation and a copy given to the shareholder with the designation that the original is kept on file with the corporation.

The process you have just gone through in this chapter is the general process for forming a corporation. In Chapter 15 you will find information on the state laws in your particular state. In addition, I have included the specific forms required in your state for meeting the filing requirement. Between these two chapters and the forms, you should be able to form your own corporation in your state with very little difficulty.

CHAPTER THREE

RAISING CAPITAL FOR YOUR BUSINESS

Sooner or later the success of your company will depend on your ability to raise capital. It would be nice to think that you can do everything on your own, but cash flow will at some point get tight, or you will need more money for expansion. In addition, if you hope someday to grow into a large corporation, eventually you will need to raise capital. Even Dreamworks, the entertainment company started by Steven Spielberg, Jeffrey Katzenberg, and David Geffen with $1 billion of their own money sought and gained outside capital from Paul Allen (cofounder of Microsoft), Chase Capital, Seagram, the Lee Family, and Microsoft to the tune of an additional $1 billion. Chances are you won't be raising that sort of capital for a while, but you will likely be raising some money in the near future, and the process is essentially the same.

Many new companies are started by the founders and their friends and relatives. In all too many cases the funding groups are put together with little formality. Whether the lack of planning and structure is from lack of knowledge, time, money, or all three is irrelevant. If the funding is not properly structured so that everyone is aware of the risks as well as the potential rewards, the result may be conflict and even potential litigation if things don't work out as everyone had hoped.

To protect yourself adequately as the founder, you must take care when you seek outside funding to structure the transaction properly. You should also know alternative financing methods so you don't give away too much of your company.

Selling Stock in Your Company

The first option most companies consider is to sell stock to outsiders in exchange for future growth of the company. This option requires careful consideration. If everything goes right and the common stock increases in value, you may have given up too much in potential profits. On the other hand, I will certainly acknowledge that giving up something is better than losing everything. The real issue perhaps is timing. Sell stock only when you have to or only if you can keep some of the money yourself.

One alternative that should be considered is to sell *preferred shares* to your investors instead of the more traditional common stock offering. Preferred shares are more like debt, except that you don't have to make a payment to the investor until you actually have the money. For example, if a stock is an 8% preferred stock, the holder will receive the first 8% of the profits of the company paid out to the shareholders. Additional profits would go to the common stockholders. Thus, the upside of preferred stock is not as large as common, but the chance of some payment is greater. In addition, preferred stock also can be cumulative. This means that the preferred stockholder must get an amount equal to the stock's stated payout before the common shareholders get anything. If the preferred shareholders don't receive the amount in one year, then the deficit is made up the next year money is available. This type of stock is encouraging to investors, who realize that they will get the first profits produced and that the only real way for a founder holding common stocks to make money is after preferred stockholders have been paid. Founders prefer to act as common stockholders because common stock controls the company, as those who own common stock usually are the only stockholders who vote. In addition, because all the profits above the stated payment to preferred shareholders go to the common stockholders, the greatest chance for growth is with the common stock. A preferred stockholder gets only a specific percentage of benefits. If a company does well, there is no such cap on how much a common stockholder can receive.

Preferred shares may be an acceptable finance structure, but other investors may be more interested in getting a bigger upside if the company really becomes successful. The answer to these investors may be to design a *convertible preferred stock*. This stock allows the investors to have preferred income treatment, but eventually convert the preferred stock to common stock if the company takes off. The conversion could be on the same dollar cost ratio the investor paid for the preferred stock or some other alternative depending on the creativity and structuring skills of the founder.

Selling Notes, Bonds, and Convertibles

Small corporations are free to issue their own debt instruments, just like large companies. Typical debt instruments issued are corporate notes (generally short term) or bonds (generally long term). As with any other debt instruments, the corporation will pay interest on the note to the investor. The problem with debt is that it has to be paid back. You can, however, structure the payments to be flexible, and theoretically, you could even make the payment conditioned on income being generated by the company. The actual term can be as creative as the mind designing the financial structure.

> **PROFIT STRATEGY:**
> A funny thing about debt—it has to be paid back. Be cautious of a lot of debt. It can stifle your company and make your life miserable.

Like stock, debt also can be jazzed up by making the security convertible to stock. This instrument is known as a *convertible debenture* and gives investors a potentially greater upside on their money. In addition, debentures could be structured with warrants or rights that allow the debt holder to buy stock in the future for a price determined today. This feature also allows the debtor to participate in the growth of the company, which theoretically came about because the investor infused capital.

Forming Corporate Partnerships

Partnerships are another technique used to raise capital for your corporation. Instead of selling stock or issuing debt instruments in the company itself, a separate entity can be formed as a general or limited partnership. Frequently, these partnerships are structured in research and development work where a certain amount of money is raised for the partnership to do research and development for the company. Whatever the research and/or development turns up, the investors who put money into this partnership will get a percentage of the income derived from that discovery. Typically, the research and development partnership would develop a license for the work created and have the company become a licensee to put it into effect.

Partnerships also are considered for other purposes. A common example is marketing, such as when a company does not have enough funds to market a particular product. For example, a new product developed by a company has the potential to be marketed successfully as a television infomercial. However, the company does not have adequate resources to develop an entire marketing strategy. Instead, it forms a separate partnership seeking funds from outside investors. These investors provide dollars to the partnership and in return receive a percentage of the profits from the sales resulting from the new marketing efforts. In this manner, the corporation benefits by being able to market its products in ways it could not currently afford, and investors receive a percentage of the profits in exchange for risking capital.

In addition to research, development, and marketing partnerships, a corporation can form joint ventures to do other particular projects. For example, your company could form a separate partnership to go into a joint venture with your company to develop, manufacture, and sell a new product. The joint venture now pays the expenses incurred on the new project as well as some percentage allocated for overhead and expenses that the company has incurred in developing the project to date. In exchange, the joint venture participates in a variety of ways that could be structured in the profits of the joint venture.

Finding Venture Capital

Once you move past your initial contacts of friends and relatives and begin to think about raising money on a broader scale, you will be exposed to the world of venture capital funds.

There are approximately 950 venture capital firms listed in *Pratt's Guide to Venture Capital Sources*. However, finding and working with the right one is an entirely different matter. Later in this chapter, I'll tell you more about what they look for and how to approach them, but for now simply understand that you must be willing to do extensive preparation work prior to contacting the venture capitalist to have any chance of success. Some people feel they can simply pick up the telephone and contact a venture capitalist with the idea of selling them on their own enthusiasm. The practicality of this is virtually nil. Venture capitalist firms receive hundreds of proposals weekly and must sort through those that appeal to them. The only way to have any realistic chance of success is first to develop an extensive business plan for your company along with an executive summary that provides specific information that the capitalist would need to determine whether they want to look further at your company.

Small Business Investment Companies

Another option to consider are small business investment companies (SBICs). Some 1,000 are operating in the United States. The SBICs are restricted to investing in small-business concerns, that is, typically companies that have less than 500 employees. You can contact either your local office of the Small Business Administration or the main office in Washington, D.C., for a list of active SBICs in your area.

A Friendly Warning

One area of extreme caution for new companies seeking financing is to realize there are many scam artists. These promoters approach companies who are doing inquiries for venture capital, promising both to raise money on their behalf and to help them with the long-term success of their company. These promoters generally require large deposits and/or prepaid fees to help the company. These fees range from $25,000 to $50,000 and are nonrefundable. There have been numerous cases around the United States where the fees have been taken and little, if no assistance, was given in helping the company raise venture capital. Many of these promoters are nothing more than shell corporations that abscond with the upfront fees and leave the area upon receiving payment. Other promoters appear to be more legitimate, continuing to operate, but in reality providing little service to the company seeking venture capital. The bottom line is to be cautious when seeking capital and to deal only with reputable firms after you have checked them out. One source of initial investigation would be through the local chamber of commerce and attorneys who may have worked with these companies.

Make sure that you ask any promoter you meet for a list of clients whom they have helped in the past, and check them out before you pay any money.

Creative Financing

Other alternatives exist. These methods normally involve using other assets that you hold in your corporation to generate cash on a quicker basis. For example, one form of financing commonly used by smaller companies is *accounts receivable financing*. In this case, a lender will provide an agreement to loan money based on a percentage of the receivables that your company has. Generally, these receivables cannot be more than sixty to ninety days old. The loans range from 70% to 85% of what the lender will describe as eligible receivables. Eligible receivables means those that the lender considers likely to be received as opposed to others, which they write off as having little chance of collecting.

Another type of financing available for manufacturing firms is *inventory financing*. In this case, the lender advances a percentage of the dollar amount of work in process to allow you to complete finished goods. This allows you to create additional dollars by using other people's money to get the final product.

Equipment financing is another form of financing available from commercial lenders. Assets that can be financed include computers, manufacturing equipment, and other fixed assets, such as office furniture. The loans will be based on a percentage of the valuation of the useful life of the equipment and usually range from 70% to 85% of the liquidation value.

Asset lenders are another type of financing company. These groups are typically individual corporations that are in the business of loaning money in exchange for interest payments, as well as some participation in the company's profits. Generally, this money is advanced to the corporation against all of the assets of the company, including receivables, inventory, and fixed assets. This is normally very expensive money particularly considering the fact that you will be paying the top lending rates as well as a percentage of your company's equity to the lender.

Factoring is another method of borrowing money based on the receivables of your company. Although the cost of lending is high, factoring allows you to cash flow your operations when you might otherwise not be able to continue. To factor your receivables, you would approach a company that specializes in this field. The lender would review your company's receivables and make allowances for collection difficulties, payment history, or the length of time the receivable is outstanding. Based on those factors, the lender would loan your company a percentage of the dollar value of those receivables. The idea is that the quicker turnover in your cash flow will allow you to increase your volume of business and make up for the added factoring expense.

Leasing equipment and other types of assets also is a way to grow a company without expending capital. Leasing arrangements normally have monthly payments with high interest rates. Once the lease is complete, the contract may allow you to buy the property based on a percentage of the original value at the end of the lease. Typically, this will range from $1.00 to as much as 5% to 10% of the original purchase price. The final payment is very negotiable and lenders will frequently put in the higher percent hoping you will either miss it or think it is the best you can do. Don't fall for the trap, or you'll have a very expensive final payment that you could have reduced or eliminated with a little work.

Securities Laws

If a company decides to raise money from outside investors by selling stock or using floating debt instruments, then it will be subject to the securities laws of both the federal government and the state in which the security is sold. Under federal securities laws, every offer or sale of a security must be registered under the Securities Act of 1933 or qualify for an exemption provided under the act. Because public registration of an offering is very expensive and time-consuming, most money raised by small companies will be done by what is called a *private offering*. The private offering is an attempt to structure the offering to meet the exemption criteria of both the 1933 Act and the state in which the security is being sold. This is a very specialized area of the law, and a company should secure the services of a lawyer who is an expert in this area to ensure that the private offering qualifies for an exemption. Failure to structure a sale properly will subject the seller of the security to rescission of the sale, as well as potential damages. In some cases, depending on the disclosure, the company could be exposed to civil and criminal fraud charges.

Federal Securities Regulations

The following material deals with federal securities laws. For information on your state's securities laws, refer to Chapter 15.

Two statutory private offering exemptions at the federal level are provided in Section 4(2) and Section 4(6) of the Securities Act of 1933. Section 4(2) of the 1933 Act provides that the registration requirements under the Act shall not apply to "transactions by an issue not involving any public offering." This exemption is unusual in that it is not specifically designed by statute or rule, but it has been interpreted in many instances by the Securities and Exchange Commission (SEC) in both advisory opinions and court cases. To qualify under this particular section, care should be used to structure your offering under the guidelines provided in the opinions and court decisions. However, because it is difficult to qualify for this exemption, most attorneys look to the other exemption, which is more specific.

Section 4(6) of the 1933 Act provides that the registration requirement shall not apply to private offerings to "accredited investors" as they are defined in Section 2(15) and Rule 501A under the 1933 Act. Because of the confusions relating to these two statutory provisions, the SEC adopted in March 1982, and later amended in 1988, Regulation D. Regulation D consists of eight rules, 501 through 508, that most people use to qualify for exemptions under the act today. They are generally specific and can be followed with adequate disclosure. In the following section we discuss the most commonly used exemptions: 504, 505, and 506.

Rule 504

One of the difficulties with federal securities laws is that, with the exception of a public offering of up to $1 million under Rule 504, all Regulation D private offerings must be accomplished without any general solicitation or advertisement. This means that a company cannot hold a seminar or meeting to which the attendees are invited by general solicitation or advertising. The result is that you can contact your friends, relatives, or people that you know, but you can't run advertisements in the newspapers to bring in new investors. In a lot of cases, that is precisely what a new company wants to do to broaden its potential source of investors. If that is the case, then the company is limited to either doing the $1,000,000 small public offering referred to as a SCOR offering under Rule 504 or moving up the ladder to public offerings under Regulation A.

Rule 504 contains an exemption for an offering of not more than $1,000,000 worth of securities of a qualified company during any twelve-month period. To qualify for a 504, the company cannot already be subject to reporting requirements of the securities act, an investment company, a blind pool, a development stage company with no specific business plan, or a company that has indicated that its purpose is to acquire an unidentified company or companies. In general, the regulation does not require disclosure documents to be used with the offerings. However, because of the antifraud provisions of the securities act, which apply to all offerings, a company would be extremely unwise to present any offer of sale of its securities without some sort of disclosure document.

The purchasers in the 504 offering do not have to meet what is referred to as a sophistication test, and there is no limitation to the number of purchasers, unlike what is required to meet some of the other exemptions. In broad terms, sophistication means that a person has the ability and experience to understand the nature and risk of the investment they are making.

PROFIT STRATEGY: U.S. security laws are likely to change in the next few years. We went from no laws to too much regulation. Now, there is a mood toward deregulating some of the laws to try to open up access to capital and expansion. This is good news for entrepreneurs.

Rule 505

Rule 505 permits private offerings up to $5,000,000 in any twelve-month period to an unlimited number of "accredited investors" and up to thirty-five nonaccredited investors. An accredited investor is specifically defined as:

1. A person with a net worth of $1,000,000 or more
2. A person who had an adjusted individual gross income over $200,000 during the last two years or joint spousal income over $300,000 in

each of those two years and who reasonably expects to reach the same income level during the current year
3. A director, executive officer, or general partner of the issuer
4. Certain institutional investors, such as banks, insurance companies, registered investment companies, business development companies, SBICs, pension plans with total assets of more than $5,000,000, corporations, partnerships, business trusts, and charitable organizations with total assets in excess of $5,000,000
5. Any entity in which all of the owners are accredited investors

Nonaccredited investors do not have to meet any sophistication test under this rule, as they do under Rule 506.

Rule 506

Rule 506 allows private offerings of an unlimited dollar amount to an unlimited number of accredited investors. Up to thirty-five nonaccredited investors can be included as well, provided that the issuer "shall reasonably believe immediately prior to making any sale that each purchaser who is not an accredited investor either alone or with his purchaser representative has such knowledge and experience in financial and business matters that he is capable of evaluating the merits and risk of the prospective investment." From a practical standpoint, this is one of the most frequently used exemptions to the Federal Securities Act because it deals with an unlimited dollar amount. However, as you can deal with only thirty-five nonaccredited investors, there is some degree of practicality as to the dollar amount of money that can be raised, unless you are dealing with the more sophisticated "accredited investor," who has a greater dollar resource that they might be willing to put in any one transaction.

Other Rules or Restrictions

In addition to the type of people and amounts of money that can be raised, the rules under Regulation D have other requirements and restrictions. For example, on offerings other than 504, the issuer must ensure that there are adequate limitations on resale of the security by requiring purchasers to sign an investment letter whereby the purchasers acknowledge that they are acquiring a security for themselves and not for other people. In addition, the legend must state that the securities have not been registered under the 1933 Act and therefore cannot be resold unless registered or sold under an exemption from registration. These legends are to be printed on stock certificates and stock order instructions notified for all transfer agents.

Rule 503 requires that a notice on Form D be filed within 15 days of the first sale of the securities of any Regulation D offering. The Form D notice is considered filed with the SEC as of the date it is received. However, since March 1989, filing a Form D no longer is a necessary condition to meet the three exemptions under Regulation D. Nevertheless, under Rule 507, the penalty for failure to file Form D is disqualification from using that exemption for future offerings by an issuer if it has been enjoined by court for violating the Form D notice requirement.

In April 1989, because of additional concerns that had been raised about the technical requirements of filing under the Regulation D, Rule 508 was created to provide that insignificant deviations from the requirements of Regulation D would not result in the loss of the exemption if: (1) the failure to comply did not pertain to a condition or requirement intended to protect a particular individual or entity; (2) the failure to comply was insignificant with respect to the offering as a whole; and (3) a good-faith and reasonable attempt was made to comply with all the conditions of Regulation D.

However, you should be cautioned that certain requirements are not deemed insignificant, including the requirements about the dollar amounts, the number of purchasers, and general solicitations.

In addition to the rules and regulations of Regulation D of the Securities Act of 1933, there is a well-known intrastate offering exemption under the act. The idea is that issuers of securities that only deal in the one state in which they are operating do not need to register federally because they are not operating across the state lines in federal commerce. Issuers attempting to qualify for this exemption, however, are required to follow the guidelines of their own states. Section 3(a)(11) of the 1933 Act provides the exemption from registration for "any security which is part of an issue offered and sold only to persons resident within a single state or territory, where the issuer of said security is a resident and doing business within the state. If the issuer is a corporation, it must be incorporated under the laws of, and be doing business within, such state or territory."

In addition, the SEC adopted Rule 147 to provide a specific safe harbor for the Section 3(a)(11) intrastate exemption. If the exemption is available, a Rule 147 offering may be made to an unlimited number of persons providing they are all residents of one state. However, under this rule, only a limited number of investors can be brought in. In addition, corporations should be careful to understand that the intrastate exemption has been very narrowly construed by both the SEC and courts. For example, a single sale to one nonresident would void the exemption.

Small public offerings also can be made under the act. One such offering is Section 3(b) of the 1933 Act and Regulation A under that section, which provides for a public offering through an offering circular, sometimes referred to as the *short form registration*. The offering cannot exceed $5,000,000. Although compliance with this offering is less burdensome than with the S-1 regulation, which is considered a full-blown public registration, it is nevertheless extensive.

As mentioned, because the major purpose of the Securities Act under federal law is to provide adequate disclosure to investors, the best way to avoid liability is to ensure that an adequate private offering memorandum is designed that provides full and accurate disclosure to anyone to whom a security is offered.

The private offering memorandum should set forth all of the risks pertaining to the investment and should be drafted to include the specific risks associated with the particular company offering the security. This might include, but not be limited to, items such as tax consequences, lack of liquidity, the fact that the venture is a start-up venture, and that there might not be a market for the

---

PROFIT STRATEGY:

Being a guarantor on a long-term note has long-term ramifications. I learned this the hard way when I got called on a large bank loan I guaranteed almost fifteen years ago. At the time I gave the guarantee, I didn't have many assets, so it didn't seem like a big deal. I was wrong. If you have to guarantee a loan, try to get released from the guarantee based on certain events, such as once the property or business produces certain income levels. The guarantee also could be released after a certain number of payments are made. You won't always be able to get the release, but you won't know unless you try.

investment when the investor is ready to sell. Great care should be taken by anyone putting projections in such a memorandum, as projections tend to be overly optimistic and could likely be considered misleading if the company does not produce the optimistic returns. In addition, to make sure that the investors who are able to afford the loss of their investment are obtained, various suitability guidelines are set up by the states in which the security is offered. Typical suitability standards would include minimum net worth and/or specific dollar amount limitations for an investment. The sponsor should design a questionnaire that solicits this type of financial information from a prospect to ensure that they are protected from the suitability sale requirements.

How to Borrow Money for Your Corporation

If you don't raise the capital you need by selling stock or borrowing money privately, then you will likely need to borrow directly from an institutional lender. If this is a new experience for you, chances are it likely will be frustrating before it is successful. It is an old story and a true one that lenders prefer to loan money when you don't need it. When you do need it, lenders are hard to find. The purpose of this section is to help you understand the process and help you sell your position to the lender.

Is Your Firm Creditworthy?

The ability to obtain money when you need it is as necessary to continue operating your business as is a good location or the right equipment. Before a bank or any other lending agency lends you money, the loan officer must feel satisfied with the answers to the five following questions:

1. What sort of person are you, the prospective borrower? By all odds, the character of the borrower comes first. Next is your ability to manage your business.
2. What are you going to do with the money? The answer to this question will determine the type of loan you would need and whether you would be eligible for short- or long-term financing. Money to be used for the purchase of seasonal inventory will require quicker repayment than money used to buy fixed assets because lenders will want to be paid back as you receive

your money. They would not like your using their money to cash flow other aspects of your business.

3. When and how do you plan to pay the loan back? Your banker's judgment of your business ability and the type of loan will be deciding factors in answering this question.
4. Is the cushion in the loan large enough? In other words, does the amount requested make suitable allowance for unexpected developments? The banker decides this question on the basis of your financial statement, which sets forth the condition of your business, and on the collateral pledged.
5. What is the outlook for business in general and for your business in particular?

Information Your Lender Will Need

The banker wants to make loans to businesses that are solvent, profitable, and growing. The two basic financial statements used to determine those conditions are the *balance sheet* and *profit-and-loss statement*. The former is the major yardstick for solvency and the latter for profits. A continuous series of these two statements over a period of time is the principal device for measuring financial stability and growth potential.

In interviewing loan applicants and in studying their records, the banker is especially interested in the following facts and figures.

1. *General information*. Are the books and records up-to-date and in good condition? What is the condition of accounts payable? Of notes payable? What are the salaries of the owner-manager and other company officers? Are all taxes currently being paid? What is the order backlog? What is the number of employees? What is the insurance coverage?
2. *Accounts receivable*. Are there indications that some of the accounts receivable have already been pledged to another creditor? What is the accounts receivable turnover? Is the accounts receivable total weakened because many customers are far behind in their payments? Has a large enough reserve been set up to cover doubtful accounts? How much do the largest accounts owe, and what per-

centage of your total accounts does this amount represent?

3. *Inventories*. Is merchandise in good shape, or will it have to be marked down? How much raw material is on hand? How much work is in process? How much of the inventory is finished goods? Is there any obsolete inventory? Has an excessive amount of inventory been consigned to customers? Is inventory turnover in line with the turnover for other businesses in the same industry? Is money being tied up too long in inventory?

4. *Fixed assets*. What are the type, age, and condition of the equipment? What are the depreciation policies? What are the details of mortgages or conditional sales contracts? What are future acquisition plans?

What Kind of Money?

When you set out to borrow money for your company, it is important to know the kind of money you need from a bank or other lending institution. There are two general categories of borrowing: *short-term* and *long-term money*.

The purpose for which the funds are to be used is an important factor in deciding the kind of money needed. But even so, deciding what kind of money to use is not always easy. It is sometimes complicated by the fact that you may be using some of the various kinds of money at the same time and for identical purposes. A very important distinction between the types of money is the source of repayment. Generally, short-term loans are repaid from the liquidation of the current assets that they have financed. Long-term loans are usually repaid from earnings.

You can use *short-term bank loans* for purposes such as financing accounts receivable for, say, thirty to sixty days. You can also use them to cover aspects of your business that take longer to pay off, such as building a seasonal inventory over five to six months. Usually, lenders expect short-term loans to be repaid after their purposes have been served. For example, accounts receivable loans are expected to be paid when the outstanding accounts have been paid by the borrower's customers. Inventory loans should be repaid when the inventory has been converted into sellable merchandise.

Banks loan money for these purposes either on your general credit reputation with an *unsecured loan* or on a *secured loan*. Obviously, your preference will be unsecured. However, this type of loan seldom comes without substantial borrowing experience and repayment record. Even then, many banks consider it poor lending practice. A *secured loan* involves a pledge of some or all of your assets. The bank requires security as a protection for its depositors against the risks involved even in business situations where the chances of success are good.

Long-term borrowing provides money you plan to pay back over a fairly long time. Some people break it down into two forms: (1) intermediate loans (longer than one year but shorter than five years); and (2) long-term loans (longer than five years). Think of long-term borrowing as money you probably will pay back in periodic installments from earnings.

> **PROFIT STRATEGY:**
> Instead of using cash value on your life insurance as collateral, you might consider just borrowing against it from the insurance company. The interest rate is lower than you can get from a bank, and if you default, you simply lose the paid-up value of your insurance.

What Kind of Collateral Will You Need?

Sometimes, your signature is the only security the bank needs when making a loan. At other times, the bank requires additional assurance that the money will be repaid. The kind and amount of security depend on the bank and on the borrower's situation.

If the loan required cannot be justified by the borrower's financial statements alone, a pledge of security may bridge the gap. The types of security requested by lenders are: endorsers, comakers, and guarantors; warehouse receipts; trust receipts and floor planning; chattel mortgages; real estate; accounts receivables; savings accounts; life insurance policies; and stocks and bonds.

Endorsers, Comakers, and Guarantors

Borrowers often get other people to sign a note to bolster their own credit. These *endorsers* are contingently liable for the note they sign. If you fail to pay up, the bank expects the endorser to make the note good. Sometimes, the endorser may be asked to pledge assets or securities, too.

A *comaker* is someone who creates an obligation jointly with you as the borrower. In such cases, the bank can collect directly from either you as the maker or the comaker.

A *guarantor* is one who guarantees the payment of a note by signing a guaranty commitment. Both private and government lenders often require guarantees from officers of corporations. Sometimes, a manufacturer will act as guarantor for you if you are a good customer to help get your goods and theirs out in the marketplace.

Warehouse Receipts

Banks also take commodities as security by lending money on a *warehouse receipt*. Such a receipt usually is delivered directly to the bank and shows that the merchandise used as security either has been placed in a public warehouse or has been left on your premises under the control of one of your employees who is bonded (as in field warehousing). Such loans are generally made on staple or standard merchandise that can be readily marketed. The typical warehouse receipt loan is granted for a percentage of the estimated value of the goods used as security.

Trust Receipts and Floor Planning

Merchandise, such as automobiles, appliances, and boats, has to be displayed to be sold. The only way many small businesses can afford such displays is by borrowing money. Such loans often are secured by a note and a trust receipt. The *trust receipt* is the legal paper for *floor planning*. It is used for serial-numbered merchandise. When you sign one, you (1) acknowledge receipt of the merchandise; (2) agree to keep the merchandise in trust for the bank; and (3) promise to pay the bank as soon as you sell the goods.

PROFIT STRATEGY:

If you have never negotiated with banks, hire a good lawyer who has, and he or she will save you a great deal of money. Most people are intimidated by banks and their lawyers. Don't be. Everything in their contracts is negotiable, but unless you know it, they'll feed you the old, "It's our standard contract" line. Don't fall for it. Banks, insurance companies, and investment banks all negotiate.

Chattel Mortgages

If you buy equipment, such as a cash register or a delivery truck, you may want to get a *chattel mortgage* loan. Basically, you give the bank a lien on the equipment you are buying. The bank also evaluates the present and future market value of the equipment used to secure the loan. How rapidly will it depreciate? Do you have the necessary fire, theft, property damage, and public liability insurance on the equipment? Bankers have to be sure that you protect the equipment as it is their security.

Real Estate

Real estate is another form of collateral for long-term loans. When taking a real estate mortgage, the bank finds out (1) the location of the real estate; (2) its physical condition; (3) its foreclosure value; and (4) the amount of insurance carried on the property. Real estate traditionally has been excellent security. Unfortunately, however, the late 1980s saw real estate values crash and the security for loans go with it. Lenders have since grown more conservative and require more equity in the real estate security.

Accounts Receivable

Many banks lend money on accounts receivable. In effect, they are counting on your customers to pay your note. The bank may take accounts receivable on a *notification* or a *nonnotification plan*. Under the *notification plan*, purchasers of the goods are informed by the bank that their account has been assigned to a notification plan, and they are asked to pay the bank directly. Under the *nonnotification plan*, your customers continue to pay you directly, and then you pay the bank.

Savings Accounts

Sometimes, you might get a loan by assigning the bank one of your savings accounts. In such a case, the bank gets an assignment from you and keeps your passbook. If you assign an account in another bank as collateral, the lending bank asks the other bank to mark its records to show that the account is frozen and held as collateral.

Life Insurance Policies

Another kind of collateral is life insurance. Banks will lend up to the cash value of a life insurance policy. You have to assign the policy to the bank.

If the policy is on the life of a small corporation executive, corporate resolutions must be made to authorize the assignment. Most insurance companies allow you to sign the policy back to the original beneficiary when the assignment to the bank ends.

Stocks and Bonds

If you use stocks and bonds as collateral, they must be marketable. To protect themselves against market declines and the possible expenses associated with liquidation, banks usually lend no more than 75% of the market value of high-grade stock. On federal government or municipal bonds, they may be willing to lend 90% or more of the market value. The bank may ask you for additional security or payment whenever the market value of the stocks or bonds drops below the bank's required margin.

What Are the Lender's Rules?

Lending institutions are not just interested in loan repayments. They also are interested in borrowers with healthy profit-making businesses. Therefore, whether or not collateral is required for a loan, banks and other lenders set loan limitations and restrictions to protect themselves from un-necessary risk. Borrowers often consider loan limitations a burden. Unfortunately, it can't be helped. Even Donald Trump has had to deal with bankers telling him how to run his business. You can either forget it and be assured you won't be loaned any more money, or go with the flow and try to learn from the experience.

In making long-term loans, both the borrower and the lender should be thinking of (1) the net earning power of the borrowing company; (2) the capability of its management; (3) the long-range prospects of the company; and (4) the long-range prospects of the industry of which the company is a part. Such factors often mean that limitations increase as the duration of the loan increases.

PROFIT STRATEGY:

Most major colleges and many cities are now holding annual venture capital forums. These sessions present excellent opportunities for networking. Contact the chamber of commerce in the largest city near you or the business school at your state university.

What Kinds of Limitations?

The limitations that you will usually run into when you borrow money are (1) repayment terms; (2) pledge or use of securities; and (3) periodic reporting.

A loan agreement, as you may already know, is a tailor-made document covering or referring to all the terms and conditions of the loan. With it, lenders do two things: (1) they protect their position as creditors; and (2) they ensure that repayment is carried out according to the terms. Lenders reason that your business should generate enough funds to repay the loan while taking care of other needs. They consider that cash inflow should be high enough to do this without hurting your working capital.

Covenants: Negatives and Positives

The actual restrictions in a loan agreement come under a section known as *covenants*. *Negative covenants* are things that you may not do without prior approval from the lender, such as restrictions on borrowing more money elsewhere, an agreement not to pledge to others any of your assets, and a restriction against your company paying dividends in excess of the terms specified in the loan agreement.

On the other hand, *positive covenants* spell out things that you must do, such as maintaining a minimum net working capital, carrying adequate insurance, repaying the loan according to the terms of the agreement, and supplying the lender with financial statements and reports.

Overall, however, loan agreements may be amended from time to time and exceptions made. Certain provisions may be waived from one year to the next with the consent of the lender.

You Can Negotiate

Next time you go to borrow money, thrash out the lending terms before you sign. It is good practice no matter how badly you may need the money. Ask to see the papers in advance of the loan closing. Legitimate lenders are glad to cooperate.

> **PROFIT STRATEGY:**
>
> If you do nothing more than study the information discussed in this chapter and answer all of the questions posed, you will know more about your business than most entrepreneurs. Once you have done the planning, keep it up. It will help you view your business from an important side—the bottom line.

Chances are that some of the lender's terms are negotiable. Keep in mind while you're mulling over the terms that you may want to get the advice of your associates and outside advisors. In short, try to get terms that you know your company can live with. Remember, once the terms have been agreed upon and the loan is made, you are bound by them. If you don't think they look good now, I can assure you that they won't look good later when you miss a payment.

Venture Capitalists

Using a "venture capitalist" to raise money is a hot topic right now, but being successful at it is a very complicated matter. Venture capital arrangements frequently involve a combination of lending and equity financing. Venture capitalists are sometimes considered angels and sometimes vultures. The truth, just like the combination financing itself, probably lies somewhere in between. If you use a venture capitalist, you will likely have to give up part of your company. What you hope for is that what you retain is ultimately much more than what you could have gotten on your own.

What Venture Capital Firms Look For

Bankers and venture capitalists tend to look at a corporation differently. Banks look at the company's immediate future, but are most heavily influenced by its past. Venture capitalists consider the past and look to its long-term future for their greatest profit.

To be sure, venture capitalists are interested in many of the same factors that influence bankers in their analysis of loan applications from smaller companies. All financial people want to know the results of past operations, the amount and intended use of the needed funds, and the earnings and financial condition of future projections. But venture capitalists also look much more closely at the features of the product and the size of the market than do commercial banks.

Banks are creditors. They're interested in the product or market position of the company to look for assurance that this service or product can provide steady sales and generate sufficient cash flow to repay the loan. They look at projections to be certain that owner-managers have done their homework.

Venture capital firms are owners. They hold stock in the company, adding their invested capital to its equity base. Therefore, they examine existing or planned products or services and the potential markets for them with extreme care. They invest only in firms they believe can increase sales rapidly and generate substantial profits. Venture capital firms invest for long-term capital, not for interest income. They commonly look for a threefold to fivefold return on their investment in five or seven years.

Of course, venture capitalists don't realize capital gains on all their investments. Certainly they don't make capital gains of 300% to 500%, except on a very limited portion of their total investments. But their intent is to find projects with this appreciation potential to make up for investments that aren't successful.

Venture capital is a risky business, because it's difficult to judge the worth of early-stage companies. Consequently, most venture capital firms set rigorous policies for venture proposal size, maturity of the seeking company, and requirements and evaluation procedures to reduce risks, because their investments are unprotected in the event of failure.

Most venture capital firms are interested in projects that require an investment of $250,000 to $1,500,000. Projects requiring under $250,000 are of limited interest because of the high cost of investigation and administration. However, some venture firms will consider smaller proposals if the investment is intriguing enough.

Most venture capital firms' investment interest is limited to projects proposed by companies with some operating history, even though they may not have shown a profit yet. Companies that can expand into a new product line or a new market with additional funds are particularly interesting. The venture capital firm can provide funds to enable such companies to grow in a spurt rather than gradually, as they would on retained earnings.

Companies that are just starting or that have serious financial difficulties may interest some venture capitalists if the potential for significant gain over the long run can be identified and assessed. If the venture firm has already extended its portfolio to a large risk concentration, they may be reluctant to invest in these areas because of increased risk of loss. However, although most venture capital firms will not consider proposals from start-up companies, a small number of venture firms does only start-up financing. The small firm that has a well-thought-out plan and can demonstrate that its management group has an outstanding record (even if it is with other companies) has a decided edge in acquiring this kind of seed capital.

Most venture capital firms concentrate primarily on the competence and character of the proposing firm's management. They feel that even mediocre products can be successfully manufactured, promoted, and distributed by an experienced, energetic management group.

They look for a group that is able to work together easily and productively, especially under stress from temporary reversals and competitive problems. They know that even excellent products can be ruined by poor management.

Venture capital firms usually require that the company under consideration have a complete management group. Each of the important functional areas, product design, marketing, production, finance, and control, must be under the direction of a trained, experienced member of the group. Responsibilities must be clearly assigned. And, in addition to a thorough understanding of the industry, each member of the management team must be firmly committed to the company and its future.

Next in importance to the excellence of the proposing firm's management group, most venture capital firms seek a distinctive element in the strategy or product/market/process combination of the firm. This distinctive element may be a new feature of the product or process or a particular skill or technical competence of the management. But it must exist. It must provide a competitive advantage.

Elements of a Venture Proposal

If you deal with a venture capitalist, come prepared. Your proposal must stand out from the crowd both in looks, presentation, and content. The following is a summary of the elements of your business you should be ready to discuss.

1. *Proposed financing.* The amount of money you'll need from the beginning to the maturity of the project proposed, how the proceeds will be used, how you plan to structure the financing, and why the amount designated is required
2. *Marketing.* A description of the market segment you have or plan to get, the competition, the characteristics of the

market, and your plans (with costs) for getting or holding the market segment you're aiming at
3. *History of the firm.* A summary of significant financial and organizational milestones, description of employees and employee relations, explanations of banking relationships, recounting of major services or products your firm has offered during its existence, and the like
4. *Description of the product or service.* A full description of the product (process) or service offered by the firm and the detailed costs associated with it
5. *Financial statements.* Both statements for the past few years and pro forma projections (balance sheets, income statements, and cash flows) for the next three to five years, showing the effect anticipated if the project is undertaken and if the financing is secured (including an analysis of key variables affecting financial performance, showing what could happen if the projected level of revenue is not attained)
6. *Capitalization.* A list of shareholders, how much is invested to date, and in what form (equity/debt)
7. *Biographical sketches.* The work histories and qualifications of key owners/employees
8. *Principal suppliers and customers.* The length of time you have dealt with the suppliers
9. *Problems anticipated and other pertinent information.* A candid discussion of any contingent liabilities, pending litigation, tax or patent difficulties, or any other contingencies that might affect the project you're proposing
10. *Advantages.* A discussion of what's special about your product, service, marketing plans, or channels and what gives your project unique leverage

Provisions of the Investment Proposal

Once a venture capital firm decides to back your business, it will prepare an equity financing proposal that details the amount of money to be provided, the percentage of common stock to be surrendered in exchange for these funds, the interim financing method to be used, and the protective covenants to be included. The final financing agreement will be negotiated and generally represents a compromise between your needs and those of the venture capital firm. The important elements of this compromise are: ownership, control, annual charges, and final objectives.

Ownership.

Venture capital financing is not inexpensive for the owners of a small business. The partners of the venture firm buy a portion of the business's equity in exchange for their investment. This percentage of *equity* varies, of course, and depends on the amount of money provided, the success and worth of the business, and the anticipated return on investment. It can range from perhaps 10% in the case of an established, profitable company to as much as 80% or 90% for beginning or financially troubled firms.

Most venture firms, at least initially, don't want a position of more than 30% to 40% because they want the owner to have an incentive to keep building the business. If additional financing is required to support business growth, the outsiders' stake may exceed 50%, but investors realize that small-business owners or managers can lose their entrepreneurial zeal under those circumstances. In the final analysis, however, the venture firm, regardless of its percentage of ownership, really wants to leave control in the hands of the company's managers, because it is really investing in that management team in the first place.

Most venture firms determine the ratio of funds provided to equity requested by a comparison of the present financial worth of the contributions made by each of the parties to the agreement. The present value of the contribution by the owner of a starting or financially troubled company is obviously rated low. Often, it is estimated as just the existing value of his or her idea and the competitive costs of the owner's time. The contribution by the owners of a thriving business is valued much higher. Generally, it is capitalized at a multiple of the current earnings and/or net worth.

Financial valuation is not an exact science. The final compromise on the owner's contribution's worth in the equity financing agreement is likely to be much lower than the owner thinks it should be and considerably higher than the partners of the capital firm think it might be. In the ideal situation, of course, the two parties to the agreement are able to do together what neither could do separately: (1) the company is able to grow fast enough with the additional funds to do more than overcome the owner's loss of equity; and (2) the investment grows at a sufficient rate to compensate the venture capitalists for assuming the risk.

An equity financing agreement with a distribution in five to seven years that pleases both parties is ideal. Because, of course, the parties can't see the outcome in the present, neither will be perfectly satisfied with the compromise reached. It is important, though, for the business owner to look at the future. You should carefully consider the impact of the ratio of funds invested to the ownership given up, not only for the present, but also for the years to come.

Control

Control is a much simpler issue to resolve. Unlike the division of equity over which the parties are bound to disagree, control is an issue in which they have a common (though perhaps unapparent) interest. Though it is understandable that the management of a small company will have some anxiety about who controls the business, the partners of a venture firm normally have little interest in assuming control. They have neither the technical expertise nor the managerial personnel to run a number of small companies in diverse industries. They much prefer to leave operating control to the existing management.

The venture capital firm does, however, want to participate in any strategic decisions that might change the basic product/market character of the company and in any major investment decisions that might divert or deplete the financial resources of the company. They will, therefore, generally ask that members of their group be made directors of the company. Venture capital firms also want to be able to assume control and attempt to rescue their investments, if severe financial, operating, or marketing problems develop. Thus, they usually will include protective covenants in their equity financing agreements to permit them to take control and appoint new officers if financial performance is very poor.

Annual Charges

The investment of the venture capital firm may be in the final form of direct stock ownership that does not impose fixed charges. More likely, it will be in an interim form—convertible subordinated debentures or preferred stock. Financing also may be straight loans with options or warrants that can be converted to a future equity position at a pre-established price.

Final Objectives

Venture capital firms generally intend to realize capital gains on their investments by providing for a stock buy-back by the firm, by arranging a public offering of stock of the company invested in, or by providing for a merger with a larger firm that has publicly traded stock. They usually hope to do this within five to seven years of their initial investment, although several additional stages of financing may be required over this period.

Most equity financing agreements include provisions guaranteeing that the venture capital firm may participate in any stock sale or approve any merger, regardless of their percentage of stock ownership. Sometimes the agreement will require that the management work toward an eventual stock sale or merger. Clearly, the owner-manager of a small company seeking equity financing must consider the future impact on his or her own stock holdings and personal ambition of the venture firm's aims, because taking in a venture capitalist as a partner may be a virtual commitment to sell out or go public.

Types of Venture Capital Firms

There is quite a variety of types of venture capital firms. They include the following:

1. *Traditional partnerships,* which often are established by wealthy families to manage aggressively a portion of their funds by investing in small companies
2. *Professionally managed pools,* which are made up of institutional money and which operate like traditional partnerships
3. *Investment banking firms,* which usually trade in more established securities, but occasionally form investor syndicates for venture proposals
4. *Insurance companies,* which often require a portion of equity as a condition of their loans to smaller companies as protection against inflation
5. *Manufacturing companies,* which sometimes have looked at investing in smaller companies as a means of supplementing their research and development programs (some Fortune 500 corporations have venture capital operations to help keep them abreast of technological innovations)

6. *Small Business Investment Corporations (SBICs),* which are licensed by the Small Business Administration (SBA), and which may provide management assistance as well as venture capital (when dealing with SBICs, the small business owner-manager should initially determine whether the SBIC is primarily interested in an equity position, venture capital, or merely in long-term lending on a fully secured basis)

The Importance of Formal Financial Planning

In case there is any doubt about the implications of the previous sections, it should be noted: it is extremely difficult for any small firm, especially the starting or struggling company, to obtain venture capital. There is one thing, however, that owner-managers of small businesses can do to improve the chances of their venture proposals at least escaping the fate of the 90% that are almost immediately rejected. In a word—*plan.*

Having financial plans demonstrates to any lender that you are a competent manager, that you may have a special managerial edge over other small business owners looking for equity money. You may gain a decided advantage through well-prepared plans and projections that include cash budgets, pro forma statements, capital investment analysis, and capital source studies.

Cash budgets should be projected for one year and prepared monthly. They should combine expected sales revenues, cash receipts, material, labor and overhead expenses, and cash disbursements on a monthly basis to anticipate fluctuations in the level of cash and planning for short-term borrowing and investment.

Pro forma statements should be prepared to plan for up to three years ahead. They should include both income statements and balance sheets. Again, these should be prepared quarterly to combine expected sales revenues; production, marketing, and administrative expenses; profits; product, market, or process investments; and supplier, bank, or investment company borrowings. Pro forma statements allow you to anticipate the financial results of your operations and to plan intermediate-term borrowings and investments.

Capital investment analyses and capital source studies should be prepared to plan for up to five years ahead. The investment analyses should compare rates of return for product, market, or process investment, and the source alternatives should compare the cost and availability of debt and equity and the expected level of retained earnings, which together support the selected investments. These analyses and source studies should be prepared quarterly so you may anticipate the financial consequences of changes in your company's strategy. They will allow you to plan long-term borrowings, equity placements, and major investments.

There's a bonus in making such projections. They force you to consider the results of your actions. Your estimates must be explicit; you have to examine and evaluate your own managerial records; disagreements have to be resolved or at least discussed and understood. Financial planning may be burdensome, but it's one of the keys to business success.

Checklist of Financing Sources for Your Business

The following list summarizes the major financing options you may wish to explore:

- ❑ Sell stock in your company
   a. Potential investors: Family, friends, and other nonprofessional investors; vendors and other suppliers of your company that profit from your being in business; venture capitalists; university business development centers; SBICs
   b. Sale of equity in the form of common stock
   c. Sale of preferred stock
   d. Sale of bonds and/or notes

- ❑ Borrow money personally
   a. Banks: Unsecured loans, loans secured by real estate, stocks and bonds
   b. Finance companies: Loans secured by real estate, personal assets
   c. Credit unions: Unsecured "signature only" loans; loans secured by real estate, personal assets
   d. Savings and loan associations: Unsecured loans (rare); loans secured by real estate
   e. Mortgage brokers and private investors: Loans secured by real estate
   f. Life insurance companies: Policy loans (borrow against cash value)

- ❑ Business loans
   a. Banks: Unsecured loans (for established, financially sound companies only); loans secured by accounts receivable, inventory, equipment; loans guaranteed by SBA
   b. Commercial finance companies: Loans secured by real estate, equipment, inventory, accounts receivable
   c. Life insurance companies: Loans secured by commercial real estate
   d. SBA: Loans secured by all available business assets, all available personal assets
   e. Suppliers: Trade credit
   f. Customers: Prepayment on orders

- ❑ Leasing
   a. Banks
   b. Leasing companies: Loans secured by equipment; sales of receivables (called "factoring")

CHAPTER FOUR

DEALING WITH THE LAW AND LAWYERS

In many cases, you may have purchased this book to avoid lawyers and attempt to do everything by yourself. In general, this is a worthy goal. However, the issue is on the word *everything*. As an entrepreneur, you'll find that to run a business in and of itself has tremendous difficulties. Sooner or later you will come to the realization that not only can't you do everything yourself, but also it probably is unwise to do so. Professional consultants not only have their value but also if they're good at what they do, be they CPA, financial consultant, or lawyer, they will bring to you more than what you are paying them. If you find that this is not the case, then obviously you have chosen unwisely, and that is the real problem.

As this book is about the law as much as anything else, we are going to look at how you as an entrepreneur should operate within the legal system, how you choose a lawyer, and how you work with your lawyer. You will learn how to handle legal issues that arise in your business and how you should handle going to court if you are ultimately forced into that situation.

How to Find a Good Lawyer

The natural first question to ask yourself in dealing with this chapter is, How do I find a good, cheap lawyer? Unfortunately, those terms don't mix. No, not the good and the lawyer part, but the good, cheap lawyer part. If you find a good lawyer who knows his way around business, he is not going to be cheap because if he is good in his area of law, then he will likely understand the value of his time and will charge accordingly. A good business lawyer can make a lot of money not only by acting as a lawyer, but also by getting involved in some of his clients' businesses. If the lawyer you are considering is not successful and making a lot of money, you probably don't want him.

The first thing that you don't do in your legal search is look in the yellow pages for an experienced attorney. First, many lawyers don't advertise. These lawyers are from the old school who don't believe in self-promotion, and you may not even find them in the yellow pages other than a one-line listing of their name and telephone number. Second, the lawyers that do advertise won't likely provide the real information you need to select a lawyer for your corporation. The key element to having a good lawyer is to select one with whom you get along. An absolute must is that your lawyer have the ability to communicate at your level, whatever that may be.

The first thing that you should do when trying to find a good lawyer is to center your search around those who have been involved in the same type of business you are in. For example, if you are forming a corporation in real estate, you want to hire a lawyer who not only is an experienced corporate lawyer, but also has been involved in real estate and has more than just some legal knowledge about it. You want someone who has been personally active in real estate or at least has represented many clients in real estate. It is not likely that this individual will have done much litigation in this field, because in the legal community it is rare to find a business lawyer who also spends time in litigation. A litigator usually is a full-time litigator and doesn't get involved in transactional work.

Let's continue using our example of forming a real estate corporation. You should approach key people in the real estate community, starting with your local real estate association, and find out whom they are using as a lawyer or advisor. It may very well be that your association has hired one of the largest law firms in town and the members in that firm may be outside your financial budget. Nevertheless, it is a good starting point. You might want to contact this attorney anyway to discuss your plans and see how he or she may be willing to assist you. This lawyer may be willing to handle your situation on a reduced fee, hoping that, as your business grows, he or she can grow with it. The other possibility is that he or she may have a good referral for you outside the firm.

One of the things that you will discover in your interview process is that large law firms are not normally good for small, start-up-companies because these firms concentrate heavily on billable hours and their fees are higher than what most start-up companies can afford. What you are searching for in the beginning of your company is likely to be either a sole practitioner or a small firm. These attorneys are not only more flexible in their billing, but also because of their own size, they will understand the difficulties of a start-up business, as they are themselves running their own businesses.

You also can contact your local chamber of commerce to find lawyers who have been involved with the chamber in any of their business functions. The chamber of commerce is obviously very pro-business oriented, and its contacts tend to be people who are at least entrepreneurially inclined. Frequently, involved lawyers will hold seminars about various legal aspects of running a business, and these would be excellent not only to attend to hear what the attorney has to say, but also to see the attorneys and how they handle themselves before a group. In this seminar context, you also frequently have an opportunity to ask an attorney questions, and see how he or she handles the situation without billing you for it.

A third option, if neither of the preceding two are successful, is to go to the library and review an information source called the *Martindale-Hubble Law Directory*. This directory contains information, including biographical sketches on lawyers in your area and is one of the few independent sources that actually awards opinion ratings on attorneys. In the directory, the ratings run from AV (the highest rating), BV, to CV (the lowest rating). The *V* stands for a general recommendation that the lawyer

---

PROFIT STRATEGY:
Five Steps to Hiring a Good Lawyer
1. Contact your trade association for referrals.
2. Contact your chamber of commerce.
3. Contact other businesses in your field.
4. Contact your leading competitor.
5. Consult the *Martindale-Hubble Law Directory* for your area.

follows professional standards of conduct. This means that all lawyers who are designated in the book will have the V rating. The A, B, and C are the only difference. Other lawyers will be listed, but not rated because the lawyer can ask not to have his rating shown. Although you should not draw the conclusion that a lawyer without a rating has one of the lower ratings, it is likely that this is the case because lawyers with the high AV rating would want to show it.

Like most directories and other methods for selecting a lawyer, this, too, has flaws. One of the major flaws is that you can advertise in the *Martindale-Hubble Law Directory*. Prominent space is purchased, as it is in the yellow pages, not based on the success or rating of the lawyer. This means that some of the larger space attributed to a law firm reflects the fact that the law firm has a lot of money and can afford to spend it to get prominently displayed in the directory. None of this means that you should exclude the directory from helping you find a lawyer. Instead, it just suggests that you need to go at it with open eyes. Understand that advertising and dollars spent for that advertising also have something to do with the prominence of the lawyer in the directory, even though it has nothing to do with his or her rating.

How to Pay a Lawyer

For those of you who have already answered this question with "as little as possible," I'll go ahead and say it for you so we can get it out of the way. I wish there was some way to overcome the expense of hiring a good lawyer. I have always discussed with my clients upfront the details of billing and the alternatives available. Sometimes hourly rates work, and sometimes it is best to quote a flat fee. Flat fees can work for both the client and lawyer. In most cases, you will generally start out on an hourly basis until you and the attorney know how you best work together. After a while, it is not unusual to establish a set monthly retainer that allows you to call the attorney at any time without getting individual bills for telephone calls and short discussions. Bills for quick phone calls tend not only to upset the client the most, but also keep them from calling when they should. Sometimes the very act of calling and checking on a situation can save everybody a lot of time, money, and effort when it's discovered that the client could have exercised another option that would have been not only more profitable, but also legally sound. A number of attorneys like retainer billing because it gives them a set amount of income each month that they know is coming in without their having to drum up new business.

The key issue involved in billing is value. If the attorney is experienced not only in the legal but also in the operation and success of businesses, then her or his counsel can prove invaluable. Consequently, I encourage you to develop a working relationship with your attorney that proves profitable to both of you.

How to Handle a Legal Dispute

I hope that by now I have convinced you to hire a business attorney. Sooner or later, a legal dispute will arise because operating a business today means conflict. In fact, I think the ability to handle conflict from both the emotional side and the business side is one of the essential elements an entrepreneur must have in today's world. There will be disagreements between you and your customers, your bank, your suppliers, landlord, and yes, perhaps even your attorney. There are many ways to handle these disputes, but I can assure you that the least effective way is to go to court. Whether you are the plaintiff or the defendant, court action is an extremely expensive proposition. This is true not only of the actual hard cost that you will expend in legal fees and other professional expenses but also of the time that it will take away from your business, the emotional drain that litigation always brings, and the lost opportunity cost of what you could be doing with your business to make more money. Sometimes the absolute best course of action in a dispute is simply to do nothing and move on. This is extremely difficult because emotions certainly get involved in making a clear business decision. Nevertheless, understand that you will be paying a lot to go through the litigation process. Weighing those costs is a very important part of the legal process today.

Alternatives to Lawsuits

Because of the tremendous cost of a lawsuit, one of the very first things I believe you should attempt to do in all legal dispute situations is to work toward a reasonable settlement. This can be done either with you acting as your own negotiator or hiring someone else to act as your intermediary. This intermediary may be your lawyer, or it may very well be someone else. One reason for selecting someone other than a lawyer to handle the negotiations is because once you have your lawyer involved, the other side is likely not to want to meet with your attorney without having their attorney present as they will feel at a disadvantage. Using a non-lawyer professional at this stage to negotiate a settlement will allow you to avoid that additional conflict.

If you are going to handle your negotiations yourself, there are many good books and courses available on negotiations that I would highly recommend. Negotiating is a great skill that is not easily mastered. I think people don't give negotiators the credit they deserve because what they do appears to be nothing more than talking through a problem. Yet, they must be skillful not only to settle the dispute but also to let both sides feel they have won something. An excellent book on the topic of negotiation is *Getting to Yes* written by Harvard professor Roger Fisher. Professor Fisher was involved in creating the Harvard University School negotiation project and teaches a week-long course to professionals at the University.

Alternative Dispute Resolution

A growing trend across the United States to settle disputes outside the court system has been labeled *alternative dispute resolution*. This system has come about primarily because of the problems we have addressed with litigation, especially the cost and time involved. The alternative dispute system has many aspects, but the two primary alternatives are *mediation* and *arbitration*.

Mediation is the process of getting the parties together with a neutral third party who serves as the mediator. This individual must, by definition, be unbiased. The parties are given the opportunity to work out their differences together and arrive at a solution that is workable for both parties, even though it may not be a perfect solution. Over the past few years, virtually thousands of people across the country have served as mediators. In many courts around the country, mediation is becoming a requirement before actually setting a court date for a trial.

The best way to find a good mediator is very similar to the search for an attorney. Start with your local industry association. If it doesn't have a recommendation, turn to your chamber of commerce or other business community group. You also can turn to the *Martindale-Hubble Directory* that lists mediators from around the country in a separate directory. A third source is with your local judges' office. Frequently they assign mediators to cases, so they should have a current list.

The second alternative dispute resolution is *arbitration*. Arbitration is very much like a private court system. Unlike mediation, where the parties are left to resolve their own dispute with the assistance of a mediator, arbitration works more like a court system, where a decision actually is handed down by the arbitrator. Generally speaking, arbitrations are conducted by either single arbitrators or three arbitrators who serve as a panel. The arbitration process is much less formal and arbitrators are free to decide a case either by using the law in their decision-making process or by weighing their decision toward what is equitable between the parties. This decision process is more akin to the old legal process of having law and equity being decided within the courts.

Arbitration is much faster and much less expensive than the court system.

> **PROFIT STRATEGY:**
> Three Alternatives to Going to Court
> 1. Negotiate
> 2. Mediate
> 3. Arbitrate

Arbitrations can frequently be arranged within several months, and neither side has to go to the expense of the discovery process involved in litigation. Normally, the parties simply meet together in one or two sessions presenting their side of the case, and then the panel reaches a decision. Although it is not necessary to be represented by an attorney at the arbitration, it is normally wise to do so, particularly if the other side is represented. The important point is to make sure that your case is presented in the best fashion. If you can cite both the equitable aspects of your argument and any relevant legal points, then you may feel comfortable presenting your case. Arbitration decisions are binding and while they may be appealed, they are rarely overturned.

Arbitration and mediation are so successful that they now frequently appear in all sorts of contracts. You may even feel that it is to your advantage to insert clauses requiring arbitration and/or mediation into any contract you enter into to help ensure that this alternative judicial process is used.

Going to Court

If you can't solve your legal disputes by negotiation, mediation, or arbitration, you will likely find yourself on the way to court. I will point out that just because a lawsuit has been filed, don't assume that you will ultimately have the case decided by the court. Ninety-five percent of all court cases are settled prior to an actual decision being rendered by the court. I think you should approach any lawsuit you are involved in with that single fact in mind and always be on the lookout for an opportunity to settle. It doesn't mean that you will be giving in to your position; it simply means that if both parties can come to some agreeable term, you are probably both better off than having the case go to a judge and letting her or him make the decision, which could dramatically and negatively affect your business.

Everyone approaches the court system thinking they are right, but in reality no one knows what decision a judge will reach. Because, although everyone would like to think the law on any issue is simple and clear, it is not. Attorneys are very skilled at finding cases to support both sides of every argument and even clouding issues in such a way that the aggressor sometimes becomes the pursued. People who bring a claim to court thinking that they will be the winner because they are the plaintiffs are not walking into a case with their eyes open. Many times plaintiffs have found themselves with not only countersuits brought against them that could potentially ruin their business, but also the discovery process might turn up other problems in their business that could even cause regulatory problems. Once you go to court, your entire business becomes open to public scrutiny, and every scrap of information about your business will become public knowledge at a potential trial.

If my comments about the judicial system sound discouraging, then you have read me correctly. I have been involved in many lawsuits from many sides of the table,

> **PROFIT STRATEGY:**
> One of the oldest and best known arbitration groups in the United States is the American Arbitration Association. This organization has arbitrators around the country, and their fees are reasonable. For more information about the arbitration process, you can contact them directly at (212) 484-4000.

but I rarely have found even the ultimate winner happy with the entire process. The victory is hollow at best.

Small Claims Court

The one area of the judicial system that I find underused is the small claims court. Small claims courts are available in all counties throughout the United States to settle disputes involving smaller amounts of money, usually up to $2,500, although the range throughout the United States can vary from a low of about $1,500 to a high of $10,000.

Small claims courts are relatively easy to use and don't require the time involved in the regular litigation process. After an initial filing of court papers, the parties are quickly given a hearing date, and each side is allowed to come into court and present its case. Normally, people appear without lawyers, although you are free to hire an attorney and have representation. If you have a collections problem or small, outstanding claims under the threshold amount, small claims court is an excellent way to get a decision. Once you have done one or two cases and understand the process, you will find that it is something you can do rather quickly and will gain the upper hand on the defendant, who, in most cases, has never been through the process. The result is that, although your experience in the process won't guarantee you a win, it will give you the advantage of having a knowledge of the process that very few people have.

For more information about small claims court, look in the local yellow pages under county municipalities. You might want to contact some of the larger counties in your state as well to see whether they have any written publications about how the small claims court operates in your state. The larger counties obviously have a better budget than smaller counties, and they may have designed their own kits, which would help walk you through the process.

In conclusion, working with lawyers and the legal system can be expensive and frustrating. It is, however, a part of every business today, and the sooner you can learn how to use the system to help your business, the better off you will be.

CHAPTER FIVE

HOW TO PREPARE YOUR OWN BUSINESS CONTRACTS AND LEASES

The entrepreneur wears many hats. Unless you can find and afford help, you must raise your own money, keep your own books, and sell your own products. Somewhere in all of those efforts you come face to face with the reality that legal contracts are a part of business and that you must now either be your own lawyer or hire one. Unless you are unlike every other business person I have ever known, ultimately you will compromise and handle some of your contracts yourself and pass others along to your lawyer.

The key to writing contracts is to cover all of the elements of dispute that could arise. Naturally, this is easier said than done, which is frequently why you may find yourself in litigation at some time or another arguing a point you thought was absolutely clear. So did the other guy, but it wasn't the same way you thought.

The Basics of a Contract

The premise of a contract is that it is an agreement between two or more parties to do or refrain from doing something. In general, the contract can be oral or written, but for our purposes, we will only deal with the written form. In today's society, it makes absolutely no sense to do business if it is not in writing, and I don't want to encourage you in any way to do otherwise. If you ever feel that you had an oral contract with someone and want to know if it's enforceable, go see an attorney. You will have to see one anyway, so you might as well do it early on.

Instead of getting yourself in that position, assume that all of your contracts have to be in writing and insist on doing them that way. If you follow this suggestion, you'll have a much better chance of having your view of a transaction enforced, which is the true purpose of doing a contract in the first place.

For a contract to be enforceable, there must be a general agreement, the contract must be considered, and the offer in the contract must be accepted. To have valid consideration, something must be given in exchange for something else. You agree to pay money, for example, and the other party agrees to buy your product. Frequently, you will see the phrase "For $10 and other good and valuable consideration." This is an expression showing that there was consideration, but it does not necessarily explain what the consideration was. The $10 should be paid between the parties, but the main thrust of the consideration was the good and valuable promises that the parties gave each other in the body of the contract.

How to Develop a Contract Strategy

Every business has unique elements. This is why we often misunderstand business jargon when we hear two people in the same business speaking to each other. Because businesses are unique, it always is best to try to find contracts that have been written specifically for your business and adapt them for your use. This alone is one of the best benefits that franchises offer new businesses. They supply a complete set of important documents that the franchisees will use.

If you're not purchasing a franchise, your next best course of action is to try to get in touch with either an attorney who has represented a business similar to yours or contact the trade association to which your business belongs. Try to obtain copies of previous contracts that have come up in the normal course of the operations of a business similar to yours. By analyzing these contracts and modifying them to suit your needs, you can create your own contract forms that can be used whenever similar situations arise in your own business.

Once you get copies of these forms, spend time going through each paragraph, making sure that you understand the points that are being made. Many times the other party involved in a negotiation won't spend as much time with clauses and paragraphs that they consider to be boiler plate and will concentrate on areas where there are blanks to be filled in. This carelessness naturally works to your advantage if you've been the party who designed the boiler plate and the language is favorable to your position.

Negotiating Your Lease

You will negotiate many contracts in the course of your business, but none is likely to be any more important than the lease you negotiate for your primary place of operation because rent today is one of the largest expenses in any business. Consequently, how you negotiate your lease terms will affect your business not only in its first year of operation, but also in many years to come. In addition, you should exert great care in negotiating the lease to protect yourself in case you are unable to meet its terms for any reason. You will naturally want to minimize your liability, restricting the lease to the business and its assets, as opposed to your personal assets.

The first general premise in signing a lease is to understand that all clauses in a lease are negotiable. This having been said, your ability to negotiate the lease will depend on many variables, including the general stability of the marketplace in which you are operating. Real estate fluctuates between owners' markets and renters' markets. By this I mean that there are times in the economy where landlords have favorable negotiating positions and other times when lots of space is available and tenants have the upper hand in the negotiations. One of the most important things you can do before you begin to negotiate is to conduct

> **PROFIT STRATEGY:**
> Create a file of contracts and forms that you use in business. Over the years this file will save you thousands of dollars in the cost of drafting new agreements.

a survey of available space to see what else is available. Knowing the strength of your bargaining position will help you determine whether you should be more flexible in your negotiation or hold your ground.

The location of your business will certainly be one of the most important business decisions you can make. Nevertheless, you cannot give up everything to get a good business location if the price you pay puts you out of business. The result is that lease negotiations are a give-and-take exchange between the parties. You will have to be flexible on certain things and expect the landlord to be flexible on other points, or you will have to walk away. Ideally speaking, you as a tenant should negotiate the shortest-term lease possible for the lowest rent as you can pay with as many options to renew as you can get. Within that framework are lots of variables and the variables do become difficult.

When negotiating the length of term, I have said that you want it to be as short as possible. As you are negotiating with the landlord, if you insist on a month-to-month lease, you will certainly show the landlord weakness because he or she will consider your desire for a short-term lease as a lack of confidence in the potential of your business. Consequently, you may feel that you need to start out with at least a minimum one-year lease. From a practical standpoint, it may very well be that the minimum acceptable lease in your area is three years or even five years. You can discover this and other typical standards by doing an early investigation. As a general rule, the three-year lease probably is a reasonable standard to expect the landlord to ask you to sign. The exceptions will vary and also depend on any improvements that the landlord had to do to make the property ready for your occupancy. If he had to expend a great amount of money to fix up the property from its preceding occupant, then he will want to make sure you are planning to be in the property for a long time, so he will be able to recoup his costs of fixing the property to meet your needs. If you sign only a three-year lease, don't expect much in terms of landlord-paid property improvements.

However, if you are willing and able to sign a longer-term lease, you can be more demanding in terms of what you expect from the owner. Perhaps one of your negotiating points would be that the owner rebuild the space more to your specifications. Another possibility if you sign a longer-term lease is that the first three to six months are free rent. Again, all of these points are negotiating items and much depends not only on your skill in handling those negotiations, but also on the competitive market for rental real estate at the time you are looking for space.

Negotiating your lease rate also is important. Again, the market will help dictate exactly the available ranges. One of the elements is the type of space. Class A office space generally is a high-rise building in a major metropolitan location. This type of space normally carries a premium because of its location and the prestige attached to it. Space of lesser class is determined both by location and the type of building. For example, a building converted from residential use generally is considered C class type space and will rent for less than the same square footage in an A or B class space. Each type of space class has its own comparables, and you should exercise care in getting quotes on space to make sure you are comparing apples to apples.

Once you have determined the type of class space you will be renting and have developed the comparables for your area, matching it to the subject space is relatively easy. If it is better space, you may be willing to pay more to have a finer-looking facility. You should exercise care to lease a space in the bottom range for the type of class you desire. This is important if you ever have difficulties in your business and are forced either to sublease or assign your space to another tenant. By having a favorable lease, you will have a built-in value if you need to get out of your lease. This occurs when tenants are able to negotiate favorable long-term leases at rates that do not have substantial escalation provisions. By locking in rates that stay below market value, you have created a built-in equity, similar to the equity in a piece of real estate you have purchased. Good leases have value and can be bargained with if you have to sell your business or move out of the property.

The third area of importance to consider when negotiating a lease is to obtain an option to renew. In many cases, landlords sometimes throw in an option to renew without much bargaining. At first blush, it might seem that the landlord should favor an option to renew because he has a reliable tenant who continues to remain in the property. The key points, however, are the terms of renewal. If the option to renew is at the current rate or at a slight increase, then the lease becomes more favorable to the tenant as time passes. Chances are that sometime during your occupancy on a long-term lease, if you can structure only slight increases in rent, the lease for your space will become more valuable to you. If it doesn't increase in value, or you decide on another location, then you simply don't exercise your option to renew. With an option to renew, a tenant has everything to gain and nothing to lose. Thus, you should always try to get as many options as is feasible without giving up on other points in your lease.

Cautions and Caveats

One problem that inevitably comes up in a lease is the landlord's request for personal guarantees of yourself and potentially others in the corporation. The guarantee could make the signer personally obligated to pay the rent if the company doesn't. It is easy for me to sit here and tell you not to sign a guarantee personally ever as personal liability protection is one of the reasons you formed the corporation in the first place. However, practically, unless your corporation has very substantial assets, the landlord is likely to ask for personal guarantees. At that point, you can either sign, walk away, or negotiate. For example, on a three-year lease you might negotiate a guarantee for only the first year. If that doesn't work, you might try limiting your guarantee to one year or six months or anything you can negotiate less than the three years. Try to restrict the guarantee to only one officer and to arrange for that officer to be indemnified by the corporation if he or she is ever asked to pay up.

There are several areas in a lease where making a small mistake can lead to a big expense. One example is common

> **PROFIT STRATEGY:**
> Landlords and lenders often ask for the joint guarantee of your spouse. Again, ultimately it will be a point of negotiation, but I encourage you to draw the line at that point. If you can't keep your personal assets from being exposed, at least protect those of your spouse.

area maintenance expenses (CAM). These charges are made in both professional office space and retail space. The CAM expense is for the maintenance and operation of the common areas of the property. For example, even though you may be occupying 2,000 square feet in a retail strip center, some spaces, such as the parking lots, walkways, grass, and landscaping, belong to the entire group because it is deemed that each tenant benefits from them. To pay for these expenses, a separate charge frequently is negotiated in the lease by the landlord, called the CAM expense.

Carefully read what these CAM expenses are. Make sure that the lease does not call for unreasonable increases in the CAM expenses. In fact, it is preferable to see it raised by set percentages rather than by actual expenses. If the actual expenses are put into the lease, then a landlord can be sloppy in her or his care of the property or overspend for maintenance without being penalized for not saving money. Another important point: if you are leasing a new property, make sure the amount of CAM the landlord is using as an initial figure is similar to that for other similar types of properties. Frequently, new landlords will put in low CAM rates in the early years of a property to entice tenants into the building. Then, tenants discover the CAM expenses go up rapidly as the property gets older and needs more improvement and because the landlord stops subsidizing some of the expenses that were artificially lower, to make them more attractive to tenants.

Be sure that the landlord is required to maintain the property in compliance with both federal and state laws. The purpose of adding this kind of language is to make sure that any change to the building to comply with the Americans with Disabilities Act (ADA), for example, would be the responsibility of the landlord. Without such language protection, you may find yourself forced by the federal government to spend a lot to comply with the act, which requires general access to *all* customers.

Another similar issue applies to the Environmental Protection Agency (EPA). In this era of environmental concerns, the EPA has some very strong laws regarding the cleanup of any property determined to have an environmental problem. To the extent this kind of legislation or regulation can be construed as enforceable against a tenant, language and protection should be inserted to guarantee that the landlord indemnify the tenant against any environmental problems that develop.

Signs sometimes are an extremely important aspect of your business. If it is important for the operation of your business to have a sign that is visible from the road, then you must insert a clause to this effect in your lease. Sign ordinances are changing all across the country, and if a sign is required for your business, you can't afford to put yourself in a position where the landlord changes his mind or a municipal ordinance changes, forcing your sign to be removed from the property. If anything like this would dramatically affect your business operation, then you need to make sure a clause is inserted in your lease that protects you, often by giving you the option to terminate your lease.

Repairs and maintenance often are a disputable point in leases because they are sometimes intentionally left vague. The thought is that if they are left vague, the pressure can be put on the tenant to pay these items because without being fixed or corrected, their business will suffer. Lack of clarity reflects both bad business practice and poor lease drafting. It should be very clear who is responsible for any repairs or maintenance to the property and who in fact must pay for repairs and maintenance. Make sure that each point is specifically itemized in your contract and don't rely on vague generalities.

One aspect that often is overlooked by tenants is a prohibition for the landlord to put in a competing business in the same facility as the one you occupy. Remember, landlords are in the business of leasing space, and whether or not they have two print shops side by side is of no real consequence to them unless they are getting a percentage of the income from the business. To make sure your competition doesn't become your neighbor, you should insert a clause into your lease that prevents the owner from leasing to another tenant in a business competing with yours.

These are some of the problems and conflicts that arise in the negotiations between a landlord and a tenant for

> **PROFIT STRATEGY:**
> If there is any creative aspect to your business, make sure it is protected in the lease. If it is important, put it in writing, or you will likely wish you had.

business space. Remember that all of these items and more have been dealt with in the past. If you are concerned or confused in this area, it may be wise to spend time with a real estate attorney that has handled the negotiation of commercial properties.

Another option is to hire a commercial real estate agent who specializes in the leasing field. Make sure you have an agreement that they are representing you rather than the landlord. Either of these two professionals, if experienced in this area, will likely be able to save you a multiple of the cost of their services. In either case, I would hire the attorney or the real estate professional on an hourly rate rather than for a percentage of the lease. If you take control of their time, this will save you money.

CHAPTER SIX

HOW TO HIRE YOUR BEST EMPLOYEES

Making the decision to hire employees will be one of your first major decisions if you want to grow. It is a difficult decision because it entails bringing on additional overhead that you may or may not have contemplated. In addition, any time you bring in new people, your work environment changes. Sometimes it's better, sometimes it's not. You need to understand that hiring employees is serious business, and you need to be prepared for how it may affect you. As soon as it is practical, you should develop a set of guidelines regarding your employees. The policies should be in writing and should cover such topics as wages, promotions, vacations, days off, sick days, and benefits.

Planning for Employees

To get the right employees for any job, the key is to match your needs to the skill of a potential employee. To determine those needs, it is always better to write them down to get them firmly in your mind. Once you have a job description on paper, decide what skills a person must have to fill the job. Make sure your prospective employees read and understand what will be expected of them. Remember that simply describing a job title can be confusing: everyone has a preconceived notion about what the title means. Spelling out the function will help clear the confusion.

There are two primary ways to find job applicants if you can't get a referral. One is to run advertisements, the second is through employment agencies. Ads are cheaper in immediate dollars, though the agencies may be less time-consuming because they screen applicants for you. I prefer to work with an agency. If you work with an agency, make sure you spend initial time with them so they will understand you and your business. The first time they send you an unqualified person, immediately sit down with your contact and explain the problem. They should be made to understand that you are using them as a time saver. If they aren't screening your applicants properly, you'll choose another agency who will. If they fail the second time, do exactly that—find another agency.

Most agencies work on either a fee basis or a "temp-to-perm" arrangement. Temp-to-perm means that the employee works for a certain number of weeks for your company on a temporary basis, and if everything works out is permanently hired. I like this arrangement because it gives you an opportunity really to get to know the employee before he or she is full-time. This way, if it doesn't work out, it's easier to say you've made a mistake and make a quick change.

Employment agencies aren't cheap, but like everything else, the price is negotiable.

> **PROFIT STRATEGY:**
> Plan before you hire. Hire only when you must, and never be afraid to let an employee who is not doing his or her job go.

If you use one agency for all of your hires, they should be willing to give you higher discounts on new employees. They have to make a living, too, but subsequent hires should be cheaper because the agency didn't have to spend more on marketing to get you as a client.

One growing trend is employee leasing. Instead of hiring full-time employees, you can lease employees from a company that pays them full-time. You pay the company by the hour, and they take care of employee benefits, wages, taxes, and the like. There can be advantages to this system, particularly if you are unsure how long you will need help in a particular area of your business. In addition, it gives you the flexibility of having employees only when you need them. Naturally, there also are disadvantages. Cost is certainly one. The leasing company also needs to make a profit, so it charges you more per hour than what the employee is really worth.

The leasing companies will say that this isn't so because they say that they can negotiate better rates on health insurance and other corporate costs. Maybe some can, but every time I've tried to cost out the benefits, it seems to cost a little more to go with a leasing company.

Another disadvantage is that it may be more difficult to create company loyalty if your employees are getting checks from a leasing company. You definitely do not have control over the talent pool, repeat employees, or personal favorites.

As a company grows, you may find that your employee needs are changing frequently. One solution is to use temporary agencies to assist you. The temporary agency charges more than you would if you hired an employee on an hourly basis, but you save money on expenses such as retirement benefits and health insurance that you don't have to pay (about 6% to 7% of the gross income you pay the employee). Typically, you also save 11% of gross income on social security, unemployment insurance, and workers' compensation. Payments for time not worked, including vacations, holidays, and sick days usually amount to about 9% of gross. That's about 26% more of the employee's wages that you can pay to the temporary agency compared to the cost of having the employee on your payroll. In addition, if you hire your own employees, it is not as easy to let them go because you know they don't have another job to go to. The employee from the agency can go back to the agency and be reassigned. The other advantage to using temporary agencies is that you can quickly gear up or down based on your specific work load. This allows you to add expenses only when you have offsetting additional income.

Temporary employees are becoming such a part of the corporate structure that you are even starting to see professionals working on a temporary basis. Attorneys, accountants, doctors, and nurses are just a few examples of how the temporary employee market is expanding.

The key to successful use of temporaries is to monitor constantly their use and cost. Be quick to stop using them

> **PROFIT STRATEGY:**
> Hiring employees is a negotiation process. If you do it yourself, set absolute criteria for salary and benefits before the interviews. If you use an agency to help you, also remember to negotiate the agency's fee.

when they aren't needed, and don't let your other employees use them simply to dump off work that they don't personally like doing.

Hiring an Employee

The first step in hiring an employee starts with the interview. This process seems innocuous enough; yet for the unsuspecting business owner, there are many potential pitfalls in the process itself. In today's society, where lawsuits are prevalent, some people actually go through employment interviews knowing that they are likely to be asked questions that are improper and thus, lay a foundation for a settlement, if not a potential discrimination lawsuit.

To the novice employer, it would seem that the process of hiring an employee and conducting an interview is a simple one. Unfortunately, it is fraught with problems. As an employer, you simply cannot ask all of the things you would like to know about an employee because the federal government, as well as the states, has determined that certain types of questions are illegal and/or improper as they may be used to discriminate or take away certain rights of the employee. You may be the employer, but you certainly do not have the rights you think you do when it comes to hiring employees.

To assist you in developing a series of questions that you may ask potential employees, I have categorized certain topics that are likely to be covered in an employment interview. In each of these topics, I will advise you on the types of questions that I feel are areas of illegality or simply improper based on an overview of employment laws.

> **PROFIT STRATEGY:**
> "Caveat employer" or "let the employer beware" should be your theme when interviewing employees. Be cautious of what you say and how you say it, or the next time you hear it could be in court.

Age

Although this topic seems rather straightforward, questions that you might normally ask someone at a cocktail party are not allowed in an interview. You cannot ask someone his or her age. You cannot ask the person's date of birth, because that would, of course, indicate age. You cannot ask questions about the age of children or of a spouse. These questions all tend to disclose the age of an individual and would be considered skirting the law. Federal and state laws are very serious about age discrimination and woe be the employer who attempts to skirt the issue by trying to be sneaky. One age-related question you can ask is whether the person is at least 18 years of age or older. Some laws cover the employment and treatment of minors. With that exception, you should avoid the age questions.

Race or Color

It should be obvious to almost any American that race or color is a protected status under the Constitution, and any questions or comments regarding them are improper, not only in the interview process, but also during employment. This question spills over to the area of photographs of prospective employees. In general, I would suggest that photographs not be requested prior to hiring. Although there could be justifiable reasons for requesting a photograph, the implications that a photograph may be used to determine race, color, national origin, or disability would all be violations of federal law.

National Origin

The national origin of an applicant for employment is a protected piece of information under the Constitution. During the interview process, employers should avoid any questions about not only the applicant's nationality, but also the origin of their parents, spouse, or relatives. This restriction also includes vague questions such as, "What is your native tongue?" Although this question in and of itself is not discriminatory, the implication is that you may be attempting to find out the national origin of the individual, and consequently, such a question would be improper. Another example of a question that could be used in an attempt to get around the law would be regarding a person's name. For example, a simple question during the interview process, such as "That certainly is an interesting name. What is its place of origin?" would be unacceptable.

Religion

You cannot ask prospective employees what their religion is, whether they observe certain religious holidays, or whether they attend religious services on any particular day.

Gender

All questions that might indicate a preference to hiring a member of a particular sex should be eliminated from the interview process. These questions would include the number and ages of children, whether child care is necessary, whether the individual is on birth control, or whether the individual is pregnant. All of these areas are extremely sensitive and can cause problems for an employer. Birth control and child care questions all center not only around gender, but also the entire issue of children and their care. These questions should be avoided.

Disability or Handicap

Under the Americans with Disabilities Act (ADA), all questions regarding whether or not a person has the physical or mental capabilities of performing a job are illegal. The only thing that you can ask a prospective employee is about his or her ability to do a certain job-related task. The best procedure in this situation is to show a list of job-related functions and ask the individual whether or not they would have any difficulty performing these functions. Any other medical examination or inquiry regarding the individual prior to hiring should be handled with great care.

Arrest Record

The key element in any questions regarding an arrest is to be sure the question asks only about convictions. In other words, "Have you ever been convicted of a crime?" would be proper, as opposed to "Have you ever been arrested?", which would be improper. Even regarding a conviction, it would be advisable to design the questions to determine whether or not the particular conviction relates to something necessary to perform the duties of the job.

Military Experience

It would be acceptable to ask an applicant whether or not they have served in the military, including which branch of service. On the other hand, it would be improper to ask about military discharge and the reasons for such a discharge.

Weight or Height

Questions to applicants regarding their weight or height should be avoided because they may be construed as posed to determine any physical handicap or disability. Many states also have passed laws covering medically related problems such as AIDS. You should review your state section of this book for any additional laws your state may have in addition to federal laws.

Economic Status

Employers should avoid any questions regarding current or past credit problems, including any liabilities, credit ratings, or bankruptcies. These questions would also include whether or not the prospective individual is a homeowner or not.

Citizenship

It is acceptable to ask someone whether he or she is authorized to work in the United States because it is illegal to hire someone who is not. However, care should be made to make sure that these questions do not go into the nature of determining where a person was born or what country they are a citizen of. It is easy to get trapped in these circumstances by asking people where they are from, or the citizenship of their relatives.

Education

Educational questions are fairly open as long as they are relevant for the position at hand.

Union Membership

All questions involving whether or not a person belongs to a union or has belonged to a union should be avoided.

References

The key to working with references is to make sure that you do not ask any question of a reference that you could not ask the individual. If you do, it will simply be determined that you are using other sources of information provided by applicants to discriminate against them. Following up on references of people who are willing to provide professional or character references is acceptable.

These issues are the main areas of concern that you should have as you handle the interview process. It is very important for you to secure a good employment application and to make sure that it is completed before you interview the prospect. The application makes an excellent starting point in your discussion interview and provides you a written record of experiences and former employers' names and addresses (see Exhibit 6-1). In addition, during the interview process, I would suggest that you take careful notes regarding questions that you ask and maintain these in a file for at least a year. These types of records, while not absolute proof of what went on in the interview process, could certainly be used as evidence in court to help sway the opinion of the judge hearing the case of any potential employee-related lawsuit.

Exhibit 6-1
Application for Employment

Name: _____ Date: _____
       Last   First   Middle

Present Address: _____ SS# _____

Telephone Number: _____ Driver's License #: _____

Indicate dates you attended school:

Elementary: From _____ to _____ High School: From _____ to _____

College: From _____ to _____

Other: (Specify type and dates) _____

Have you been bonded? _____ If yes, in what job? _____

List below all present and past employment, beginning with most recent (include military service, if relevant):

Name and address of company	From Mo./Yr.	To Mo./Yr.	Name of Supervisor	Reason for Leaving	Weekly Salary	Describe the work you did:

May we contact the employers listed? _____ If not, indicate which ones you do not wish us to contact: _____

Remarks: _____
_____
_____
_____
_____

One of the important aspects of a successful interview is preparation. Prior to the interview, develop a list of open-ended questions to ask your prospects. Try to get them involved in the discussion. Although communications skills are not always important for every job, what the applicant does communicate can give you insight as to who the prospective employees are, how experienced they are, and whether they can do the work you need done in the manner you expect. Let the employee talk, and listen to the responses.

Most employees are honest in the interview process. However, honesty should not be taken for granted, and references should be checked. Hiring an employee is an extremely expensive proposition, and the time spent to check the references is well worth it. Generally, the most reliable references are from previous employers. Personal references will obviously be biased. I can't imagine anyone listing a personal reference that would give anything but a glowing report.

Make sure you don't make any promises in the interview that you can't keep. This would include making statements that could later be construed to imply that something would be done or a needed benefit added. For example, a statement such as, "We are looking into getting insurance for our employees and expect to have it shortly" could be considered a promise that insurance was forthcoming in the near future. It always is a good idea to have an employee manual in which you state policies that are acceptable and those that are not. These manuals, as well as signed statements by employees regarding certain policies, will help you in any situation if you might find yourself having to let one of your employees go.

I think that any time you hire an employee you must think about the possibility that sometime you and this employee will part ways. How you have conducted yourself within that time and documented the employment will help you in case any lawsuit ensues. If an employee must be disciplined, care should be taken to document the employment file as to the specifics for the discipline.

Working with New Employees

A new job is a stressful situation for any employee. To get maximum efficiency, you should try to make the employee feel as comfortable as possible from the beginning. One of the best ways to accomplish this is to explain clearly what is expected. I think that everyone operates better once he or she understands the rules and the parameters to follow. Some offices are formal and strict about everything, from the clothes you wear to how you deal with your time. These companies have strict limitations on personal calls and chatting with fellow employees. You can imagine the stress a new employee coming from a casual atmosphere might feel in this type of environment.

Consider assigning a "buddy" to help the new employee settle in. This "buddy" can help the new person feel more like part of the team and clue her or him in on everything from lunch shifts to coffee breaks. In addition to making the new employee feel comfortable, it is a good idea to explain again the job they were hired for. People who understand their responsibilities are much more likely to perform in the manner you expect.

The final step in dealing with a new employee is re-evaluation. It is important to determine as quickly as possible if you have hired the right person for the job. If you haven't, the faster you correct the situation, the better off you and the new employee will be. Everyone makes mistakes in hiring. Don't increase your mistake by keeping the person simply because he or she is new. If you determine that the employee isn't right for the job for whatever reason, change direction. Keeping the employee and hoping things will improve are a waste of everyone's time.

CHAPTER SEVEN

MASTERING EMPLOYMENT LAWS

I wish I could make this chapter go away, but I can't. Employment law isn't easy, but it is important. Once you have employees, your control over your business changes, and you must subrogate your own ideas to the law or suffer its consequences. In this chapter, I have attempted to summarize the major laws that govern the actions of an employer. It may not be a "fun" read, but it will likely be a profitable one.

The Fair Labor Standards Act

The Fair Labor Standards Act (FLSA) is a federal law that defines the minimum wage, equal pay, overtime, child labor, and recording requirements that a company must keep. As a general rule, a business comes under the FLSA if it is engaged in commerce or the production of goods for commerce or if it is handling, selling, or producing goods that have already been moved or produced for commerce with a minimum gross sales volume of $500,000. Even if your business is not considered covered under the act, individual employees may be separately covered under the act if they are somehow engaged in interstate commerce. The bottom line, as you might guess, is that, if anything in your business has to do with interstate commerce, you're probably going to come under the act.

The FLSA requires payment to individuals of a minimum wage standard for each hour worked. The minimum wage was changed in August of 1996 to $4.75 per hour beginning October 1, 1996, and is increasing to $5.15 per hour on September 1, 1997. Individuals who receive tips may be credited with up to 50% of the minimum wage for the tips they receive, but the employer must be able to prove that they received at least the minimum wage.

The federal act requires that employees who work more than forty hours in a work week be paid an overtime rate calculated at one and one-half times the employee's regular hourly rate. There are numerous exceptions to this rule based on the specific classification of the employee. The best way to make any kind of final determination for overtime payment is to contact the federal Department of Labor and obtain a copy of their bulletin describing in complete detail all of the rules and regulations regarding it. I got in trouble with these rules one time when I let an employee work additional hours at the same rate instead of hiring someone else. I thought it reasonable to let someone make more money who wanted to work more.

PROFIT STRATEGY:
Keeping employee records and time cards are a pain, and employees hate punching in. Unfortunately, only your good records will save you in an audit.

Unfortunately, our firm got audited, and the Labor Department told me that, "No one in America has the right to work more than forty hours per week because it keeps others from getting a job." I learned that you can't always do what you think is right for your business or your employees.

Two of the most commonly asked questions regarding work time and the minimum wage are whether or not rest periods and meal periods are covered. Generally speaking, rest periods are considered to be primarily for the benefit of the employer (yes, that's right, I said employer, not employee). Thus, short periods (less than 20 minutes) for breaks are considered payable by the employer. Meals are different. If the employee is relieved of all duties during that time, the employer does not have to pay.

The act requires close recordkeeping for all employees. The records are divided into two separate periods: one three years in length, the other two years. The three-year record requirements are for employee payroll records, including W-2s and ledgers.

Included under this category would be any employment contracts and purchase and sales records for the company. Records that must be kept for two years include time cards, work schedules, any deductions, or any records regarding the employment time of the individuals.

In maintaining payroll records, it is important to include several items, such as the time and day of week the employee worked, the regular pay rate, any overtime pay rate that was authorized and the amount paid during that period of time, dates of each payment, the gender of the individual, as well as the specific work requirements and the actual wages paid during that period. The FLSA regulations require that you display an official wage and hour poster in a conspicuous place in your office. The posters are provided free from the Department of Labor. Although the rule seems simple enough to understand, many small businesses hate to clutter their facilities with regulatory posters. I would recommend that you comply because the poster is one of the first things that the Labor Department checks if it ever investigates you. The thought is that if you don't comply with the simplest things, you're probably sloppy in your other recordkeeping.

PROFIT STRATEGY:
The Labor Department is serious about child labor. It doesn't matter whether kids want to work for you or are friends of your family. I was fined once when a sixteen-year-old who wanted to make some extra money for Christmas was not a person to hire.

Child Labor Laws

The Federal Labor Standards Act, as well as the various state laws, regulates and prohibits the employment of children in businesses, although the children of the owner are usually exempt. With that exception, the business owner should avoid hiring any children in the business. As a general rule, the definition of a *child* would be somebody sixteen years of age or younger. However, there are exceptions to this, depending on your state. Check the state's rules regarding child labor laws in Chapter 15.

In addition to the general prohibition against hiring children, some laws also govern hiring underage individuals to do hazardous work. In this category, children under the age of eighteen are considered protected. Hazardous employment would include places where there is heavy manufacturing, mining, powerful machinery, or work in transportation, warehousing, or construction.

Discrimination

The major law governing the rights of employees to be free of discrimination in the workplace is Title VII of the Civil Rights Act of 1964. This act governs employees in public and private work and includes provisions on discrimination for race, color, religion, gender, or national origin. The Civil Rights Act applies to businesses who employ fifteen or more people in each of twenty consecutive weeks. The act is enforced by the federal Equal Opportunity Employment Commission (EEOC), which has district offices throughout the United States.

Under the Civil Rights Act, an employer cannot treat an individual who is within a group designated as a protected class differently. Examples commonly heard about are the hiring of one individual of one race over another individual of a different race. The act also prohibits reverse discrimination equally. The act protects not only the employee who was discriminated against, but also anyone who might raise the issue when looking after the employee. This portion of the act is referred to as Retaliation and would keep someone who has raised the issue of discrimination from being fired.

> **PROFIT STRATEGY:**
> Sexual harassment is a problem, and it should be stopped. Having said that, I also am aware of how charges of sexual harassment are being used as extortion against companies. Be very careful. Document your actions and those of your managers.

Sexual harassment in the workplace has become more newsworthy because of the increase of women in the workplace. Basically two types of sexual harassment are illegal under the act. The first type is referred to as the *quid pro quo*, where an employer looks for sexual favors in exchange for employment. The other type of sexual harassment is less obvious, but no less a violation under the act. This type of harassment includes the creation or continued operation of a hostile work environment that is considered offensive under the sexual harassment guidelines.

Employers used to believe that discrimination that went on in the workplace that did not involve officers or directors of the company would keep the company from being involved in a discriminatory lawsuit. This is no longer the case. Employers must make sure that the workplace is safe, and this includes freedom from working in an environment in which sexual harassment exists.

One of the less known aspects of the act is that it also protects women from discrimination because of pregnancy, childbirth, or any similarly related condition under a specific Pregnancy Discrimination Act. The act keeps an employer from using any element of the pregnancy to keep an individual from either holding or getting a certain job. This would include requiring someone to leave the employment at a certain stage of the pregnancy. An employer can, however, stop a pregnant individual from doing certain types of work if she is not performing up to certain standards. This would be true of any individual, so it is not a particular bias against women in general or a pregnant individual.

The Civil Rights Act also prohibits discrimination against applicants based on any religious belief. In fact, an employer is required to make some accommodations to allow an individual to exercise religious belief. The issue always arises as to how far that should be extended. Most recently, a problem arose with regard to the religious belief of a basketball player in the NBA and whether or not he should be required to stand during the playing of the U.S. national anthem. Under his religious belief that act constituted a worship of something other than his higher authority. The issue was what accommodations should or could be made to that individual regarding allowing him to participate in his own faith, even though the standing for the national anthem was required under his contract. Fortunately, for both the NBA and the individual, a mutually satisfactory settlement was reached that allowed the individual to stand quietly during the anthem but not participate. However, the case shows a clear example of where confusion can arise within the law. If an individual desires to file a charge for violation of the Civil Rights Act, the charge must be filed within 180 days of the wrongful act.

Age Discrimination and Employment Act

The Age Discrimination and Employment Act (ADEA) was adopted as additional protection for individuals who were not covered under the Civil Rights Act because age was not considered a protected class. With the ADEA, employers who have twenty or more employees working for twenty consecutive weeks cannot discriminate when hiring or firing individuals because of their age. This act has been expanded to include the treatment that individual employees might receive within a company based on their age, even though they are not dismissed. For example, an employer cannot offer people who are under thirty-five better job opportunities than people who are fifty or older. Otherwise, that employment act would be considered discriminatory.

The act prohibits the mandatory or involuntary retirement of an employee, but certain compulsory retirement is permissible for executive-level employees in three cases: (1) for the two years immediately preceding their retirement they've been employed in an executive position; (2) they must be at least 65 years of age at retirement; and (3) they must be entitled upon retirement to immediate, nonforfeitable income of $44,000 per year.

Americans with Disabilities Act

The Americans with Disabilities Act (ADA) of 1990 prohibits discrimination against any person with disabilities. As of July 26, 1994, the act covers all private employers with fifteen or more employees. To be protected under the act, the employee must meet certain statutory definitions as to disability. These are defined as: (1) a physical or mental impairment that substantially limits one or more major life activities; or (2) the record or history of such an impairment; or (3) being regarded by the employer as having such an impairment. The act lists the following conditions to be considered as disabilities under the act: blindness, deafness, speech impediments, cerebral palsy, epilepsy, muscular dystrophy, multiple sclerosis, AIDS, cancer, heart disease, diabetes, mental retardation, and emotional illness.

To be protected under the act, an individual must be considered specifically "qualified" for the work to be performed. This means that, with reasonable accommodations, they can do the essential functions of the job. This raises the importance for employers of defining in writing the specific qualifications and duties of a certain position for which they are looking to hire an individual. Written job descriptions will help prove what the requirements are for a particular job. One of the tricky areas of the law is the requirement to provide reasonable accommodations to a qualified individual that lets them perform the job function. These reasonable accommodations might very well require an employer to make changes in the physical construction of his facilities, such as adopting a ramp within the office to allow wheelchair access to certain areas. Modifying work schedules to allow a person to take extra breaks or use computer equipment that has been adapted to a certain disability would all qualify as reasonable accommodations. Failure to make these accommodations is a discriminatory act under the law.

A major exception to the Disabilities Act comes under the "undue hardship" rule. This rule as expressed by states that the accommodation required under the act is not necessary if it can be shown that it creates an undue hardship on behalf of the employer. An example of such an undue hardship would be an extremely costly alteration far beyond the value of the work to be performed. It is obvious that this is an imprecise rule, but various factors such as the financial resources of the employer can be considered in making that determination.

This section was one of the major concerns that small businesses had when the act was adopted.

The Occupational Safety and Health Act

The Occupational Safety and Health Act (OSHA) of 1970 was established to provide safe and healthy working conditions for every employee. All employers are required to provide a workplace free of safety and health hazards and to comply with the various rules and regulations established by the administration.

Primary responsibility for governing the act lies with the secretary of labor. OSHA's national headquarters are located at the following address: Occupational Safety and Health Administration, 200 Constitution Avenue, N.W., Washington, DC 20210; telephone: (202) 523-6091.

OSHA is a broad act that covers a variety of workplace safety- and health-related problems. In general, normal office environments are not concerned with OSHA regulations unless they operate under what are reasonably unsafe conditions. If, however, you are in the manufacturing business, a restaurant, or any business involving food, agriculture, or medical byproducts and waste, you should know that these types of industry are of greater concern to the federal government because of potential health problems.

In general, OSHA conducts spot investigations of businesses throughout the country, which is one of their most effective means of determining whether or not violations occur. These inspections are made at the open request of employers, and if they object, it is up to OSHA to determine whether or not they want to seek a search warrant to conduct the investigation. The on-the-spot checks are conducted based on a certain procedure that OSHA maintains regarding office inspections. You are allowed to be advised of your rights during any inspection.

To assist the government in protecting the public against unsafe working hazards, all employers must keep records as to any injuries and illnesses that occur at the place of employment. The employers must maintain a record of any injury or illness that results in a fatality, lost work days, or transfer to another job or medical treatment other than minor first aid.

Workers' Compensation Law

The purpose of workers' compensation is to pay injured workers benefits for accidents that occur on the job regardless of fault. With the exception of intentional injuries and violations of safety rules, including the use of drugs or alcohol, most job-related injuries are covered under workers' compensation, and the employee is protected from the expense.

All employers are required to have workers' compensation. If you are in the construction industry, you are required to have workers' compensation for all your employees.

Employers can fulfill the requirements of workers' compensation law in several ways. (1) They can obtain an insurance policy, probably the most widely used method of complying with workers' compensation rules, (2) by establishing individual self-insurance funds. Groups of employers may collectively get together to establish funds for workers' compensation. The State Department of Insurance governs these self-insurance funds. If there is a deficiency in the fund, the employer would be responsible for any deficiency over and above what he has paid into the pool. (3) Individual self-insurance. Certain individual employers with a net worth of at least $250,000 may insure themselves as self-insured under the workers' compensation rules.

If an employer fails to obtain coverage and an accident occurs, the employee can require the employer to pay the workers' compensation benefits directly to the individual, or he can sue the employer to collect. In addition to this civil action, the Department of Labor also can assess penalties of up to $100 per day as well as lump-sum penalties for each employee who has not been properly covered under the act.

One of the biggest issues under workers' compensation rules revolves around employers who try to classify employees as independent contractors or subcontractors to skirt the requirements of paying the unemployment compensation costs. As workers' compensation laws hold individual employers personally responsible for the cost of any injury to an employee, I would recommend that any employer attempting to classify employees into exempted categories should do so only under the review and advice of an attorney who specializes in workers' compensation law.

The Employee Polygraph Protection Act of 1988

The Employee Polygraph Protection Act (EPPA) of 1988 makes lie detector testing of employees and applicants for a job illegal. The purpose of the law is to protect employees from being forced to take a test that has not been proven to be completely accurate. As with many of the other laws we have discussed, there are various exemptions. Employers who are involved in the distribution of certain controlled substances may administer polygraph tests in limited circumstances. The act is authorized and enforced by the secretary of labor, and specific information as to whether or not you may qualify for an exception can be determined by contacting that office directly.

The Electronic Communications Privacy Act of 1986

The Electronic Communications Privacy Act (ECPA) of 1986 prohibits the use of wire or other electronic communications to intercept information regarding an employee. The general guidelines under this act allow certain monitoring of employees if they are aware of it. In addition, monitoring and taping by telephone are allowed so long as all of the parties are informed that monitoring is going on and a "beep" tone is placed on the recording every so often to remind all of the parties that the conversation is being recorded.

The Family and Medical Leave Act

The Family and Medical Leave Act (FMLA) went into effect on June 30, 1995. It allows eligible employees to take up to twelve weeks of unpaid leave in each year for family or medical reasons. The act requires all employers to grant such leave and allow employees to return to a position equivalent to the one that they had when they left. Employers are covered under the act if they have fifty or more employees during twenty or more consecutive weeks.

The act covers leave for the birth or adoption of a child, the care of an immediate family member with a serious health condition, or inability to work because of a serious health condition. The act is sometimes thought to apply only to women as it relates to the birth of a child, but as this would be discriminatory under the Civil Rights Act, the act specifically includes both men and women.

Employers who come under the act must post a notice explaining the rights to their employees. Employees who desire to qualify or to exercise their rights under the act must advise their employer at least thirty days in advance of their desire to take leave.

This chapter has given you an overview of federal employment laws, but you are cautioned to check your state laws as well. These are covered in Chapter 15.

CHAPTER EIGHT

BUYING AN EXISTING BUSINESS

Starting a new business from the ground up is not for everyone. You must be creative enough to design a workable plan, including having a product that both has value and is marketable. You must be extremely organized and have the ability to put together a variety of elements in a timely fashion to launch the business. Finally, you must be dependable enough to manage the business once the initial start-up phase is over.

Because of these diverse talents and requirements, many people find that they would rather purchase an existing business instead, particularly one that is already operating and successful. However, doing so also is more easily said than done. For every successful business that is available there are many that appear to be successful but in reality are operating on a thin line of profitability. Part of the problem that creates this situation is the conflicting nature between the buyer and the seller. The seller may be very interested in selling his business, but only at a price and on the terms which he considers to be fair. Frequently, his definition of fairness does not necessarily include profitability for the next individual. The seller frequently establishes a price based on what a new buyer could do to improve the business and make it more profitable. This idea may have merit, but this natural conflict between the buyer and seller must be resolved before a sale can take place. In the end, you need people who are willing to give and take to accomplish the objective that both parties have.

Where Do You Find Good Businesses for Sale?

I thought I would start this section out with the $64,000 question. Where do you find good businesses to buy? The most common place everybody immediately turns to is the newspaper and/or business brokers. Unfortunately, these are the least likely businesses to have long-term profitability. Not because there is anything wrong with either source, but because sellers who can't otherwise sell their businesses, always turn to the newspapers and/or business brokers. I am not going to suggest that you can never find a good deal from either of these two sources, because you can. But you will have to weed through a lot of businesses that are not good and you will have to be careful not only when investigating the business, but also when negotiating to make sure that you don't overpay for the business.

Well, if the first two sources are not the best place to look for businesses, where would I suggest that you turn? Before you start looking for a business to buy, you should first determine the specific type of business that you are most interested in. It really doesn't do any good to find a business that is for sale at a great price if you really aren't interested in operating it. Sure, you may be able to find a manager and operate it as an absentee owner, but I don't know of many. Most successful businesses today require a heavy time commitment on the part of the owner, or sooner or later there won't be a business to manage.

With that in mind, I'd like to suggest that you start with something that you are interested in. Once you know that, the best place to start is to look for a business that fits your needs. For example, if you wanted to buy a printing business, instead of looking in the newspaper for those that are available, I would make a list of every printing business within your general location. Then, I would contact the businesses in person and explore whether they are interested in selling. Surprisingly, in most cases, you will find a lot of people interested in selling their business, depending on the price and terms. In a relatively short amount of time you can discover the people operating the kind of business you want, in the area you want, and those who are interested in selling their business. From that point, it is a matter of negotiation. By contacting the owners directly, you have eliminated middle-man charges and you have demonstrated to the owner that you are a self-starting individual who may be able to continue to operate his or her business. This, of course, is one of the greatest fears a seller has in selling his business. He is afraid that the new owner will come in and mess up the business and never fully pay all of the amount owed. By demonstrating early on your confident attitude and ability to handle a situation, you may be more likely to hold some of the financing on the business as well.

Personal contact directly with the sellers is the best way to build rapport and open the door for arrangements. Many owners are in essence stuck in their business. They have no confidence in a purchaser, but they don't have anyone to leave the business to when they retire. These situations create the potential for the best type of business deal. You may have the opportunity to acquire a very successful business without a lot of cash upfront and with a smooth transition between the current owner and yourself. The owners will not only want you succeed but also help you to succeed because they have a vested interest in your future.

Trade sources are another good place to find businesses for sale. Key people within an industry or in companies on the periphery of the industry, such as suppliers, often know when businesses come up for sale. Every industry has a trade association and the association's official publication may hint of businesses for sale.

Pricing the Business

Determining the value of a business is the part of the buy–sell transaction most fraught with potential for differences of opinion. Buyers and sellers usually do not share the same perspective. Each has a distinct rationale for the price they think is right for the business, and that rationale may be based on logic or emotion.

The buyer may believe that the purchase will create synergy or an economy of scale because of the way the business will be operated under new ownership. The buyer also may see the business as an especially good lifestyle fit. These factors are likely to increase the amount of money a buyer is willing to pay for a business. The seller may have a greater than normal desire to sell because of financial difficulties or the death or illness of the owner or a member of the owner's family. Ultimately, however, for the transaction to come to conclusion, both parties must be satisfied with the price and be able to understand how it was determined.

Factors That Determine Value

The topic of business evaluation is so complex that any explanation short of an entire book does not do it justice. The process takes into account many, many variables and requires that a number of assumptions be made. To help with a good overview of the subject, the Small Business Association quotes six factors to use in determining the value of a business:

1. *Profit history.* How has the company performed over its historical life? A balance sheet and operating statement would help determine this.
2. *Current condition of the company* (facilities, completeness and accuracy of books and records, morale and so on). Will the new owner need to spend a lot of money? If so, the price will go down.
3. *Market demand.* How many other people would be interested in this type of business? The higher the demand, the higher the price.
4. *Economic conditions* (especially cost and availability of capital and any economic factors that directly affect the business). Businesses are much easier to buy at low prices during depressions or recessions. A robust economy will drive the price up.
5. *Ability to transfer goodwill or other intangible values to a new owner.* Is a CPA's practice sellable if you take away the person everyone has dealt with? Does a designer's company have the same value when the designer is dead?
6. *Future profit potential.* What can be changed to increase profits?

Businesses rarely change hands at fair market value because other factors often come into play in arriving at an agreed-upon price. Examples of these would include: special circumstances of the particular buyer and seller, terms of the sale, and tax consequences for the buyer and seller, which depend on how the transaction is structured.

Rule-of-Thumb Formulas

The problem with rule-of-thumb formulas is that they don't address all of the factors that have an impact on a business's value. They rely on a "one size fits all" approach when, in fact, no two businesses are identical. Rule-of-thumb formulas do, however, provide a quick means of establishing whether a price for a certain business is "in the ballpark." They normally are calculated as a percentage of either sales or asset values or a combination of both.

Comparables

Using comparable sales as a means of valuing a business has the same inherent flaw as rule-of-thumb formulas. Rarely, if ever, are two businesses truly comparable. However, businesses in the same industry do have some common characteristics, and a careful contrasting may allow a conclusion to be drawn about a range of value.

Balance Sheet Methods of Valuation

This approach calls for the assets of the business to be valued. It is most often used when the business being valued generates earnings primarily from its assets rather than the contributions of its employees, or when the cost of starting a business and getting revenues past the break even point doesn't greatly exceed the value of the business's assets.

There are a number of balance sheet methods of valuation, including book value, adjusted book value, and liquidation value. Each has its proper application. The most useful balance sheet method is the adjusted book value method. This method calls for the adjustment of each asset's book value to equal the cost of replacing that asset in its current condition. The total of the adjusted asset values is then offset against the sum of the liabilities to arrive at the adjusted book value.

Adjustments are frequently made to the book values of the following items:

1. *Accounts receivable.* Often adjusted down to reflect the lack of collectability of some receivables
2. *Inventory.* Usually adjusted down as it may be difficult to sell off all of the inventory at cost
3. *Real estate.* Frequently adjusted up because it often has appreciated in value since it was placed in service

4. *Furniture, fixtures, and equipment.* Adjusted up if those items in service (probably more than a few years) have been depreciated below their market value or adjusted down if the items have become obsolete

Income Statement Methods of Valuation

Although a balance sheet formula sometimes is the most accurate means to value a business, it is more common to use an income statement method. Income statement methods are most concerned with the profits or cash flow produced by the business's assets. One of the more frequently used methods is the discounted future cash flow method. This method calls for the future cash flows (before taxes and before debt service) of the business to be calculated using the four-step formula that follows.

Step 1

Historical cash flows are a good basis from which to project future cash flows. Cash flows are computed to include the following:

1. The net profit or loss of the business
2. The owner's salary (in excess of an equivalent manager's compensation)
3. Discretionary benefits paid to the owner (such as automobile allowance, travel expenses, personal insurance, and entertainment)
4. Interest (unless the buyer will be assuming the interest payment)
5. Nonrecurring expenses (such as nonrecurring legal fees)
6. Noncash expenses (such as depreciation and amortization)
7. Equipment replacements or additions (this figure should be deducted from the other numbers because it represents an expense the buyer will incur in generating future cash flows)

The future cash flows may be projected for a number of years, but for many small businesses it is not possible to project very far into the future before the projections become meaningless. Even with somewhat larger and more substantial businesses, it is difficult to project cash flows for more than five years.

Step 2

Once future cash flows have been projected, they must be discounted back to their present value by selecting a reasonable rate of return or capitalization rate for the buyer's investment. The selected rate of return varies substantially from one business to the next and is largely a function of risk. The lower the risk associated with an investment in a business, the lower the rate of return that is required. The rate of return required is usually in the 20% to 50% range and, for most businesses, it is in the 30% to 40% range. The present value of future cash flows can then be determined by using a financial calculator or a set of present value tables, which are available in most bookstores. Table 8-1 demonstrates how the conversion is made with a 40% rate of return.

Table 8-1. Calculating Future Cash Flows with a 40% Rate of Return

Year	Projected Cash Flow ($)	Discount Factor *	Present Value ($)
Year 1	360	0.714	257
Year 2	383	0.510	195
Year 3	397	0.364	145
Year 4	413	0.260	107
Year 5	438	0.186	81
			785†

* Based on 40% rate of return. The discount factor declines in each succeeding year.

† Present value of the sum of discounted projected cash flows. This figure is added to the residual value of the business to arrive at the total value of the business.

Step 3

One more calculation must now be done, the residual value of the business. The residual value is the present value of the business's estimated net worth at the end of the period of projected cash flows (in this example, at the end of five years). This is calculated by adding the current net worth of the business and future annual additions to the net worth. The annual additions are defined as the sum of each year's after-tax earnings, assuming no dividends are paid to stockholders. These additions are added to the current net worth, and that total is discounted to its present value to yield the residual value.

Step 4

The residual value is added to the present value sum of the projected future cash flows previously computed to arrive at a price for the business. Table 8-2 shows an example.

Table 8-2. Calculating the Residual Value

Year	Income after Tax ($)
Year 1	125
Year 2	131
Year 3	138
Year 4	144
Year 5	152
Total additions to net worth	690
Current net worth	910
Total net worth	1,600
Residual value (1,600 x 0.186)	298*

* Multiplying the total net worth by the discount factor used in the final year of projected cash flows yields the residual value. Adding the residual value of $298 to the present value sum of projected cash flows of $785 yields a value for the business of $1,083.

Although this formula is widely used, it cannot be applied in this simplistic form to arrive at a definitive value conclusion. It fails to address issues such as the buyer's working capital investment, the terms of the transaction, or the valuing of assets such as real estate that may not be needed to produce the projected cash flows. However, it is useful in establishing a price range for negotiation purposes.

Whatever multiplier you finally arrive at, the day eventually comes when you must arrange with the seller to prove his numbers. Never, and I repeat, never buy a business based on a double set of books. I am constantly amazed at hearing stories of people who are working with sellers who are showing them different sets of books between their profit and loss sheets supplied to the Internal Revenue Service and the ones which they say they operate on. If a business owner is willing to cheat the IRS out of taxes and risk the penalties and possible jail sentences for fraud, think about the type of honesty that he will likely be showing you as it relates to the numbers. If the seller has two sets of books, he probably has three and you won't be getting anything near what you think you're buying.

To evaluate what a business is producing, you should look at minimum at the following kinds of documents:

1. Tax returns for the previous five years, including all schedules that go with the returns.
2. The current lease on the property the business is occupying.
3. Any documentation on loans that you may be assuming.
4. Any documents on contracts, including both those that have liabilities attached as well as those that are the basis for corporate revenues. If the contracts are not properly drafted, you may find that you are paying for something that isn't binding once you take over.
5. Employment agreements and personnel files.
6. Any official papers relating to assets such as purchase contracts, and so on.

In addition to these items, I would ask for a right to speak to the individual who is involved in filing the corporate tax return. This would normally be the CPA of the company, either in-house or from an outside company. I would ask the seller to give that individual a waiver so they may speak directly with you regarding any aspect of the company's finances. If possible, I would also seek to get the same type of waiver from the corporate attorney as it relates to disclosures of any outstanding lawsuits and/or information that may not have been disclosed by the seller but is considered material to a transaction. This may be very difficult to obtain, but it never hurts to try. If you get a strong objection, the conclusion may be that there is a problem.

If you aren't experienced in looking over the books and records of a company, there is no use in pretending that you are. In this case, make sure you have a very experienced business CPA who has been involved in valuations of businesses or contact someone who is appropriately certified. One group of individuals is the American Society of Appraisers, headquartered in Washington, D.C. These individuals are all over the country, and the association will provide you with a list of those available in your area.

Whatever method you select to review the corporate records, be thorough. The following section discusses the specific items that should be requested.

Balance Sheet

Accounts Receivable

1. Obtain an accounts receivable aging schedule, and determine whether there is a high number of receivables among a few accounts.
2. Determine the reasons for all overdue accounts.
3. Find out whether any amounts are in dispute.
4. Are any of the accounts pledged as collateral?
5. Is the reserve for bad debt sufficient, and how was it established?
6. Review the business's credit policy.

Inventory

1. Make sure the inventory is determined by physical count and divided by finished goods, work in progress, and raw materials.
2. Assess the method of valuation and why it was used (Last In First Out, LIFO; First In First Out, FIFO; etc.).
3. Determine the age and condition of the inventory.
4. How is damaged or obsolete inventory valued?

5. Is the amount of inventory sufficient to operate efficiently and for how long?
6. Should an appraisal be obtained?

Marketable Securities
1. Obtain a list of marketable securities.
2. How are the securities valued?
3. Determine the fair market value of the securities.
4. Are any securities restricted or pledged?
5. Should the portfolio be sold or exchanged?

Real Estate
1. Obtain a schedule of real estate owned.
2. Determine the condition and age of the real estate.
3. Establish the fair market value of each of the buildings and land.
4. Should appraisals be obtained?
5. Are repairs or improvements required?
6. Are maintenance costs reasonable?
7. Do any of the principals have a financial interest in the company(s) that perform(s) the maintenance?
8. Is the real estate required to operate the business efficiently?
9. How is the real estate financed?
10. Are the mortgages assumable?
11. Will additional real estate be required in the near future?
12. Is the real estate adequately insured?

Machinery and Equipment
1. Obtain a schedule of machinery and equipment owned and leased.
2. Determine the condition and age of the machinery and equipment and the frequency of maintenance.
3. Identify the equipment and machinery that is state-of-the-art.
4. Identify the machinery and equipment that is obsolete.
5. Identify the machinery and equipment that is used in compliance with Environmental Protection Agency (EPA) or Occupational Safety and Health Act (OSHA) standards, and determine whether additional equipment and machinery is needed to comply.
6. Should an appraisal be obtained?
7. Will immediate repairs be required and at what cost?

Accounts Payable
1. Obtain a schedule of accounts payable, and determine whether there is concentration among a few accounts.

2. Determine the age of the amounts due.
3. Identify all amounts in dispute, and determine the reason.
4. Review transactions to spot undisclosed and contingent liabilities.

Accrued Liabilities
1. Obtain a schedule of accrued liabilities.
2. Determine the accounting treatment of: unpaid wages at the end of the period; accrued vacation pay; accrued sick leave; payroll taxes due and payable; accrued federal income taxes; other accruals.
3. Search for unrecorded accrued liabilities.

Notes Payable and Mortgages Payable
1. Obtain a schedule of notes payable and mortgages payable.
2. Identify the reason for indebtedness.
3. Determine terms and payment schedule.
4. Will the acquisition accelerate the note or mortgage? Is there a prepayment penalty?
5. Determine whether there are any balloon payments to be made and the amounts and dates due. A Balloon Payment is a single payment on all the remaining balance of a loan. These payments are used when a loan has been only partially amortized.
6. Are the notes or mortgages assumable?

Income Statement

The potential earning power of the business should be analyzed by reviewing profit and loss statements for the past three to five years. The income statement gives you much more detail about cash flow. The balance sheet won't tell you whether you are making money, but the income statement will. It is important to substantiate financial information by reviewing the business's federal and state tax returns. The business's earning power is a function of more than bottom line profits or losses. The owner's salary and fringe benefits, noncash expenses, and nonrecurring expenses also should be calculated.

Financial Ratios

While analyzing the balance sheet and the income statement, sales and operating ratios should be calculated to identify areas that require further study. Key ratios are the current ratio, quick ratio, accounts receivable turnover, inventory turnover, and sales/accounts receivable. The significance of these ratios, the methods for calculating them, and industry averages are available through special research by companies such as Dun & Bradstreet. In addition, you could contact the trade association for the particular industry you are involved in. Look for trends in the ratios over the past three to five years.

Leases

1. What is the remaining term of the lease?
2. Are there any option periods, and if so, is the option exercised only by the choice of the tenant?
3. Is there a percent of sales clause?
4. What additional fees (such as a common area maintenance or merchants association dues) are paid over and above the base rent?
5. Is the tenant or landlord responsible for maintaining the roof and the heating and air conditioning system?
6. Is there a periodic rent increase called for to adjust the rent for changes in the consumer price index or for an increase in real estate tax assessments?
7. Is there a demolition clause?
8. Under what terms and conditions will the landlord permit an assumption or extension of the existing lease?

Personnel

1. What are the job responsibilities, rates of pay, and benefits of each employee?
2. What is each employee's tenure?
3. What is the level of each employee's skill in their position? Do they have an employment contract?
4. Will key employees stay after the business is purchased?
5. Are any employees part of a union, or is any union organizing effort likely?

Marketing

1. Are any of the products proprietary?
2. Describe any new upcoming products and projected sales.
3. What is the business's geographic market area?
4. What is the business's percentage of market share?
5. What are the business's competitive advantages?

6. What are the business's annual marketing expenditures?

Patents

A list of trade names, trademarks, logos, copyrights, and patents should be obtained, noting the period of time remaining before each expires.

Taxes

1. Are FICA, unemployment, and sales tax payments current?
2. What were the date and the outcome of the last IRS audit?

Legal Issues

1. Are there any suits now or soon to commence?
3. Are all state registration requirements and regulations being met?
4. Are all local zoning requirements being met?
5. Review the articles of incorporation, minute books, bylaws, and/or partnership agreements.
6. What are the classes of stock and the restrictions of each, if any?
7. Has any stock been canceled or repurchased?
8. Is the business a franchise? If so, review the franchise agreement.

Competitors

1. Who are the business's competitors?
2. What is their market share?
3. What are each competitor's competitive advantages and disadvantages?

All the factors identified in this section on evaluating a business have to be carefully scrutinized. Some factors will have a positive influence on the decision to buy. Others will have a negative influence. Seek out professional assistance if help is needed in interpreting any of the information you are getting.

As you get to the final stage of the negotiating process, try to secure an option to purchase the business within the next ninety days subject to inspection of the books. You can either establish a price at this time based on an assumed price, but subject to verification, or you can structure an option to purchase at a price and terms that are "satisfactory to both parties and to be mutually agreed to within the future." Obviously, this sort of option has little teeth to it other than making it somewhat more difficult for the seller to sell the property out from under you. However, what you are attempting to do is tie up the property so that you don't spend a great deal of time, money, and effort looking over a business only to find out that it is later bought by someone else for a higher price.

One of the things to determine early on is what you actually are going to be buying. If you are buying the stock in a corporation, then you are buying all of the assets as well as the liabilities of the corporation. That is normally less attractive unless you are dealing with a large company that has good audited financials by one of the big eight accounting firms. If you are dealing with a small business, it would be much safer if you simply buy the assets of the company and let all the liabilities remain with the company. Under this circumstance, you may have to comply with what are referred to as *bulk sales laws* in the state in which you are operating. This law simply requires you to disclose to all of the creditors of a company that the assets are being sold in bulk. If they have any rights to those assets, they need to notify you ahead of the purchase. Failure to comply with the bulk sales act would allow a creditor who was not properly notified to have the potential right of coming back against you in the future as a creditor. At least half of the states have altered their bulk sale transfer act substantially, and some have totally eliminated the statute. It would be wise to contact the Secretary of State to determine whether or not the bulk sale act still applies in your state and what the requirements are for compliance.

One area of particular concern if you are considering buying the entire business is workers' compensation insurance and unemployment taxes. In certain circumstances, individual officers and directors can become liable for workers' compensation claims and unemployment taxes if the corporation doesn't pay them. If you purchase a business and there are outstanding debts of this type, you may become personally liable for those claims, which could exceed what you are buying. Consequently, you want not only to see affidavits of payment, but also to verify in writing with the appropriate governmental authority that such debts have been paid.

It is likely that in any business sale, some personal property will be involved. If this is the case, make sure that you or your attorney contacts the state to see whether there are any Uniform Commercial Code (UCC) filings against those assets. These UCC filings are done by lenders who have claims on the personal property that would be superior to yours. If there are UCC filings, make sure that your purchase price is adjusted downward to reflect the debt owed on the filings.

If by now you have a lawyer involved in the transaction, make sure that she or he checks with the various local courthouses to determine whether litigation has been filed against the company that was not reported to you. If you don't have an attorney at this time, you should contact the courthouses directly, explaining your situation and asking them to let you know how to go through the process of checking to see whether any litigation has been filed. Normally, it is a very simple process and the court documents are maintained in alphabetical order based on the names of the parties.

Determining if there are any lawsuits filed against the company is important, not only from the standpoint of assessing potential additional dollars that may have to be expended because of the lawsuit, but also because they give you some hint as to the operation of the company. For instance, if the company has several lawsuits pending regarding the same type of things, such as a defective product, it may raise a flag that there is some truth behind the lawsuits. Don't automatically assume that lawsuits are being filed for frivolous reasons. The company may very well be operating in a manner that is improper, and in fact the product they may be selling to you may have a defect. Obviously reading the complaints of others could give you a greater understanding of what problems the company is facing and a glimpse at another side to their story.

If you are buying a franchise or a business that requires a license, check with the franchisor or licensing agent that the franchise and/or license is in fact assignable. Many times these agreements have clauses that require that the franchise revert to the franchise company on the sale of the business, unless a certain payment is made and/or the approval of the purchaser by the franchisor. If such is the case, you would want to make sure that you received approval prior to paying any money to the seller.

Drafting the Purchase Agreement

After you have inspected the books and records of the company, you will want to move to the contract phase. At this point, unless you are an experienced buyer, I would strongly encourage you to have an attorney who is experienced in this area of acquisitions. The cost that you incur will be more than offset by the savings that they can get for you in terms of negotiations and protections.

In drafting the contract, many parties attempt to have the other create the initial contract and then make counteroffers and changes. I prefer to do the initial drafting and take control of what is in the base of the contract. Just as with negotiating a lease, if you control the structure of the body of the contract, then you control the basic framework for the purchase of the business, and many items that will be slightly to your advantage will never be negotiated.

Closing Date

Once you have signed a formal contract with the seller of the business, you will set a closing date similar to one you may have had when you purchased a piece of real estate. On the closing date, all items of ownership are assigned to you as the new owner, and a bill of sale for all the personal property should be executed along with an assignment of various leases. It is important that, immediately prior to the closing, a walk-through be allowed to inspect the business. This specifically applies to businesses in which a great deal of inventory is involved because that will necessitate the proper accounting for inventory and offsetting of payments by the buyer to the seller. If you are using an attorney experienced in this area, she or he will know how it is traditionally set up in your local community and establish safeguards to make sure that inventory does not leave the property during the change of owners.

On the day of the closing, you are now the proud new owner of a business. With some luck, it will be everything you thought it was going to be. If it isn't, don't be afraid to go back to the seller and try to get modifications to your purchase price. A performance guarantee is a clause you should put in your purchase contract to allow you to negotiate if the business doesn't perform like the seller suggested.

Buying a business is loaded with potential land mines. However, properly structured with the right legal assistance, your investment should be protected, and you can create great sources of income for you and your family.

Financing the Purchase

As a buyer, your source of financing will depend in part on the size of the business being purchased. The vast majority of businesses are purchased with a significant portion of the purchase price financed by the owner. You must make a down payment and be sure that adequate working capital sources are available.

If the funds needed for the down payment are not readily available, then you must look for financing from an outside source. To grant such financing, an institutional lender is almost certain to require personal collateral for the loan as well as a compendium of financial and operating data of the business to be acquired. It is rare indeed to be granted a loan to purchase a smaller, privately held business when the loan is secured only by the assets of the business. The most attractive types of personal collateral from the lender's point of view are real estate, marketable securities, and the cash value of life insurance. In addition to personal collateral, it also must be demonstrated to the lender that you are of good character, have a clear source of repayment, and have a good business plan. The most common sources for such loans are financial institutions, such as banks and consumer finance companies.

The chances of obtaining outside financing improve with the size of the business being acquired. Not only does the willingness of the lender to participate in the transaction increase, but the number of potential lenders increases. Banks, insurance companies, commercial finance companies, and venture capital companies all may be interested in lending money for an acquisition of some size. Again, you must be of good character, have a clear source of repayment, and have a good business plan.

Lenders for larger transactions may or may not require personal collateral from the purchaser; however, they will require a personal guarantee. Collateral for larger loans generally will consist of a first lien security interest in the tangible assets of the business, such as accounts receivable, inventory, equipment, and real estate. The lender will set loan conditions and restrictions regarding certain activities of the business. In the case of insurance companies and venture capitalists, the lender may insist on an equity position in the business and a role in major management decisions. Insurance companies typically only participate in transactions above $10 million. Commercial finance companies make loans on much the same basis as banks. The interest rate such companies charge usually is higher than that charged by a bank, but they often are willing to take more risk.

It is rare for a privately held business to be acquired without leveraging the business's assets in some manner, pledging them as collateral for a loan made either by the owner of the business or an outside lender. The owner has a strong incentive to provide financing if he feels it is necessary to get the price he wants for the business and has confidence in the buyer. An outside lender must be convinced that the loan's risk of failure is minimal and represents a profitable transaction. Institutional lenders are generally conservative and concentrate primarily on repayment. To obtain outside financing, it is important to be well prepared and have the information that a lender needs to make a decision. These data should be submitted in the form of a loan proposal and should contain all of the items discussed.

Leveraged Buyouts

Just as in an installment sale, a leveraged buyout uses the assets of the business to collateralize a loan to buy the business. The difference is that you typically invest little or no money of your own, and the loan is obtained from a lending institution or venture capital firm.

This type of purchase is best suited to asset-rich businesses. A business that lacks the assets needed for a completely leveraged buyout may be able to put together a partially leveraged buyout. In this structure, the seller finances part of the transaction and is secured by a second lien security interest in the assets. Because leveraged buyouts place a greater debt burden on the company than do other types of financing, you and the seller must take a close look at the business's ability to service the debt.

Stock Exchanges

In some instances a business owner may want to accept the stock of a purchasing corporation as payment for the business. Typically, the stock he receives (if it is the stock of a publicly held company) may not be resold for two years. If the stock may not be freely traded, it is not as valuable as freely traded stock, and its value should be discounted to allow for this lack of marketability.

There is an advantage to the seller in this kind of transaction. Taxes incurred by the seller on the gain from the sale of the business are deferred until the acquired stock is eventually sold. This kind of transaction is termed a *tax-free exchange* by the IRS. Several tests must be met to qualify for this tax treatment. Check with a competent accountant or tax attorney, or request a ruling from the IRS Reorganization Branch in Washington, D.C.

Making and Evaluating Offers

Making the Offer

Before making an offer, you will have typically investigated a number of businesses. At some point in the investigation process, it may be necessary to sign a confidentiality agreement and show the seller a personal financial statement. A confidentiality agreement pledges that you will not divulge any information about the business to anyone other than immediate advisors.

You should determine a range of value for the business. An appraisal of the business "as is" can be used to establish a pricing floor. A pricing ceiling can be established by using an appraisal that capitalizes projected future cash flows under new management. You should have access to all records needed to prepare an offer. If some information is lacking, you must make a decision either to discontinue the transaction or make an offer contingent on receiving and approving the withheld information. The nature and amount of withheld information determine which course of action to take.

An offer may take the form of a purchase and sale contract or a letter of intent. Purchase and sale contracts usually are binding on the parties, whereas a letter of intent often is nonbinding. The latter is more often used with larger businesses. Regardless of which form of the agreement is used, it should contain the following:

1. Total price to be offered.
2. Components of the price (amount of security deposit and down payment, amount of bank debt, amount of seller financed debt).
3. A list of all liabilities and assets being purchased. The minimum amount of accounts receivable to be collected

and the maximum amount of accounts payable to be assumed may be specified.
4. The operating condition of equipment at settlement.
5. The right to offset the purchase price in the amount of any undisclosed liabilities that come due after settlement and in the amount of any variance in inventory from that stated in the agreement.
6. A provision that the business will be able to pass all necessary inspections.
7. A provision calling for compliance with the Bulk Transfer provisions of the Uniform Commercial Code. (This does not apply to sales of the stock of the corporation.)
8. Warranties of clear and marketable title, validity and assumability of existing contracts if any, tax liability limitations, legal liability limitations, and other appropriate warranties.
9. A provision (where appropriate) to make the sale conditional on lease assignment, verification of financial statements, transfer of licenses, obtaining financing, or other provisions.
10. A provision for any appropriate prorations, such as rent, utilities, wages, and prepaid expenses.
11. A noncompetition covenant. This document is sometimes part of the purchase and sale agreement and is sometimes a separate exhibit to the purchase and sale agreement.
12. Allocation of the purchase price.
13. Restrictions on how the business is to be operated until settlement.
14. A date for settlement.

The purchase and sale agreement is a complex document, and it is a good idea to get a professional to draft it.

Closing the Transaction

Meeting Conditions of Sale

After you have entered into a binding contract, several conditions may need to be met before the sale is closed. Such conditions often address issues such as assignment of the lease, verification of financial statements, transfer of licenses, or obtaining financing. Usually a date is set for meeting the conditions of sale. If a condition is not met within the specified time frame, the agreement is invalidated.

Types of Settlements

Business settlements or closings, as they are also called, are usually done in one of two ways. First, an attorney performs the settlement. In this procedure, your attorney or an independent attorney acting on behalf of both buyer and seller draws up the necessary documents for settlement. These documents may include deeds to transfer property, bills of sale for personality, and assignments of contracts that may already be in existence. You and the seller meet with the settlement attorney at a predetermined time (after all conditions of sale have been met). Documents are signed at the meeting by you and the seller. A good settlement attorney also is a good problem solver. He can help find creative ways to resolve differences of opinion. The settlement attorney holds money in escrow and disburses it when all the appropriate documents are signed.

Second, in an escrow settlement, the money to be deposited, bill of sale, and other documents are placed in the hands of a neutral third party or escrow agent. The escrow agent usually is an escrow company or the escrow department of a financial institution. You and the seller sign escrow instructions that name the conditions to be met before completion of the sale. Once all conditions are met, the escrow agent disburses both previously executed documents and funds. There usually is no formal final meeting at which the signing of the documents takes place. You and the seller usually sign them independently of one another.

Regardless of whether escrow or a settlement attorney is used, the requirements of the bulk sales act must be met if the assets (not the stock of the corporation) of the business are being sold. This law calls for the business's suppliers to be notified of the impending sale. The supplier must respond within the allowed time frame if money is owed by the seller. A lien search also is performed by the attorney or escrow agent. This determines whether any liens against the business's assets have been filed with the local courthouse.

Documents

A number of documents are required to close a transaction. The purchase and sale agreement is the basic document from which all the documents used to close the transaction are created. The documents most often used in closing a transaction are described in the following. Other additional documents also may be needed depending on the particulars of the transaction:

1. *Settlement sheet.* Shows, as of the date of settlement, the various costs and adjustments to be paid by or credited to each party. It is signed by you and the seller.
2. *Escrow agreement.* Is used only for escrow settlements. It is a set of instructions signed by you and the seller in advance of settlement that sets forth the conditions of escrow, the responsibilities of the escrow agent, and the requirements to be met for the release of escrowed funds and documents.
3. *Bill of sale.* Describes the physical assets being transferred and identifies the amount of consideration paid for those assets. It must always be signed by the seller and is often also signed by the buyer.
4. *Promissory note.* Used only in an installment sale. It shows the principal amount and terms of repayment of the debt to the seller. It specifies remedies for the seller in the event of default by the buyer. It is signed by the buyer, and the buyer often must personally guarantee the debt.
5. *Security agreement.* Creates the security interest in the assets pledged by the buyer to secure the promissory note and underlying debt. It also sets forth the terms under which the buyer agrees to operate those assets that constitute collateral. It is used only in an installment sale. It is signed by both parties.
6. *Financing statement.* Creates a public record of the security interest in the collateral and therefore notifies third parties that certain assets are encumbered by a lien to secure the existing debt. The cost to record the financing statement varies by jurisdiction. It is used only in installment sales. It is signed by you and the seller.
7. *Covenant not to compete.* Protects you and your investment from immediate competition by the seller in your market area for a limited amount of time. The scope of this document must be reasonable for it to be legally

enforceable. The covenant not to compete sometimes is included as a part of the purchase and sale agreement and is sometimes written as a separate document. It is signed by both parties. It is not required in every transaction.

8. *Employment agreement.* Specifies the nature of services to be performed by the seller, the amount of compensation, the amount of time per week or per month the services are to be performed, the duration of the agreement, and often a method for discontinuing the agreement before its completion. Employment agreements are not required in all transactions, but they are used with great frequency. It is not uncommon for the seller to remain involved with the business for periods of as little as a week or as much as several years. The length of time depends on the complexity of the business and the experience of the buyer. For periods of more than two to four weeks, the seller often is compensated for his services. The agreement is signed by both the buyer and the seller.

Contingent Liabilities

Contingent liabilities must be taken into account and provided for when a business is sold. This type of liability is unsure and contingent on an event. For example, a lawsuit is a contingent liability. If the company loses, it becomes a liability based on a judgment. Contingent liabilities can be handled by escrowing a portion of the funds earmarked for disbursement to the seller. The sum escrowed then can be used to pay off the liability as it comes due. Any remaining money can then be disbursed to the seller.

CHAPTER NINE

PROVIDING CREDIT FOR YOUR CUSTOMERS

Let's face it. America is both a consumer society and a debtor society. What we get or what we buy is controlled in part by the amount of credit that we are extended. Very few Americans don't have credit cards today, and most of them are extended to the hilt. The result of this debtor society is that new businesses must understand that to succeed, they will have to offer methods of payment for their products other than cash. Mastercard, Visa, Discover, and American Express are all the leaders in the credit card field. If you are offering purchases on credit cards to your customers, you will need to use at least one of these options, and the better approach is to have several available.

To secure the right to use credit cards in your business, you will need to have a merchant account. If you are operating your business out of a storefront, merchant accounts can be obtained by working through your local lender. If you do not have a storefront and if you are involved in the direct mail business, merchant accounts are much more difficult to obtain because of the exposure that the credit card lender has to chargebacks against the credit card. A chargeback occurs when a consumer has purchased a product and returns it to the place purchased within the return period. In that situation, the merchant is required to give credit back (chargeback) against the consumer's credit card rather than to pay the customer cash for the returned goods.

Companies in certain direct mail order businesses are known for very high chargebacks. These chargebacks are expensive for the credit card companies. Consequently, they are extremely reluctant to extend merchant accounts to new companies, particularly ones that have no storefront operation. The result of this is a sort of catch-22. You need to be able to offer credit card purchases to your consumers; yet you need to be in business for a while to be able to establish credibility with the merchant account providers.

To counter this catch-22 and make credit cards available, a mini-industry has been established by banks and some financial institutions who are willing to take a higher risk in dealing with merchants who are in this category. These lenders require that you place cash deposits in advance in your merchant account to offset potential chargebacks. In the beginning, higher than normal deposits may be required based on the expectancy of the amount of charges that will take place in the account. Later through negotiations you may be able to get the deposits reduced. Although this may be an extremely expensive form of credit supply for your company, the alternative of not having credit available probably is not an acceptable option. Once you start dealing in consumer debt a whole array of new laws come into affect. You must understand how they apply to your business and what you can do to simplify their requirements.

PROFIT STRATEGY:
In the early days of my publishing business, I had trouble getting a merchant account because we operated primarily by direct mail. Ultimately, we had to find a specialty provider. They required a large deposit, but we have had a successful relationship for many years. Their name and address are: Cardservice International, P.O. Box 2310, Aguora Hills, CA 91376-2310; telephone (800) 456-5989.

Credit Law

Consumer credit, as you may guess, is a major concern to the federal government. Consequently, the extension of credit and the collection of debts owed to you are all governed by a variety of federal laws. The major governmental agency governing the extension of credit is the Federal Trade Commission (FTC), who not only who regulates the creation of the laws, but also enforces them. Included within their review are the federal Truth in Lending Act, the Fair Credit Billing Act, the

Equal Credit Opportunity Act, and the Fair Credit Reporting Act.

Truth in Lending Act

The purpose of the Truth in Lending Act is to allow consumers an easy way to shop for credit and compare the costs. Before this act, it was practically impossible to compare one financing method to another because of a variety of terms as well as mathematical gyrations used to compound interest on interest. The result was that a consumer found it almost impossible to understand exactly the amount of interest they were paying, and this was, of course, found to be misleading.

The act controls two major components of financing. One is the actual financing charge, and the second is the annual percentage rate. By knowing these numbers, it makes comparative shopping for financing terms relatively easy. The financing charge is the total dollar amount that the borrower will be paying to the lender for the use of the credit. Included in this charge are interest costs as well as all other costs of borrowing such as service charges, appraisal fees, or setup costs. The annual percentage rate (APR) is the percentage of those costs on the credit that you are paying on a yearly basis. By converting all credit costs to an annual base as a standard, consumers are allowed to compare that number offered by each lender.

Who Must Comply with the Truth in Lending Act?

The Truth in Lending Act applies to any extension of credit where a financing charge is imposed. In addition, the law applies where there is no financing charge but payments will be made in more than four installments. To come under the provisions of the act, the consumer transaction being considered must contain four specific criteria:

1. The transaction must fall under the definition of a credit transaction; that is, it must be a credit sale giving the consumer the right to defer payment on the debt or the right to incur debt and defer payment.
2. Credit must be offered by a creditor. A creditor is defined under the act as one who regularly extends credit. This means one who extends credit more than twenty-five times in any calendar year.

3. The extension of credit must be payable by written agreement in more than four installments or with the finance charge.
4. The transaction must fall under the definition of a consumer credit transaction, which is any credit offered to a consumer primarily for personal, family, or household purposes.

If not all four of these criteria are met, then the federal act does not cover you. If you do meet the four criteria, then you will be covered under the Truth in Lending Act and must comply. In addition, you should review your state law to determine whether the type of business you are involved in may fall under the Truth in Lending Act and local law. I would advise you to speak specifically with an attorney who works within this area. The law is very complicated with its multilayered disclosure requirements, and compliance is strictly construed against the business owner.

Fair Credit Billing Act

The Fair Credit Billing Act was an amendment made to the Truth in Lending Act and is enclosed with every consumer credit card bill. The purpose of the act was to protect customers against unfair practices of issuers of open-ended credit, including all of those who issue credit cards. The act requires that people who extend credit inform the debtor of their rights and responsibilities in the case of a billing dispute and requires the creditor to resolve the dispute within a certain time. If you are involved in open-ended credit, then you will have to comply with this element of the Truth in Lending Act. Open-ended credit applies when the creditor expects the customer to make repeated transactions rather than a one-time credit purchase. The creditor is allowed to impose a financing charge from time to time on the unpaid balance and as the customer pays the balance due, the amount of credit is once again available to the customer.

If you fall under the criteria of the act, you will be required to distribute a notice in a specific form prescribed in the act informing all of your customers of their rights. You will have to set up specific procedures to handle customer disputes that comply with the act. Again, as cautioned, if you feel that you are extending this type of credit to customers, it is important that you consult with an attorney to make sure that your procedures are properly established.

Equal Credit Opportunity Act

The purpose of the Equal Credit Opportunity Act (ECOA) is to benefit primarily married women. At the time of the enactment of the act, many creditors would not extend credit to a married woman based on her own credit, even if she had income separate from her husband. Frequently, these lenders required either an account be opened in the husband's name or joint accounts at a minimum.

The act makes it illegal for any creditor to discriminate in the extension of credit based on race, color, religion, national origin, gender, marital status, or age. It also makes it illegal to deny credit because part or all of an individual's income comes from public assistance or because the person is known to have exercised their rights under the Credit Protection Act. This act, unlike the other acts mentioned, governs both commercial credit and consumer credit. One of the areas that can easily get you in trouble with this act is credit prescreening procedures. You must be very careful not to ask questions having to do with race, color, religion, national origin, gender, or age. This includes the problems associated with questions on normal applications where you are asked to indicate whether you are Mr. or Mrs. If these terms are contained in the form, you must indicate somewhere that the completion of these terms is optional and is not necessary to receive credit. Another tricky area of the law is that you must be cautious to apply the same criteria to engaged couples who apply for joint credit as you would to a married couple. This rule also applies to unmarried couples who live together.

Just to put this law into perspective for you, any individual or business found in violation of this act is subject to actual and punitive damages up to $10,000 per violation. In addition, a class action will likely be filed against a company if it can be shown that there was a pattern to the discrimination. As you can see, this aspect should not be taken lightly.

Fair Credit Reporting Act

We live in the information age, and we are all listed on a multitude of computers throughout the world. The potential for misuse of all of this information increases as the Internet and other general access information become widely available. If you have ever obtained credit, including a charge account, home mortgage, or even a life insurance policy, it is certain that there will be a credit file on some computer showing how you pay your bills, whether you have filed for bankruptcy, and the like. Such a file will contain a variety of demographic information about you, including where you live and work. The problems with this type of information start when it is inaccurate. For example, people who were not the right person have been hounded by creditors. Others have been denied credit because they were told they had high debts or a poor pay record, even though it was someone with a similar name or social security number who actually had bad credit.

The result of these potential problems was the creation in 1971 of the Fair Credit Reporting Act. At present, it is one of the few federal laws available that regulate the collection and use of personal information about you. It was designed by Congress to protect you against the dissemination, maintenance, circulation, and even retention of inaccurate or old credit information and to ensure that consumer reporting agencies adopt procedures that are fair regarding the maintenance of information about individuals. The act gives specific rights for you to dispute information on your credit file, and when there is a disagreement between you and the agency, the law gives consumers equal access and allows them to write a one-hundred-word explanation on their credit file.

One of the key elements of the Fair Credit Reporting Act is that it provides methods for consumers to clear their credit files. Under the act, if a consumer is affected by any information that a creditor finds in a credit report, that potential creditor must give to the consumer denied credit the name and address of the reporting agency. The reporting agency is then required to make available to the consumer without charge a complete copy of the credit report. If the consumer disputes the accuracy of the credit report, then such disputes must be verified

> **PROFIT STRATEGY:**
> Unlimited liability is a major reason why you should be cautious about ATMs. Review all your bank statements monthly; if something doesn't look right make sure you report it. Remember, don't just call, put it in writing and even consider sending it by registered mail.

within a reasonable time to determine whether or not the report is accurate. If, after such investigation, the information is found to be inaccurate or can no longer be verified, then the information must be taken off the consumer's file. If the information is verified, but you don't agree with the information, then you are allowed to add up to one hundred words on your credit report to explain the specific information in their file. This right is frequently used by consumers when there is a dispute on a particular item or there was a particular time in which they had bad credit caused by unusual circumstances, such as a health problem. The explanation is sometimes enough for an understanding lender to go along with a borderline case. Finally, all adverse information must be deleted from your file after seven years to allow you a fresh start.

Credit Card and Electronic Funds Transfer Fraud

The purpose of this amendment to the Truth in Lending Act was to prohibit the unsolicited distribution of credit cards, to make the fraudulent use of credit cards a federal crime, and to limit an individual's liability to $50.00 on the unauthorized use of their credit cards.

Although the amendments to the Truth in Lending Act cover credit card liability, ATM machines and other similar devices did not come under the act until the passage of the Electronic Funds Transfer Act in 1978. The purpose of that act was to protect consumers who use ATM machines. The act specifically restricts the liability of consumers when someone uses their credit card without authority at either an ATM machine or certain point-of-purchase machines, such as those now being used in grocery stores throughout the country. The basic protection under the act allows the cardholder who notifies the financial institution within two business days of an unauthorized use of his card, protection of a maximum liability of $50.00. If the cardholder reports the unauthorized transfer within sixty days of his receipt of his billing statement, the

> **PROFIT STRATEGY:**
> Don't be harassed by creditors and don't let someone you know be either. This is one thing you can fight and win. If you have a problem, contact the Federal Trade Commission in Washington, D.C., at (203) 326-2222.

maximum liability is $500.00. Finally, if the cardholder fails to notify the institution within sixty days, then liability is unlimited. It should be noted that the banks and major lending institutions were much better protected under this act than they were for unauthorized credit card use because of the time requirements placed on consumers to notify the bank of unauthorized use. It is unlikely, except in the case of a stolen credit card, that a consumer would be able to notify the lender within the two-day period. Thus, more than likely, the liability limitation would fall under the $500 rule instead of the $50 rule, as with credit cards.

Fair Debt Collection Practices Act

The Fair Debt Collection Practices Act (FDCPA) was an amendment to the Consumer Credit Protection Act in 1977. Its purpose was to eliminate abusive and unfair collection practices by independent debt collectors. Although most of this act applies directly to specific collection agencies and not to a private company that has an outstanding debt, the rules and regulations are useful because they help you understand what may be construed as improper or illegal acts under other consumer protections. In addition, states have adopted their own consumer protection laws modeled after the federal act, and some of these laws are broader and apply to all creditors, not just collection agencies. Although the act is specifically directed to a debt collector, there are some very broad exclusions: banks, credit unions, loan companies, and retailers are excluded from the act's definition of a debt collector because the primary purpose of the business is the extension of credit rather than the collection of debt. Likewise, the statute does not apply to people or businesses collecting debts on their own accord.

The first type of illegal activity is any threat of or actual harassment or abuse, including abusive language, racial or religious slurs, or profanity. You can't solicit checks postdated by more than five days unless the agency notifies the debtor in writing at least three days before it intends to deposit the check. The idea is that you cannot create a situation where an individual can become liable for criminal penalty for writing an illegal check simply to get your debts collected.

False or misleading threats also are confusing. Credit agencies frequently write letters that threaten action against creditors if they don't pay their debts. An example is a threat to file a lawsuit. If it can be shown that the agency does not really file lawsuits or even that they never intended to file a lawsuit, that activity is considered illegal because it is misleading. Likewise, threats that imply some criminal prosecution or threats of using other legal authorities also can get the collection agency in trouble. For more information about credit card laws, contact the Federal Trade Commission in Washington, D.C., at (202) 326-2222.

The following are major credit reporting services that will provide you with credit information on any potential customer. I encourage you to establish a relationship with these reporting entities prior to starting your business.

1. Equifax Information Service Center
   P.O. Box 40241
   Atlanta, GA 30375-0241
   telephone: 1 (800) 685-1111.

2. TRW
   505 City Parkway West
   Orange, CA 92863
   telephone: (714) 385-7000.

CHAPTER TEN

PROTECTING YOUR BUSINESS WITH INSURANCE

You know you're going to have a bad day when you walk into your office and find that all of your computers have been stolen. I know because I've been there. The first thing you'll do is see whether you and everyone else followed your procedures for backing up everything on your computer. If you have, the damage will be contained by what you learn in this chapter. If you haven't, it's going to be a very long day.

The theft of business equipment is unfortunately a growing business. Our company has been hit four times in the last six years. Each time, the thefts were selectively done. One time they went for all of the printers; another time they went for the computers. It was almost as if they were taking orders. The good news for our company was that in every case, we had insurance—good coverage from a stable company that paid off timely. By now, you can probably guess I believe in insurance.

Where Do You Find a Good Agent?

If you don't know anyone in the business, check with your local business association for agent referrals. Another source is your chamber of commerce, which also most likely has an arrangement with a company that offers a special discount to its members. Perhaps the best method is to contact the largest business in your field. They are obviously successful and likely to have already gone through a claim. Call them, and ask whom they use and would recommend. Don't be shy about calling your competition. In most cases, particularly if they are successful, you also will find they are helpful, and this also will give you a good opportunity to meet them. There are plenty of businesses out there, and a great deal of time and money can be saved by working together.

What Type of Coverage Should You Get?

If you own the property where your business is located, you definitely need to be concerned about insurance coverage for the building itself. If your business is conducted in your home or in a converted residential house, make sure the insurance company knows you are conducting business at that location. Residential insurance is normally cheaper than commercial insurance, but it would be foolish to think that you will be able to get by on residential coverage if you also are operating a business. Insurance companies are experienced at writing language that excludes coverage when they aren't given the complete picture. Trying to get by might result in having paid premiums and then ultimately not being covered because you had the wrong type of insurance. You won't get the premiums back and the insurance company won't pay your claim.

PROFIT STRATEGY: Insurance is definitely important, but don't forget to protect your business with security alarms and fire alarms. They'll lower your premium and protect you better.

How Much Coverage Should You Get?

When you own a piece of property, part of the value of that property is allocated to land and part to the building. You want to have enough insurance to cover 100% of the value of the building or improvements. Your insurance agent will work with you to determine this amount, and although the natural tendency is to try to arrive at a low figure that also would lower your premiums, this isn't necessarily the best approach because insurance policies have a clause called coinsurance. This clause requires you to insure the value of your property within a percentage (normally 80%) of its total value (land and building). If you fail to meet that requirement, you will not receive the full amount of your claim because the insurance company will pay only on a prorated valuation. You can imagine that the formula wasn't structured to your advantage. Remember also that your valuation is likely to rise over the years, so you should discuss how the company determines the increase. Sometimes it is done on an actual value adjustment, but more than likely it will be calculated on an inflation factor.

Replacement Cost versus Current Value

Another insurance coverage to be careful of is the type of value the insurance company will be paying on. Replacement coverage is the best because the insurance company is in essence agreeing to replace your property, without regard to depreciation, wear and tear, or even the changing value of materials.

Current value on the other hand would allow the insurance company to reduce the amount they pay you based on changed circumstances such as depreciation. This would be a considerably lower amount on older property. By now you should be getting the idea that the insurance companies know exactly what they are doing, and you should too, or your premiums will be wasted.

PROFIT STRATEGY:
If you have an insurance claim you are going to need the records of all of your purchases. This is just another reminder why good records are so important.

Types of Policies

There are three basic types of policies: basic, broad form, and special. Based on their names, it would seem the broad form would be the best. Unfortunately, labels can be misleading. The most extensive coverage is produced by the special form because it covers everything *unless* specifically excluded. The basic and broad form policies cover only items stated in the insurance contract. As you may well guess, it's the little things that can kill you, and remembering everything to cover is just too difficult. Like most lessons, I also learned this one the hard way when one of my properties was damaged by water coming in from a hard rain. I knew I had water coverage and rain was something I had been specifically interested in because we live in Florida (the wet state). You can imagine my dismay when the insurance adjustors said, "Sorry, but you aren't covered from rising water." It seemed my policy only covered falling water. Once it hit the ground, I needed different coverage. In short, the special form will cost more, but try to figure out how you can afford it.

One final comment on coverage. Insurance contracts are getting easier to read, but they still are confusing. As an added precaution, write a letter to your agent stating anything you wanted to make sure that you are covered for. Ask him or her to notify you specifically if anything in your letter is not covered and to advise you of any changes in this coverage. The letter isn't a perfect solution, but keeping a strong paper trail can help you tremendously if you ever have to go to court.

Personal Property Protection

In addition to real estate insurance, you will need separate protection for the contents or personality. Just as important as it was with your real estate, you want replacement coverage on your personal property even if it is more expensive. I hate to tell you how fast computers and other equipment drop in value after you buy them, and anything electronic has very little value after a year because of changing technology advances.

The best way to make sure all of your property is covered is to do an extensive inventory. If you aren't a detailed person, make sure someone who is performs the inventory. Small businesses need to be careful to make sure that the owners' own property is accounted for. For example, if you purchased your desks or computer and are now using them in your incorporated business, then neither the desk nor the computer will be covered if the policy is a company policy. Either have your company purchase the item from you, or check to see if a rider can be placed in the policy to cover the item.

If you are a tenant, most likely nothing you have will be covered by the landlord's policy. Plan to get your own. Even if you find you may be included in the landlord's policy, you will be better off if you can negotiate a rent reduction and get your own because you don't want to be worrying about your landlord's cash flow. If he doesn't make a payment on his insurance and you have a loss, all of a sudden it becomes *your* loss. Sure you may have rights to sue the landlord, but I guarantee you that you don't want that battle.

Liability Insurance

You will recall that one of the reasons for forming a corporation was liability protection. You wanted to insulate your personal assets from your business. One of the best ways to protect the business and its assets is through liability insurance protection. Liability insurance protects your business if someone is injured. This includes the normal slip and fall type of injury and also less common, but no less expensive, injuries for libel, slander, defamation, false imprisonment, and other similar claims that someone wants to hold your company responsible for. This type of coverage is important whether you are the owner or the tenant because in case of injury both will be named in a lawsuit.

One of the important reasons for liability insurance is the legal assistance it also provides you. The insurance company takes on your role in defending the suit because they have to pay if the plaintiff wins against you. Consequently, you will have the company's team of legal experts representing you from the beginning. This alone is probably worth the cost of insurance when you factor in the cost of litigation today.

> **PROFIT STRATEGY:**
> Every state has specific protections for certain property from creditors in a bankruptcy proceeding. I strongly encourage you to find out these exemptions. If those protections are not adequate for you, either seek asset protection advice or buy insurance. Any other position is too great a risk.

Another form of liability insurance not covered under the standard policy is products liability insurance. As the name implies, it covers injuries caused by products you manufacture or supply. Products liability insurance is expensive because the injuries normally sustained in these types of cases often are extensive and frequently involve multiple parties who have been similarly injured by your product. How much products liability insurance you need will require careful work on the part of you and your agent.

Professional Liability Insurance

The counterpart in the professional world to a products liability claim is professional malpractice. Coverage is available, but like products liability insurance, it is expensive. Many doctors retire early rather than continue part-time because they cannot afford the insurance coverage.

One option some professionals have adopted is to go naked. This means that they elect not to have any insurance and believe that fact may even prevent some people from trying to bring a claim because they don't have a "deep pocket." This is a risky position for anyone who has any assets to take because professionals are held personally liable for their professional acts, even if they are operating in a corporation. The result of this position is that all of your personal assets are directly at risk in addition to those of your corporation. Think carefully about all of the potential ramifications to this choice if you elect to go that way.

Business Interruption Insurance

Business interruption insurance is a type not normally thought about by small businesses. It protects your lost income while your business has been stopped by certain events such as fire or other disaster. Naturally, there are limits on how much the insurance company will pay you and for how long. The idea is to tide you over until you can get started again, the same way disability insurance protects individuals if they are injured.

> **PROFIT STRATEGY:**
> While doing a risk analysis, take it a step further, and find out how you could operate your business if different types of disasters struck. Where would you go if you had a fire? How could you get immediate phone service at another location? Preplanning is profitable planning.

The only way you can determine whether this type of insurance makes sense for you is to do your own risk analysis. If disaster struck, what would you do? Could you get back in business fairly quickly, or would you have a long down time to restock materials? If time is a major factor, then you may want to consider such a policy.

As with investing, there is a risk-to-reward ratio associated with insurance. You can get protection for continuing higher risk, but how bad do the premiums affect your cash flow? Sometimes you will reach the conclusion that you are better off being self-insured simply by understanding that if something goes wrong, that's just part of your risk for being in business. One compromise that we have frequently found helpful is to raise your deductible as high as possible. This shifts some of the burden to you and also gets the insurance company involved if a disaster strikes. It's not ideal, but neither are high premiums that eat away at your profits.

Answering your insurance needs is a hard issue. Unfortunately, you may have the tendency to second-guess your decisions. Don't. It is one of those situations where there is no "right" answer. Take your best educated choice, and move on.

The following checklist is provided to help you recall important items to consider when shopping for insurance. As you learn more, add your own questions and develop an extensive list.

Business Insurance Checklist

1. What points are covered in your policy?
   - ❑ Windstorm ❑ Hail ❑ Smoke ❑ Explosion
   - ❑ Vandals ❑ Malicious Mischief ❑ Fire ❑ Theft
2. How much is your deductible? $_____
   What happens if you increase it?
3. Is your insurance: ❑ Repair ❑ Replace
4. In case of fire, does the policy cover important papers such as bills, accounts receivables, and evidence of debt?
5. If your property is unoccupied, is it still covered?
6. What documentation is required to show proof of loss? Do you need original receipts?
7. Are you covered for the full market value of your property?
8. Do you have at least a $1,000,000 liability protection?
9. Does your liability policy cover libel and slander?
10. If your insurance company settles for the deductible amount, do you have to pay?
11. Who pays the court cost to defend a lawsuit?
12. Do your employees have car insurance? Are you protected if they are driving during employment?
13. Do you need work interruption insurance?
14. Does a burglar alarm reduce your premiums?
15. Do you need special glass breakage protection?
16. Are you required to have any insurance for your employees?
17. Do you need key-person insurance on someone in your company? This type of insurance protects your company if the key person dies.

CHAPTER ELEVEN

COPYRIGHTS, TRADEMARKS, PATENTS, AND LICENSES

Copyrights, trademarks, patents, and licenses are collectively referred to as *intellectual property*. As the owner and creator of intellectual property, you have the right to protect it from unauthorized use. This right is even codified as a constitutional protection, specifically enumerated "to promote the progress of science and useful arts by securing for limited times to authors and inventors the exclusive right to their respective writings and discoveries." Having announced those rights, let me hasten to add that their protection is easier said than enforced. The courtroom halls are filled with battles between those who have attempted to secure intellectual property protection and those who pirate that property for their own gain. Entire countries have been embroiled in the attempts to circumvent U.S. laws protecting our creative artists. International treaties governing such rights often are ignored with little consequence. The practical aspect of the complicated issues surrounding intellectual property is that, although you can seek to protect your creations, it is likely that the more valuable they are, the more likely you will have to spend time in court protecting those rights.

In this chapter, I give you an overview of the laws governing the protection of intellectual property. In addition, I'll give the name of resources to contact when you are ready to structure your legal protection. For those of you who have created a work that can be loaned out to others, I have included a discussion on licenses.

Copyrights

Copyright laws are designed to protect originality in expression. This means that, although an idea cannot be copyrighted, the exact way in which you express the idea in oral or written form can be protected under the Copyright Act.

There are two ways to copyright your work. The first is to make sure that three things are included on every piece of material that you want to copyright. (1) The symbol © or the word *copyright*, or the abbreviation corp., (2) the year of first publication, and (3) the name of the owner of the copyright. The second method of creating copyright protection is to register the copyright with the federal government. Registration is simple and involves sending in the official registration Form TX along with $10.00 to the Register of Copyrights. Once your form is accepted, you have created a legal registration of your work.

The difference between the two methods of creating copyright protection is significant. The first method of simply labeling your work as copyrighted creates legal protection but it does not allow you to sue in court. To have the right to sue and protect your copyright in court, you must register the work with the Copyright Office. Therefore, full registration is the only real protection for your work. For your convenience and to protect any work that you have, I have included a copy of Form TX at the end of this chapter. In addition, I would suggest that you write to the register of copyrights for one of their copyright kits: Register of Copyrights, Copyright Office, Library of Congress, Washington, DC 20559; telephone (202) 707-9100.

Although you will need to register the copyright to be able to sue in court and protect your interest, you should also go through the process of meeting the common law test of copyright protection by putting the three items previously discussed on any work that you seek to have protected. From the common law view, copyright protection attaches when the work is "fixed" in its medium. This means that, once it is published in its particular medium, it will be protected under common law. Thus, to protect it, a video should be produced to an audience and a written work should be published.

Although most people understand the necessity to protect through copyright registration any book that they might be the author of, other works in a business may ultimately become more valuable than a book. For example, advertisements that you create may prove to be a huge success. By copyrighting the advertisement itself, you prohibit other businesses from lifting that material and copying it for their own use. There is nothing more frustrating than creating a public relations or advertising campaign only to find that your competitors simply steal your idea and use it for their own purpose to compete against you. In this case, you have been doubly violated. Your competitor has saved all of the time and money that you spent developing the advertisement, plus you will be out all of the lost dollars that the competitor captured by using your successful advertising campaign.

Another area that is beginning to get respect under copyright protection is your customer list. Compilations of specific lists are protected under the copyright laws. Consequently, as you develop a customer base, you may want to copyright the entire list as your own property. This becomes important when you have employees who leave your company and take a list of your customers for their own use. By copyrighting the list, you will be able to pursue for collection of damages under not only trade secret laws, but also copyright laws.

Trademarks

One of the identifiable marketing trends in business today is the shift away from competitive pricing or quality toward creating brand loyalty. All major companies today attempt to create a brand that at least a segment of the market can identify with. The "Pepsi Generation" is a direct targeted effort to get a certain segment of the population (the "younger" crowd) to identify with Pepsi as its drink of choice.

The importance of brand marketing in our society has now increased the importance of exercising trademark protection for the brands and slogans surrounding the products. The term *trademark* includes "any word, name, symbol or device, or any combination thereof, adopted and used by manufacturer or merchant to identify his or her goods and distinguish them from those manufactured or sold by others."

Whereas a trademark identifies a tangible, a service mark is used to identify the services of one person and distinguish them from the services of others. For example, the Sesame Street characters are service marks created and registered by public television. This denotation creates the ownership of the actual group of characters, so that they can then be licensed out to others for use. In our example of the Sesame Street characters, millions of dollars are generated for public television by licensing out these characters for toys, T-shirts, and even ice shows.

The trademark process seems simple enough, but it is one area of the law that I would not recommend attempting without an attorney that has specific experience in this area. Not all marks (trademarks or service marks) are protectable, and developing and advertising to promote a mark is extremely expensive. It certainly doesn't do anybody any good to spend a lot of time, money, and effort creating a trademark or service mark only to find out that the mark is being used in other parts of the country by someone else. Should that occur, depending on who used the mark first and how it is being used, one of you would likely have to stop using it. This can obviously affect your entire operation, not to mention the money that you have spent attempting to develop brand loyalty.

Once you have selected a mark, you need to conduct a search in the U.S. Patent and Trademark Office to determine whether or not the mark is being used anywhere else in the country. This search of all major databases in the United States is a science in itself. If during the search it is discovered that a word or similar word to your desired trademark is being used elsewhere, then your attorney will need to work with the staff counsel in the trademark division to determine whether or not your trademark is distinguishable from the other's use. For example, a word could be trademarked in conjunction with restaurant businesses and not be trademarked for use as a particular product. Distinguishing between uses is not only complicated but also requires a skillful attorney who is able to negotiate fine points with trademark staff counsel.

There are three key elements to think about with trademarks: (1) Is the mark generic? (2) Is it descriptive? (3) Is it distinctive? The elements will be used by your attorney and the trademark staff to determine whether your trademark can be registered and protected. A generic term cannot be used as a trademark because it does not specifically identify goods and distinguish them from those which are produced by others. Therefore, you cannot trademark a name of an article that is in the English language. For example, you cannot trademark the word *coat* for a product that you put on if you are cold. Obviously, whether or not something is generic or not often becomes a question of use. At one time, the words *aspirin* and *thermos* were all privately used, but over time the words became the meaning for the products. Once that occurs, the product loses its distinguishable characteristic, and the word becomes generic and is no longer trademarkable. Great care should be used to make sure that your trademarked term is used only as an adjective and not a noun.

Another confusing area in trademark law is to pick a word that you desire to trademark that clearly describes or identifies the product or service. You cannot use a descriptive term because it will not, by its use, advise the public that you are talking about a particular product or service instead of the general product or service in the marketplace. For example, a bank cannot trademark the term *savings account*. Because the two words *savings* and *account* are descriptive of an account in which you put your money to save, they are descriptive of the product and thus are not trademarkable.

The best way to get a trademarkable word is to make it distinctive. Words that are made up and/or arbitrary are good examples. For example, *Exxon* is a totally made up word and cannot be found in the dictionary. Consequently, it was a good word for a trademark.

Once you have selected your trademark and you have done a trademark search to determine whether it is relatively free in the marketplace, you will want to do a trademark registration with the U.S. Patent and Trademark Office. By registering the mark, you will be giving constructive notice to the world that the mark belongs to you. This will give you rights to sue anyone who uses the mark without your authorization. The registration of your mark is good for twenty years from the date of registration and can be renewed for periods of twenty years thereafter.

A practical problem arises from the creation of a trademark. A good mark will attract the attention of others. To protect it, you must police it by filing a suit against abusers and stop them from using your mark. If you do not police your mark, you can lose it to general use in the public domain. This requirement of policing the mark creates a disadvantage to a small company. It's one thing for IBM to file a suit to protect the use of its "Big Blue" logo and another thing for a small, one-person operation to try to take on giant companies that may be attempting to pirate a trademark. This aspect is unfortunate, but it is one of the practicalities of the law and one that you must be aware of as you spend the money to develop your mark.

Patents

If you think that the laws for copyright and trademark are complicated, patent laws are even more so. A lot of companies promote taking your product and for a fee getting you a patent. These companies, for the most part, should be avoided. I would encourage you to work only with an attorney who specializes in patent law. Attorneys' expertise is easy to check out, and if you have a problem with the attorney from an ethical point of view, you have a powerful ally in a State Bar Association that governs the licensing of attorneys. Although the patent process is difficult, it would be unfair if I didn't also note the tremendous monetary possibilities of securing a patent on a process or product that proves marketable. If you can secure your patent, you will be given a virtual monopoly of ownership during the period of your patent that could result in financial security.

Patent law is found in Title 35 of the U.S. Code and through the Manual of Patent Office Procedures at the U.S. Patent Office. Three basic types of patents are granted: (1) a utility or functional patent, which governs the workings of the article themselves and protects their actual function rather than their look; (2) a design patent for creating new designs in an existing product; and (3) a plant patent, which can be obtained for creating a new variety of plant. In addition, the patent also must be (1) novel; (2) nonobvious; and (3) useful. Assuming that your creation falls within those categories, you can obtain a patent for your invention.

There are alternatives to the patent process. One of the major options is to continue to remain secret about your product. If you get a patent, you will have to disclose the precise workings of your product, including the drawings. A competitor can take these drawings, modify them, and depending on the degree of modification, may be able to use them with immunity to your patent. In addition, supplying your competitor with the exact drawings may allow more unscrupulous competitors to operate by ignoring your patent. Of course, such a course of action allows you to sue the violator, but the cost of enforcing your patent could be prohibitive in and of itself. In addition, like the problem of piracy with trademarks, patents also have been pirated overseas, and, although the inventor has the rights to sue to protect it, the cost involved in an international patent lawsuit may prove prohibitive for the individual inventor.

The first thought that most people have regarding the failure to file the patent is that you may lose all of your work. This is true, but you also have to weigh the possibility of people copying your work and producing something similar. This was obviously the thinking of Coca-Cola when they selected neither to copyright, trademark, or patent their formula for Coca-Cola. That recipe is kept a secret and thus, prevents anyone from copying it directly from the patent filing.

It usually takes two to three years to obtain a patent. Once you receive the patent, it is issued generally for a period of either three and one-half, seven, or fourteen years, depending on the patent office and your negotiation with them for that protected period. One possibility to consider if you receive a patent is to license a patent to a larger company who would be able to spend the money to enforce and protect your patent in the general marketplace. Selling off a license interest to a major company might decrease some of your profit, but it would likely provide you with steady income and assurance that your patent is protected in the long run.

Licenses

It isn't often that entire new industries are created by a marketing concept. However, in the case of licensing of products, that is exactly what happens. According to the *Licensing Letter*, total retail sales of licensed products in the United States and Canada tripled from $20.6 billion to $70 billion from 1982 to 1994. In addition, $31.2 billion of licensed merchandise is sold each year overseas. The result of these rather startling statistics is that the licensing industry has come of age big time.

The concept of licensing is in essence the leasing of legal rights from one entity to another entity. These legal rights are typically the use of property, which covers everything from the name of a company, a design, a logo, or a concept, such as the design of clothes. The license is typically granted for a specific use and for a certain period. Sometimes there also is a geographic limitation. In exchange for this right, the person granting the right (the licensor) receives a fee from the licensee, which typically is based on a percentage of the wholesale price of every product actually sold, which offers the advantage to the licensor of receiving a stream of payment without any overhead or additional costs other than what it took originally to develop the licensed property.

Licensing is not a new concept. It dates back to the 1800s, when the British characters Punch and Judy were licensed out to banks and other companies. However, it hasn't been until the recent surge and success in the sports world that we have seen such a massive proliferation of the concept. Although licensing is not limited to the sports world, I think it can certainly be credited with having brought to the forefront the notion of licensing and the dollars that it can generate. The result of that success has brought licensing into all other types of fields, from Hollywood studios, to major corporations such as Coca-Cola and Ford Motor Company, to fashion designers such as Oleg Cassini or Ralph Lauren.

In addition to providing an outlet for the licensor's products and assisting in product cross-merchandising, the licensing of concepts also helps corporate marketers test new products in a relatively risk-free way. By licensing the products instead of creating their own marketing force, the licensor can determine the success potential of the product or product line without risk. In addition, for some corporations licensing can actually be a more cost-efficient method of generating profits than creating and manufacturing a new product line.

Licensors receive benefits as well. In many cases, the licensor may be new in a particular market, and by purchasing licensing rights, can immediately create name awareness and establish a brand line. For example, licensees who produce educational products for children can enjoy instant name recognition if they can obtain the license rights to use the Sesame Street association. By gaining immediate name recognition, the product becomes one immediately known in the marketplace.

There are ten major categories of licensing products:

1. *Entertainment and character licensing.* Entertainment and character licensing includes long-term standard properties, such as the Sesame Street characters and more short-term properties, such as those generated by the latest Disney movie. Common examples of licensing

in this area feature the characters of the movie that generate a toy sold by one of your favorite hamburger chains. In this matter it is sometimes said that licensing has become more successful than the sale of the hamburger itself.

2. *Sports licensing*. This category of licensing has evolved as sports organizations have looked to other avenues to generate more dollars to pay the rising salaries that players are demanding. In addition, since the mid-1980s, the use of licensing by colleges and universities has increased in an unprecedented way. Universities are recognizing that they have a superior product, which because of brand loyalty can generate a great deal of additional dollars for the university. Although they are not in the business of selling clothes and other products, licensing offers them the advantage of being able to receive proceeds off the products that are endorsed with their name. It is now estimated that colleges alone are responsible for $1 to $3 billion in retail sales.

3. *Fashion licensing*. This category includes not only clothing lines, but also jewelry and cosmetics. In a growing number of cases, licensing has become so successful that some major name brands have dropped their own production of merchandise manufacturing and have converted to full-time licensing.

4. *Corporate trademark and brand licensing*. This category includes most of the household names that you would be familiar with. Harley Davidson, Betty Crocker, Coca-Cola, Pizza Hut, and Disney are all examples of companies that are heavy into licensing their corporate logo and name in addition to brand licensing of additional products themselves.

5. *Toy companies*. Toy companies have entered the licensing business to extend their product lines. They will take a product character, such as GI Joe, and extend it beyond a toy into books, video games, and even movies.

6. *Music licensing*. Music licensing is another successful category in brand licensing. This category includes not only the performers themselves who are endorsing products, but also record companies. Unique examples of product extension in the music area are the licensing by musicians who

produce music, comic books, or clothing apparel.

7. *Publishing.* The publishing world is another area where licensing has certainly expanded. Sports Illustrated, Playboy, and Better Homes and Gardens, are all examples of companies who have taken their name and extended it into other product areas. Better Homes and Gardens has licensed its name to Wal-Mart for use in an entire line of hardware and gardening products. Better Homes and Gardens benefits by the income produced solely by their respected name, and Wal-Mart achieves instant name recognition for an entire line of products.

8. *Nonprofit licensing.* Nonprofit licensing is one of the newest areas in licensing. The National Audubon Society and the Sierra Club have made major inroads into creating product lines around their respected areas of concentration or specialty. I think that we will see more active participation by nonprofit organizations as they begin to see cutbacks from the federal government in both grants and donations. These organizations realize that they must begin to find other avenues to receive income, and licensing is an option that gives them that kind of potential.

9. *Celebrity licensing.* Celebrity licensing is a common way of receiving endorsements. Celebrities release the use of their famous name or picture to appear with a product or a company in exchange for a marketing or promotional fee. It is becoming more common with the growth of the entire licensing industry.

10. *Art licensing.* Art licensing is a relatively new concept for the licensing industry. Some of the major museums throughout the world are licensing successful art and reproducing it in various collections sold by the museum in the form of greeting cards, gift items, and other similar types of products.

How Profitable Is Licensing?

Licensing can be extremely profitable for the licensor, particularly considering that it is an extension of something they already have. Royalty percentages are the most common method of compensation and range between 5% and 12% of the wholesale price of each item sold. Depending on how well-known and successful the license already is, the licensor may ask for a guarantee against future sales. In this case, the risk of success is shifted totally to the licensee, who either must produce a minimum sale volume or is out of the game. For example, if you had a rock band and you were selling your rock band's name or likeness on a T-shirt, you might contract to receive a royalty of 10% of the wholesale price of the T-shirt. Assuming the sale of one million T-shirts at a retail price of $15.00 and a wholesale price of $5.00, your royalty for the use of your name would be $500,000. Not bad pay for doing nothing more than lending your name or likeness. Of course, your name and likeness have to be worth something for you to be able to command this kind of payback.

he Disadvantages?

antages for the licensor revolve ensing success. You may have problem the United States expe- h the trade agreements with was not doing anything to keep pirating down in the record industry. For every record or other product that is pirated away, neither the original creator nor the licensor receives any royalty on the product. The result is that millions, if not billions, of dollars have been lost overseas because of the lack of ability of U.S. companies to enforce their patents and trademarks and make the license worthwhile. In addition, even in the United States, licensors must be diligent to make sure they enforce and protect their trademark, patent, or copyright interest to be able to keep that product from entering the public domain and from losing its licensing value.

How Do I Get Started?

After reading this overview on licensing, if you think that licensing is a possibility for your business, I would suggest that you consider contacting some of the leaders in the industry. There are two major licensing trade shows each year, one by the Licensing Industry Merchandisers Association, normally held in June (they can be reached at 212-244-1944), or the World Wide Licensing Exposition, normally held in April (call 212-545-4510). For additional information, you might consider contacting the *Licensing Letter* (212-941-0099) or requesting information about purchasing the *Licensing Book* (212-575-4510).

FORM TX
For a Literary Work
UNITED STATES COPYRIGHT OFFICE

REGISTRATION NUMBER

_____
TX   TXU
EFFECTIVE DATE OF REGISTRATION

_____
Month   Day   Year

DO NOT WRITE ABOVE THIS LINE. IF YOU NEED MORE SPACE, USE A SEPARATE CONTINUATION SHEET.

1 TITLE OF THIS WORK ▼

PREVIOUS OR ALTERNATIVE TITLES ▼

PUBLICATION AS A CONTRIBUTION If this work was published as a contribution to a periodical, serial, or collection, give information about the collective work in which the contribution appeared. **Title of Collective Work ▼**

If published in a periodical or serial give: Volume ▼   Number ▼   Issue Date ▼   On Pages ▼

2 a NAME OF AUTHOR ▼   DATES OF BIRTH AND DEATH
                                                            Year Born ▼   Year Died ▼

Was this contribution to the work a   AUTHOR'S NATIONALITY OR DOMICILE   WAS THIS AUTHOR'S CONTRIBUTION TO
"work made for hire"?   Name of Country   THE WORK   If the answer to either
  ☐ Yes   OR ┌ Citizen of ▶ _____   Anonymous?   ☐ Yes ☐ No   of these questions is
  ☐ No   └ Domiciled in ▶ _____   Pseudonymous? ☐ Yes ☐ No   "Yes," see detailed
                                                                                                            instructions.
NATURE OF AUTHORSHIP Briefly describe nature of material created by this author in which copyright is claimed. ▼

NOTE
Under the law, the "author" of a "work made for hire" is generally the employer, not the employee (see instructions). For any part of this work that was "made for hire" check "Yes" in the space provided, give the employer (or other person for whom the work was prepared) as "Author" of that part, and leave the space for dates of birth and death blank.

b NAME OF AUTHOR ▼   DATES OF BIRTH AND DEATH
                                                          Year Born ▼   Year Died ▼

Was this contribution to the work a   AUTHOR'S NATIONALITY OR DOMICILE   WAS THIS AUTHOR'S CONTRIBUTION TO
"work made for hire"?   Name of Country   THE WORK   If the answer to either
  ☐ Yes   OR ┌ Citizen of ▶ _____   Anonymous?   ☐ Yes ☐ No   of these questions is
  ☐ No   └ Domiciled in ▶ _____   Pseudonymous? ☐ Yes ☐ No   "Yes," see detailed
                                                                                                            instructions.
NATURE OF AUTHORSHIP Briefly describe nature of material created by this author in which copyright is claimed. ▼

c NAME OF AUTHOR ▼   DATES OF BIRTH AND DEATH
                                                          Year Born ▼   Year Died ▼

Was this contribution to the work a   AUTHOR'S NATIONALITY OR DOMICILE   WAS THIS AUTHOR'S CONTRIBUTION TO
"work made for hire"?   Name of Country   THE WORK   If the answer to either
  ☐ Yes   OR ┌ Citizen of ▶ _____   Anonymous?   ☐ Yes ☐ No   of these questions is
  ☐ No   └ Domiciled in ▶ _____   Pseudonymous? ☐ Yes ☐ No   "Yes," see detailed
                                                                                                            instructions.
NATURE OF AUTHORSHIP Briefly describe nature of material created by this author in which copyright is claimed. ▼

3 a YEAR IN WHICH CREATION OF THIS   **b** DATE AND NATION OF FIRST PUBLICATION OF THIS PARTICULAR WORK
        WORK WAS COMPLETED This information   Complete this information Month ▶ _____ Day ▶ _____ Year ▶ _____
                            must be given   ONLY if this work
                            ◀ Year in all cases. has been published.   _____ ◀ Nation

4 COPYRIGHT CLAIMANT(S) Name and address must be given even if the claimant is the same as   APPLICATION RECEIVED
      the author given in space 2. ▼   _____
                                                                                                    ONE DEPOSIT RECEIVED
See instructions   _____
before completing   TWO DEPOSITS RECEIVED
this space.   _____
      TRANSFER If the claimant(s) named here in space 4 is (are) different from the author(s) named in   FUNDS RECEIVED
      space 2, give a brief statement of how the claimant(s) obtained ownership of the copyright. ▼ _____

MORE ON BACK ▶ • Complete all applicable spaces (numbers 5-11) on the reverse side of this page.   DO NOT WRITE HERE
                • See detailed instructions.   • Sign the form at line 10.   Page 1 of ____ pages

COPYRIGHTS, TRADEMARKS, PATENTS, AND LICENSES

EXAMINED BY _____ FORM TX

CHECKED BY _____

☐ CORRESPONDENCE
   Yes

FOR
COPYRIGHT
OFFICE
USE
ONLY

DO NOT WRITE ABOVE THIS LINE. IF YOU NEED MORE SPACE, USE A SEPARATE CONTINUATION SHEET.

PREVIOUS REGISTRATION Has registration for this work, or for an earlier version of this work, already been made in the Copyright Office?
☐ Yes ☐ No If your answer is "Yes," why is another registration being sought? (Check appropriate box) ▼
a. ☐ This is the first published edition of a work previously registered in unpublished form.
b. ☐ This is the first application submitted by this author as copyright claimant.
c. ☐ This is a changed version of the work, as shown by space 6 on this application.
If your answer is "Yes," give: **Previous Registration Number** ▼   **Year of Registration** ▼

5

DERIVATIVE WORK OR COMPILATION Complete both space 6a and 6b for a derivative work; complete only 6b for a compilation.
a. **Preexisting Material** Identify any preexisting work or works that this work is based on or incorporates. ▼

b. **Material Added to This Work** Give a brief, general statement of the material that has been added to this work and in which copyright is claimed. ▼

6

See instructions
before completing
this space.

—space deleted—

7

REPRODUCTION FOR USE OF BLIND OR PHYSICALLY HANDICAPPED INDIVIDUALS A signature on this form at space 10 and a check in one of the boxes here in space 8 constitutes a non-exclusive grant of permission to the Library of Congress to reproduce and distribute solely for the blind and physically handicapped and under the conditions and limitations prescribed by the regulations of the Copyright Office: (1) copies of the work identified in space 1 of this application in Braille (or similar tactile symbols); or (2) phonorecords embodying a fixation of a reading of that work; or (3) both.

a ☐ Copies and Phonorecords   b ☐ Copies Only   c ☐ Phonorecords Only

8

See instructions.

DEPOSIT ACCOUNT If the registration fee is to be charged to a Deposit Account established in the Copyright Office, give name and number of Account.
Name ▼   Account Number ▼

CORRESPONDENCE Give name and address to which correspondence about this application should be sent.   Name/Address/Apt/City/State/ZIP ▼

Area Code and Telephone Number ▶

9

Be sure to
give your
daytime phone
◀ number

CERTIFICATION* I, the undersigned, hereby certify that I am the
                                          ☐ author
                     Check only one ▶   ☐ other copyright claimant
                                          ☐ owner of exclusive right(s)
                                          ☐ authorized agent of _____
of the work identified in this application and that the statements made
by me in this application are correct to the best of my knowledge.   Name of author or other copyright claimant, or owner of exclusive right(s) ▲

Typed or printed name and date ▼ If this application gives a date of publication in space 3, do not sign and submit it before that date.
_____   date ▶

Handwritten signature (X) ▼

10

MAIL CERTIFI-CATE TO	Name ▼	YOU MUST: • Complete all necessary spaces • Sign your application in space 10 **SEND ALL 3 ELEMENTS IN THE SAME PACKAGE:** 1. Application form 2. Nonrefundable $20 filing fee in check or money order payable to *Register of Copyrights* 3. Deposit material **MAIL TO:** Register of Copyrights Library of Congress Washington, D.C. 20559-6000
Certificate will be mailed in window envelope	Number/Street/Apartment Number ▼ City/State/ZIP ▼	

11

The Copyright Office has the authority to adjust fees at 5-year intervals, based on changes in the Consumer Price Index. The next adjustment is due in 1996. Please contact the Copyright Office after July 1995 to determine the actual fee schedule.

*17 U.S.C. § 506(e): Any person who knowingly makes a false representation of a material fact in the application for copyright registration provided for by section 409, or in any written statement filed in connection with the application, shall be fined not more than $2,500.

July 1993—400,000   ✿ PRINTED ON RECYCLED PAPER   ☆U.S. GOVERNMENT PRINTING OFFICE: 1993-342-582/80,020

CHAPTER TWELVE

YOUR BUSINESS AND TAXES

There are two major types of corporations: the regular corporation or C corporation, which is an individual entity and taxed as a separate taxpayer, and the Sub Chapter S corporation, which is an entity that does not pay taxes at the corporate level, but passes all income and losses directly to its shareholders. To understand fully the ramifications of paying corporate tax, you should review the schedule of taxation (Exhibit 12-1). In addition, states have their own tax schedules, and you should know the requirements for state income tax.

Estimated Tax Returns

A corporation is required to file quarterly an estimate of the taxes that will be owed for the total year. The purpose of this filing is to get money to the IRS before the end of the year. To assist you in completing your estimated calculations, I would suggest you use Form 1120-W, "U.S. Corporation Work Sheet for Computation of Estimated Income Tax." A copy of this form is provided for your convenience at the end of this chapter.

All estimated tax payments are deposited into local commercial banks in an account specially designated for that purpose and the payment is accompanied

Exhibit 12-1
Federal Tax Schedules for a C Corporation

If taxable income (line 30, Form 1120, or line 26, Form 1120-A) on page 1 is:

Over—	But not over—	Tax is:	Of the amount over—
$0	$50,000	15%	$0
50,000	75,000	$7,500 + 25%	50,000
75,000	100,000	13,750 + 34%	75,000
100,000	335,000	22,250 + 39%	100,000
335,000	10,000,000	113,900 + 34%	335,000
10,000,000	15,000,000	3,400,000 + 35%	10,000,000
15,000,000	18,333,333	5,150,000 + 38%	15,000,000
18,333,333	—	35%	0

by Form 503, "The Federal Tax Deposit, Corporation Income Tax." A corporation that fails to pay the correct installment of estimated tax in full by the due date is likely to be subject to a penalty. The penalty rate applies to the period of underpayment on any installment due. The penalty is calculated at a rate of interest published by the Internal Revenue Service.

Dividend Reporting Forms

In addition to the tax forms that you are required to file, a corporation that pays dividends during the year is required to notify the Internal Revenue Service by using Form 1099-DIV for each shareholder who was paid. For your convenience, a copy of this form is included at the end of this chapter.

Employment Taxes

A corporation is responsible for paying employment taxes on each and every employee by withholding a portion of each employee's wages. This amount is calculated using the withholding allowance exemptions that the employee supplies to the corporate employer. The exemptions are based on the number of dependents that the employee has. To determine the correct amount, each employee should complete a W-4 form, Employee Withholding Allowance Certificate, at the beginning of employment. Should the number of dependents change during the course of employment, this form can be changed and the withholding taxes adjusted.

In addition to employment taxes, the corporation is responsible for withholding from the employee's wages social security taxes and contributing in equal part to social security payments. The tax is based on a percentage of the employee's salary up to a certain maximum figure. The corporation files quarterly returns disclosing the amount of tax paid on Form 941. These deposits for social security are placed in a special depository in a local bank. Finally, the corporation also must file an unemployment tax return, Form 940, that calculates the amount of unemployment tax that it is required to pay. This tax is charged directly to the corporation, not to the individual employee.

> **PROFIT STRATEGY:**
>
> As an employee, adjust your withholding allowance if you are getting refunds each year. The adjustments give you more cash flow each month by not taking out excess withholding payments. Use the additional cash flow to buy something that will grow in value.

Care in handling employment taxes is extremely critical for new businesses. Many businesses use the taxes due to assist with cash flow during difficult times. This is not only unwise, but also extremely dangerous because under the Internal Revenue Code, the employer's officers and directors can be held personally liable for unpaid employment taxes. Under those circumstances, the IRS can pierce the corporate veil, going directly to the officers' and directors' personal assets for the payment of employment taxes. In addition, the penalties for failure to pay can dramatically increase the overall amount due, resulting in tremendous hardships for not only the new company, but also the individual officers and directors.

The following publications produced by the IRS should be ordered by all new businesses to assist you with compliance: Circular E, *Employers Tax Guide*, *A Business Tax Kit*, Publication 454, and *A Tax Guide for Small Businesses*. These may be obtained by calling the IRS at (800) TAX-FORMS.

Taxpayer Identification Number

The ID number for individual taxpayers is their social security number. If you are operating as a sole proprietorship, you can continue to use your social security number for your business. However, if you operate as a partnership or corporation, you must have a separate employer ID number (EIN) to use as your taxpayer identification number. In addition, sole proprietors must have EINs if they pay wages to one or more employee or are required to file any pension or excise tax returns.

To obtain an EIN, use Form SS-4, and file it with the Internal Revenue Service. You should do this as quickly as possible when starting your business because it may take thirty to sixty days to get the EIN. Between applying and receiving the number, you can simply put "applied for" on any official correspondence that would require this number.

Recordkeeping Requirements

Now that you have formed your own business, you are subject to all sorts of new regulatory constraints, including recordkeeping. Unfortunately, entrepreneurs are notoriously poor recordkeepers. Yet to justify and preserve many of the deductions that you will attempt to receive as benefits from operating your business, records are a necessity. In addition, you will find that, as your company grows larger and becomes subject to other regulations and/or potential lawsuits, keeping accurate corporate records is necessary to prove your positions.

Records monitor how your business is actually doing. Records can be used for inventory control and to determine which products and services may need to be either increased or decreased. At some point in your business growth, you will likely need to borrow money. All lenders require accurate financial statements of your business. It would be impossible to construct accurate profits and losses of your company without having consistent records.

As your business begins to develop, you will receive money from a variety of sources. Your records will need to identify specifically where this money has come from and whether or not it is income or contributions of capital. Without adequate records, this money could be improperly allocated, and thus, you would be required to pay income tax on money that has come into the business and should have been nontaxable.

Last, you will need the records to prepare your tax return. If you ever are audited by the IRS, the records will establish the deductibility of any item. Failure to have proper records will allow the IRS to reconstruct the potential deduction in a manner that is less favorable to you.

What Type of Records Are You Required to Keep?

The law does not require any specific type of records to keep. You should adopt a system that is best suited for you and that you feel will clearly show your income and expense deductions. One area of concern to the Internal Revenue Service when they are reviewing a business is travel and entertainment deductions. Consequently, a business should be careful to maintain accurate records in this area. For special assistance on the rules and regulations governing these kinds of deductions, you should refer to Publication 463, *Travel, Entertainment, and Gift Expenses* (call 800-TAX-FORM). In addition, you may want to consider ordering Publication 917, *Business Use of a Car*. These publications are available free from the IRS and clearly disclose the type of deductions that are allowed and the records that are necessary to preserve those deductions.

Another area of great concern to the Internal Revenue Service is employment taxes and income tax withholding. Once you have employees, your responsibilities heighten with the IRS, and you should take great care to pay the appropriate tax and to withhold the correct amount of money from an employee. I would recommend that you maintain separate files on each employee showing his or her name, address, and social security number. In addition, you should use a table to show the amount of wages earned and the amount of withholding done for each employee. You also should keep the W-4 forms that establish the number of allowances your employees elected to take based on their individual circumstances.

As your corporation begins to expand, you will begin to acquire assets such as furniture and machinery. You must keep records about these assets to depreciate them and take deductions, along with reporting gain or loss when you actually sell the asset. As a general guideline, your records should show:

1. When and how you acquired the asset
2. Purchase price
3. Cost of any improvements

4. Whether you amortized or expensed the deduction (Section 179)
5. Deductions taken for depreciation
6. Deductions taken for casualty losses
7. How you use the asset
8. When and how you disposed of the asset
9. Selling price
10. Expenses of sales

It is always advisable to keep separate receipts for any assets purchased and to maintain those records for any audit review. How long should you keep the records? The Internal Revenue Service has no set guidelines for the length of time you are required to keep business records. The general rule is that you must keep them as long as necessary to provide backup information that the Internal Revenue Service might need. That statement being vague and unhelpful, the most prudent method is to keep the records for the duration of the statute of limitations, the time during which you can amend your return to claim a credit refund or the IRS can assess additional tax, which is generally the later of three years after the date your return is due or filed or two years after the date the tax is paid. Returns filed before the due date are treated as filed on the due date. The Internal Revenue Service has three years from the date you file your return to assess any additional tax. If you file a fraudulent return or no return at all, the IRS has a longer time to assess the tax.

You must keep employee records at least four years after the date taxes become due or are paid, whichever is later. This includes all of the records previously discussed, maintaining a separate file on each employee. Regarding assets purchased by your business, you should keep records relating to the property until the statute of limitations expires for the year in which you sell the property.

Accounting Periods and Methods

All businesses must calculate their taxable income and file an income tax return on the basis of their annual accounting period. Your "tax year" is the annual accounting period you use for recordkeeping purposes and for reporting your income and expenses. You have two alternatives that you can use: (1) a calendar year or (2) a fiscal year.

If you adopt the calendar year for an annual accounting period, you must maintain your books and records and report your income and expenses for the period of January 1 through December 31 of each year. A fiscal tax year is twelve consecutive months ending on the last day of any month except December. If you adopt a fiscal tax year, you must maintain your books and records and report your income and expenses using that same tax year every year. As a general rule, most businesses now adopt the calendar year because employment taxes and other records must still be maintained on a calendar year basis, and many of the advantages that were once available for income shifting between different entities based on various tax reporting years are no longer available. Consequently, unless you get specific advice from your tax advisor to adopt a fiscal year, it is likely that the calendar year will be best for your purposes.

Accounting Methods

In addition to selecting an accounting period, you also must determine which accounting method your business will follow. In general, the two primary accounting methods are the cash method and the accrual method. For certain depreciable items, there will be exceptions to this rule, but these two methods are by far the most widely used.

The cash method of accounting is the primary method used by most businesses. However, if inventories are necessary in accounting for your income, you must use a separate accrual method for sales and purchases. If you do not have to keep inventories, you usually will use the cash method. With the cash method you report income when you get it as opposed to earned but not received yet. Expenses are deducted when actually paid as opposed to billed.

Under the accrual method of accounting, income generally is reported in the year earned and expenses or deductions are capitalized in the year incurred. Although the purpose of an accrual method of accounting is to match your income and your expenses in the correct year. The accrual method is the most accurate method to reflect the actual flow of your

> **PROFIT STRATEGY:**
> Section 179 allows you to expense up to $25,000 of equipment purchased in your business instead of amortizing it. Use this faster method to increase your deduction.

income and expenses, it is generally considered more cumbersome and difficult for small businesses than the cash method.

Travel, Entertainment, and Gift Expenses

This category of business deductions is the one favored by most entrepreneurs. The reason, of course, is because by structuring it properly, you can both enjoy yourself and take deductions on things that would normally not be deductible. This does not imply that you should take deductions when they are not allowed, but to encourage you to structure your travel and entertainment to involve your business and make the expense deductible.

Travel Expenses

For tax purposes, travel expenses are ordinary and necessary expenses that you pay while traveling away from home for your business or profession (Table 12-1). An ordinary expense is one that is common and accepted in your field of business, trade, or profession. A necessary expense is one that is helpful and appropriate to your business. An expense does not have to be indispensable to be considered necessary. However, you cannot deduct expenses that are lavish or extravagant.

Traveling away from Home

You are traveling away from home if: (1) your duties require you to be away from the general area of your tax home substantially longer than an ordinary day's work; and (2) you need to get sleep or rest to meet the demands of your work while away from home.

Tax Home

To deduct travel expenses, you must first determine the location of your tax home. Generally, your tax home is your regular place of business or post of duty, regardless of where you maintain your family home. It includes the entire city or general area in which your business or work is located. If you have more than one regular place of business, your tax home is your main place of business. If you do not have a regular or a main place of business because of the nature of your work, then your tax home may be the place where you regularly live.

If you do not fit any of these categories, you are considered a transient (an itinerant), and your tax home is wherever you

Table 12-1. Deductible Travel Expenses

Expense	Description
Transportation	The cost of travel by airplane, train, or bus between your home and your business destination.
Tax, commuter bus, and limousine	Fares for these and other types of transportation and limousine between the airport or station and your hotel, or between the hotel and your work location away from home.
Baggage and shipping	The cost of sending baggage and sample or display material between your regular and temporary work locations.
Car	The costs of operating and maintaining your car when traveling away from home on business. You may deduct actual expenses or the standard mileage rate, including business-related tolls and parking. If you lease a car while away from home on business, you can deduct business related expenses only.
Lodging	The cost of lodging if your business trip is overnight or long enough to require you to stop to get substantial sleep or rest to perform your duties properly.
Meals	The cost of meals only if your business trip is overnight or long enough to require you to stop to get substantial sleep or rest. Includes amounts spent for food, beverages, taxes, and related tips.
Cleaning	Cleaning and laundry expenses while away from home overnight.
Telephone	The cost of business calls while on your business trip, including business communication by fax machine or other communication devices.
Tips	Tips you pay for any expenses in this chart.
Other	Other similar ordinary and necessary expenses related to your business travel, such as public stenographers' fees and computer rental fees.

work. As a transient, you cannot claim a travel expense deduction because you are never considered away from your home.

Once you have determined that you are traveling away from your tax home, you can determine what travel expenses are deductible. You should keep records of all the expenses you incur. You can use a log, diary, notebook, or any other written record to keep track of your expenses.

Deductible Travel Expenses

Deductible travel expenses include those ordinary and necessary expenses you incur while traveling away from home or business. The type of expense you can deduct depends on the facts and your circumstances.

Travel Expenses for Another Individual

If a spouse, dependent, or other individual goes with you (or your employee) on a business trip to a business convention, you generally cannot deduct their travel expenses. You can only deduct the travel expenses you pay or incur for an accompanying individual if that individual (1) is your employee; (2) has a bona fide business purpose for the travel; and (3) would otherwise be allowed to deduct the travel expenses.

A bona fide business purpose requires a real business purpose for the individual's presence. Incidental services, such as typing notes or assisting in entertaining customers, are not enough to warrant a deduction.

New Business

You cannot deduct amounts you spend for travel to conduct a general search for, or preliminary investigation of, a new business.

Travel in the United States

The following discussion applies to travel in the United States, that is, the fifty states and the District of Columbia. The treatment of your travel expenses depends on how much of your trip was business related and how much of your trip occurred within the United States.

Trip Primarily for Business

You can deduct all your travel expenses if your trip was entirely business related. If your trip was primarily for business and, while at your business destination, you extended your stay for a vacation, made a nonbusiness side trip, or had other nonbusiness activities, you can deduct only your business-related expenses. These expenses include the travel costs of getting to and from your business destination and any business-related expenses at your business destination.

Trip Primarily for Personal Reasons

If your trip was primarily for personal reasons, such as a vacation, the entire cost of the trip is a nondeductible personal expense. However, you can deduct any expenses you have while at your destination that are directly related to your business.

A trip to a resort or on a cruise ship may be a vacation even if the promoter advertises that it is primarily for business. The scheduling of incidental business activities during a trip, such as viewing videotapes or attending lectures, will not change what is really a vacation into a business trip. If you attend an event at a resort or other luxury type location, make sure you are very careful to keep accurate records of all business or courses attended. Any auditor will look carefully at this item, and the way to getting a successful deduction is to be able to show the business value or purpose of the trip. Keep in mind the specific reasons why you intended to take the trip for business. Perhaps it was the end of the year and you needed continuing educational credits, so you had to take the course in Hawaii. Whatever the reason, document everything.

Travel Outside the United States

If any part of your business travel is outside the United States, some of your deductions for the cost of getting to and from your destination may be limited. How much of your travel expenses you can deduct depends in part on how much of your trip outside the United States was business related.

Travel Entirely for Business

If you travel outside the United States and you spend the entire time on business activities, all your travel expenses of getting to and from your business destination are deductible. In addition, even if you do not spend your entire time on business activities, your trip is considered entirely for business and you can deduct all of your business-related travel expenses if you meet at least one of the following four conditions:

1. You did not have substantial control over arranging the trip. You are not

considered to have substantial control merely because you have control over the timing of your trip. A self-employed person generally is regarded as having substantial control over arranging business trips.
2. You were outside the United States for a week or less, combining business and nonbusiness activities. One week means seven consecutive days. In counting the days, do not count the day you leave the United States, but count the day you return to the United States.
3. You were outside the United States more than a week, but you spent less than 25% of the total time you were outside the United States on nonbusiness activities. For this purpose, count both the day your trip began and the day on which it ended.
4. You can establish that a personal vacation was not a major consideration, even if you have substantial control over arranging the trip.

If you do not meet any of these conditions, you may still be able to deduct some of your expenses. The key will be documentation and consideration of these rules.

Travel Primarily for Business

If you traveled outside the United States primarily for business purposes, but spent 25% or more of your time on non-business activities, your travel expense deductions are limited unless you meet one of the four conditions listed. If your deductions are limited, you must allocate your travel expenses of getting to and from your destination between your business and non-business activities to determine your deductible amount. These travel allocation rules are discussed in IRS Publication 463.

Trip Primarily for Vacation

If your travel was primarily for vacation or for investment purposes and you spent some time attending brief professional seminars or a continuing education program, the entire cost of the trip is a nondeductible personal expense. You may, however, deduct your registration fees and any other expenses incurred that were directly related to your business.

Conventions

You can deduct your travel expenses when you attend a convention if you can show that your attendance benefits your trade or business. You cannot deduct the travel expenses for your family. If the convention is for investment, political, social, or other purposes unrelated to your trade or business, you cannot deduct the expenses. Nonbusiness expenses, such as social or sightseeing expenses, are personal expenses and are not deductible. Your appointment or election as a delegate does not, in itself, entitle you to or deprive you of a deduction. Your attendance must be connected to your own trade or business.

The agenda of the convention does not have to deal specifically with your official duties or the responsibilities of your position or business. If the agenda is related to your active trade or business and your responsibilities, attendance for business purposes is justified.

> **PROFIT STRATEGY:**
> Don't be afraid to maximize your travel and entertainment deduction. Just follow the guidelines, keep good records, and you will have nothing to fear from the IRS.

Entertainment Expenses

You may be able to deduct business-related entertainment expenses. These include entertaining a client, customer, or employee. To be deductible, the expense must be both ordinary and necessary. An ordinary expense is one that is common and accepted in your field of business, trade, or profession. A necessary expense is one that is helpful and appropriate for your business. An expense does not have to be indispensable to be considered necessary.

In addition, the entertainment expense must either be *directly* related to your business, such as entertaining a specific customer, or *associated* with your business. The associated test allows you to be a little creative, but the expenses still need a connection to your business: (1) directly related test; or (2) associated test.

Even if you meet all the requirements for claiming a deduction for entertainment expenses, the amount you can deduct may be limited. Generally, you can deduct only 50% of your nonreimbursed entertainment expenses.

Club Dues and Membership Fees

You are not allowed a deduction for dues (including initiation fees) for membership in any club organized for business, pleasure, recreation, or other social purpose. This applies to any membership organization if one of its principal purposes is to conduct entertainment activities for members or their guests, or to provide members or their guests with access to entertainment facilities.

Entertainment

Entertainment includes any activity generally considered to provide entertainment, amusement, or recreation. Examples include entertaining guests at nightclubs; at social athletic and sporting clubs; at theaters; at sporting events; on yachts; or on hunting or fishing vacations, and similar trips. You cannot deduct expenses for entertainment if they are lavish or extravagant. If you buy a ticket to an entertainment event for a client, you generally can take into account only the face value of the ticket, even if you paid a higher price. Entertainment also may include meeting the personal, living, or family needs of individuals, such as providing food, a hotel suite, or a car to business customers or their families.

A Meal as a Form of Entertainment

Entertainment includes the cost of a meal you provide to a customer or client whether the meal is a part of other entertainment or by itself. A meal sold in the normal course of your business is not entertainment. Generally, to deduct an entertainment-related meal, you or your employee must be present when the food or beverages are provided. A meal expense includes the cost of food, beverages, taxes, and tips for the meal.

Expenses Not Considered Entertainment

Entertainment does not include supper money you give your employees who are working overtime, a hotel room you keep for your employees while on business travel, or a car used in your business (even if it is used for routine personal purposes, such as commuting to and from work). However, if you provide a hotel suite or a car to an employee who is on vacation, this is entertainment of the employee.

Fifty Percent Limit

In general, you can deduct only 50% of your business-related meal and entertainment expenses. This limit applies to employees or their employers, and to self-employed persons (including independent contractors) or their clients, depending on whether the expenses are reimbursed. The 50% limit applies to business meals or entertainment expenses incurred while: (1) traveling away from home (whether eating alone or with others) on business; (2) entertaining business customers at your place of business, a restaurant, or other location; or (3) attending a business convention or reception, business meeting, or business luncheon at a club.

Taxes and tips relating to a business meal or entertainment activity are included in the amount that is subject to the 50% limit. Expenses such as cover charges for admission to a nightclub, rent paid for a room in which you hold a dinner or cocktail party, or the amount paid for parking at a sports arena are subject to the 50% limit. However, the cost of transportation to and from a business meal or a business-related entertainment activity is not subject to the 50% limit.

If you pay or incur an expense for goods and services consisting of meals, entertainment, and other services (such as lodging or transportation), you must allocate that expense between the cost of meals and entertainment and the cost of the other services. You must have a reasonable basis for making this allocation. For example, you must allocate your expenses if a hotel includes one or more meals in its room charge, or if you are provided with one per diem amount to cover both your lodging and meal expenses.

Application of 50% Limit. The 50% limit on meal and entertainment expenses applies if the expense is otherwise deductible and is not exempted (see IRS Publication 335). The 50% limit also applies to activities that are not a trade or business. It applies to meal and entertainment expenses incurred for the production of income, including rental or royalty income. It also applies to the cost of meals included in deductible educational expenses.

You apply the 50% limit after determining the amount that would otherwise qualify for a deduction. You first determine the amount of meal and entertainment expenses that would be deductible under the rules discussed in this chapter. If you are self-employed, figure the limit on Schedule C. If you file Schedule C-EZ, enter the total amount of your business expenses on line 2. You can include only 50% of your meal and entertainment expenses in that total.

Business Gift Expenses

If you give business gifts in the course of your trade or business, you can deduct the cost subject to the limits and rules in this section.

Limit on Business Gifts

You can deduct no more than $25 for business gifts you give directly or indirectly to any one person during your tax year. A gift to a company that is intended for the eventual personal use or benefit of a particular person or a limited class of people will be considered an indirect gift to that particular person or to the individuals within that class of people who receive the gift.

If you and your spouse both give gifts, both of you are treated as one taxpayer. It does not matter whether you have separate businesses, are separately employed, or whether each of you has an independent connection with the recipient. If a partnership gives gifts, the partnership and the partners are treated as one taxpayer.

Gift or Entertainment

Any item that might be considered either a gift or an entertainment expense generally will be considered an entertainment expense. However, if you give a customer packaged food or beverages that you intend the customer to use at a later date, treat it as a gift expense.

If you give tickets to a theater performance or sporting event to a business customer and you do not go with the customer to the performance or event, you can choose to treat the tickets as either a gift or entertainment expense, whichever is to your advantage.

You can change your treatment of the tickets at a later date, but not after the time allowed for the assessment of income tax. In most instances, this assessment period ends three years after the due date of your income tax return. But if you go with the customer to the event, you must treat the cost of the tickets as an entertainment expense. You cannot choose, in this case, to treat the tickets as a gift expense.

PROFIT STRATEGY: The 50% limitation may cramp your style, but don't take the attitude that the deduction is not worth keeping records for. It is.

Local Transportation Expenses

Local transportation expenses include the ordinary and necessary expenses of getting from one workplace to another in the course of your business or profession when you are traveling within your tax home area. Local transportation expenses also include the cost of getting from your home to a temporary workplace when you have one or more regular places of work. These temporary workplaces can be either within the area of your tax home or outside that area.

Local business transportation does not include expenses you incur while traveling away from home overnight. Transportation expenses you can deduct while traveling away from home overnight are discussed earlier in this chapter under Travel Expenses. Local business transportation expenses include the cost of transportation by air, rail, bus or taxi, and the cost of driving and maintaining your car. You can deduct your expenses for local business transportation, including the business use of your car, if the expenses are ordinary and necessary.

Commuting Expenses

You cannot deduct the costs of taking a bus, trolley, subway, or taxi or of driving a car between your home and your main or regular place of work. These costs are personal commuting expenses. You cannot deduct commuting expenses no matter how far your home is from your regular place of work. You cannot deduct commuting expenses even if you work during the commuting trip.

Parking Fees

Fees you pay to park your car at your place of business are nondeductible commuting expenses. You can, however, deduct business-related parking fees when visiting a customer or client.

Hauling Tools or Instruments

If you haul tools or instruments in your vehicle while commuting to and from work, this does not make your commuting costs deductible. However, you can deduct additional costs, such as renting a trailer that you tow with your vehicle for carrying equipment to and from your job.

Advertising Display on Car

The use of your car to display material that advertises your business does not change the use of your car from personal use to business use. If you use this car for commuting or other personal uses, you cannot deduct your expenses for such uses.

Office in the Home

If you have an office in your home that qualifies as a principal place of business, you can deduct your daily transportation costs between your home and another work location in the same trade or business (see IRS Publication 587, *Business Use of Your Home*, for information on determining whether your home office qualifies as a principal place of business). Note that the home office deduction requires strict compliance to a set of rules. Make sure you read the publication and understand the requirements prior to taking a deduction.

Examples of Deductible Local Transportation

The following examples illustrate when you can deduct local transportation expenses based on the location of your work and your home:

1. Your office is in the same city as your home. You cannot deduct the cost of transportation between your home and your office. This is a personal commuting expense. You can deduct the cost of round-trip transportation between your office and a client's or customer's place of business.
2. You regularly work in an office in the city where you live. You attend a one-week training session at a different office in the same city. You travel directly from your home to the training location and return each day. You can deduct the cost of your daily round-trip transportation between your home and the training location.

Car Expenses

If you use your car for business purposes, you may be able to deduct car expenses. You generally can use one of two methods to figure your expenses: actual expenses or the standard mileage rate.

Whether you use actual expenses or the standard mileage rate, you must keep records to show when you started using your car for business and the cost or other basis of the car. Your records also must show the business miles and the total miles you drove your car during the year.

Actual Expenses

If you deduct actual expenses, you must keep records of the costs of operating the car. If you lease a car, you also must keep records of that cost. If you choose to deduct actual expenses, you can deduct the cost of the following items: depreciation, lease fees, rental fees, garage rent, licenses, repairs, gas, oil, tires, insurance, parking fees, tolls.

Business and Personal Use

If you use your car for both business and personal purposes, you must divide your expenses between business and personal use. For example, you are a contractor and drive your car 20,000 miles during the year, 12,000 miles for business use and 8,000 miles for personal use. You can claim only 60% (12,000 ÷ 20,000) of the cost of operating your car as a business expense.

PROFIT STRATEGY:
There also are tax ramifications for taking a home office deduction that may be unfavorable. For example, if you set up a portion of your home as an office and take depreciation, you will have to recapture on that portion when you sell your home. In addition, as part of your home was used for business, that portion will not qualify for the $125,000 capital gains exclusion of the sale of your home.

Taxes Paid on Your Car

You cannot deduct luxury or sales taxes, even if you use your car 100% for business. Luxury and sales taxes are part of your car's basis and may be recovered through depreciation.

Fines and Collateral

Fines and collateral expenses such as traffic school imposed for traffic violations are not deductible.

Leasing a Car

If you lease a car that you use in your business, you can deduct the part of each lease payment that is for the use of the car in your business. You cannot deduct any payments you make to buy a car even if the payments are called lease payments.

Depreciation and Section 179 Deductions

If you use your car for business purposes, you may be able to recover its cost by claiming a depreciation or Section 179 deduction. The amount you may claim depends on the year you placed the car in service and the amount of your business use.

Standard Mileage Rate

Instead of figuring actual expenses, you may be able to use the standard mileage rate to figure the deductible costs of operating your car, van, pickup, or panel truck for business purposes. You can use the standard mileage rate only for a car that you own. Since 1997 the standard mileage rate has been 31.5¢ a mile for all business miles.

If you choose to take the standard mileage rate, you cannot deduct actual operating expenses. These include depreciation, maintenance and repairs, gasoline (including gasoline taxes), oil, insurance, and vehicle registration fees. You generally can use the standard mileage rate regardless of whether you are reimbursed.

Choosing the Standard Mileage Rate

If you want to use the standard mileage rate for a car, you must choose it in the first year you place the car in service in business. Then in later years, you can choose to use the standard mileage rate or actual expenses.

If you choose the standard mileage rate, you are considered to have made an election not to use the accelerated cost recovery system (ACRS) or the modified accelerated cost recovery system (MACRS) because the standard mileage rate allows for depreciation. You also cannot claim the Section 179 deduction. If you change to the actual expenses method in a later year, but before your car is considered fully depreciated, you have to estimate the useful life of the car and use straight-line depreciation. For information on how to figure that depreciation, see the exception in Methods of Depreciation under Depreciation Deduction in Publication 917.

Standard Mileage Rate Not Allowed

You cannot use the standard mileage rate if you (1) do not own the car; (2) use the car for hire (such as a taxi); (3) operate two or more cars at the same time (as in fleet operations); or (4) claimed a deduction for the car in an earlier year using ACRS or MACRS depreciation or a Section 179 deduction.

Two or More Cars

If you own two or more cars that are used for business at the same time, you cannot take the standard mileage rate for the business use of any car. However, you may be able to deduct a part of the actual expenses for operating each of the cars. See Actual Car Expenses in Chapter 2 of Publication 917 for information on how to figure your deduction. You are not using two or more cars for business at the same time if you alternate using (use at different times) the cars for business.

Parking Fees and Tolls

In addition to using the standard mileage rate, you can deduct any business-related parking fees and tolls. (Parking fees that you pay to park your car at your place of work are nondeductible commuting expenses.)

Recordkeeping

This section discusses the written records you need to keep if you plan to deduct an expense discussed in this chapter. By keeping timely and accurate records, you will have evidence to show the IRS if your tax return is ever examined. Or, you may require proof of expenses for which you are reimbursing your employees under an accountable plan.

If you reimburse employees for business expenses that they incur on your behalf, this section applies to your employees as well as to you, the employer. Your employees must submit the proper records to you, and you must retain these records to support your deductible business expenses.

Proof

You must be able to prove (substantiate) your deductions for travel, entertainment, business gift, and transportation expenses. You should keep adequate records or have sufficient evidence that will support your own statement. Estimates or approximations do not qualify as proof of an expense.

Timely Recordkeeping

You do not need to write down the elements of every expense at the time of the expense. However, a record of the elements of an expense or of a business use made at or near the time of the expense or use, supported by sufficient documentary evidence, has more value than a statement prepared later when generally there is a lack of accurate recall. A log maintained on a weekly basis, which accounts for use during the week, is considered a record made at or near the time of the expense or use.

Duplicate Information

You do not have to record information in your account book or other record that duplicates information shown on a receipt as long as your records and receipts complement each other in an orderly manner.

Adequate Records

You should keep the proof you need for these items in an account book, diary, statement of expense, or similar record and keep adequate documentary evidence (such as receipts, canceled checks, or bills) that together will support each element of an expense.

Separating Expenses

Each separate payment usually is considered a separate expense. If you entertain a customer or client at dinner and then go to the theater, the dinner expense and the cost of the theater tickets are two separate expenses. You must record them separately in your records.

Totaling Items

You may make one daily entry for reasonable categories, such as taxi fares, telephone calls, gas and oil, or other incidental travel costs. Meals should be in a separate category. You should include tips with the costs of the services you received.

Expenses of a similar nature during the course of a single event are considered a single expense. For example, if during entertainment at a cocktail lounge, you pay separately for each serving of refreshments, the total expense for the refreshments is treated as a single expense.

Documentary Evidence

You generally must have documentary evidence, such as receipts, canceled checks, or bills to support your expenses. However, this evidence is not needed if (1) you have meal or lodging expenses when you travel away from home and you use a per diem allowance method for claiming these expenses; (2) you use the standard mileage rate to claim business car expenses; (3) your expense, other than lodging, is less than $25.00 (less than $75.00 for expenses incurred after September 30, 1995); or (4) you have a

> **PROFIT STRATEGY:**
> Recordkeeping for an automobile is a big hassle, but also a big deduction. Buy a small memo book, and keep it in your car to record expenses. You'll be amazed at the deduction if you keep records.

transportation expense for which no receipt is readily available.

Adequate Evidence

Documentary evidence ordinarily will be considered adequate if it shows the amount, date, place, and essential character of the expense. For example, a hotel receipt is enough to support expenses for business travel if it has: (1) the name and location of the hotel; (2) the dates you stayed there; and (3) separate amounts for charges such as lodging, meals, and telephone calls.

A restaurant receipt is enough to prove an expense for a business meal if it has: (1) the name and location of the restaurant; (2) the number of people served; and (3) the date and amount of the expense.

If a charge is made for items other than food and beverages, the receipt must show these.

Canceled Check

A canceled check, together with a bill from the payee, ordinarily establishes the cost. However, a canceled check by itself does not prove a business expense without other evidence to show that it was for a business purpose.

Business Purpose

A written statement of the business purpose of an expense generally is needed. However, the degree of proof varies according to the circumstances in each case. If the business purpose of an expense is clear from the surrounding circumstances, a written explanation is not needed. For example, a sales representative who calls on customers on an established sales route does not have to submit a written explanation of the business purpose for traveling that route.

Confidential Information

Confidential information relating to an element of a deductible expense, such as the place, business purpose, or business relationship, need not be put in your account book, diary, or other record. However, the information has to be recorded elsewhere at or near the time of the expense and be available to prove that element of the expense.

Inadequate Records

If you do not have adequate records to prove an element of an expense, then you must prove the element by (1) your own statement, whether written or oral, containing specific information about the element; and (2) other established evidence sufficient to establish the element.

Additional Information for the IRS

You may have to provide additional information to the IRS to clarify or to establish the accuracy or reliability of information contained in your records, statements, testimony, or documentary evidence before a deduction is allowed.

How Long to Keep Records and Receipts

You must keep proof to support your claim to a deduction as long as your income tax return can be examined. Generally, it will be necessary for you to keep your records for three years from the date you file the income tax return on which the deduction is claimed. A return filed early is considered as filed on the due date.

> **PROFIT STRATEGY:**
> The biggest thing going for the IRS is a taxpayer's fear of an audit. If you're honest and you keep good records, you should have no fear. Don't lose valuable savings because of fear.

Additional Information

See Chapter 5 of Publication 463 for more information on recordkeeping, including a discussion on how to prove each type of expense discussed in this chapter.

Summary

Mastering business taxation does not happen overnight. As soon as possible you will want to get a good accountant to help you maximize your deductions. Still, many deductions available will be up to you and your understanding of the general laws and how to take advantage of them.

Throughout this chapter I have referred to various tax publications available from the IRS. They are free, and I encourage you to order them.

Your Business and Taxes

Form 1120-W (WORKSHEET)
Department of the Treasury
Internal Revenue Service

Estimated Tax for Corporations

For calendar year 1998, or tax year beginning _____ , 1998, and ending _____

(Keep for the corporation's records - Do *not* send to the Internal Revenue Service.)

OMB No. 1545-0975

1998

1	Taxable income expected in the tax year	1
	(Qualified personal service corporations (defined in the instructions), skip lines 2 through 13 and go to line 14.)	
2	Enter the smaller of line 1 or $50,000. (Members of a controlled group, see instructions.)	2
3	Subtract line 2 from line 1	3
4	Enter the smaller of line 3 or $25,000. (Members of a controlled group, see instructions.)	4
5	Subtract line 4 from line 3	5
6	Enter the smaller of line 5 or $9,925,000. (Members of a controlled group, see instructions.) ..	6
7	Subtract line 6 from line 5	7
8	Multiply line 2 by 15%	8
9	Multiply line 4 by 25%	9
10	Multiply line 6 by 34%	10
11	Multiply line 7 by 35%	11
12	If line 1 is greater than $100,000, enter the smaller of 5% of the excess over $100,000 or $11,750. Otherwise, enter -0-. (Members of a controlled group, see instructions.)	12
13	If line 1 is greater than $15 million, enter the smaller of 3% of the excess over $15 million or $100,000. Otherwise, enter -0-. (Members of a controlled group, see instructions.)	13
14	**Total.** Add lines 8 through 13. (Qualified personal service corporations, multiply line 1 by 35%.)	14
15	Estimated tax credits (see instructions)	15
16	Subtract line 15 from line 14	16
17	Recapture taxes	17
18	Alternative minimum tax (see instructions)	18
19	**Total.** Add lines 16 through 18	19
20	Credit for Federal tax paid on fuels (see instructions)	20
21	Subtract line 20 from line 19. **Note:** *If the result is less than $500, the corporation is not required to make estimated tax payments*	21
22 a	Enter the tax shown on the corporation's 1997 tax return. **CAUTION: See instructions before completing this line**	22a
b	Enter the smaller of line 21 or line 22a. If the corporation is required to skip line 22a, enter the amount from line 21 on line 22b	22b

		(a)	(b)	(c)	(d)
23	**Installment due dates.** (See instructions.) ▶	23			
24	**Required installments.** Enter 25% of line 22b in columns **(a)** through **(d)** unless the corporation uses the annualized income installment method, the adjusted seasonal installment method, or is a "large corporation." (See instructions.)	24			

For Paperwork Reduction Act Notice, see the instructions on page 6.

Form **1120-W** (1998)

Form 1120-W (WORKSHEET) 1998   Page 2

Schedule A   Annualized Income Installment Method and/or Adjusted Seasonal Installment Method. (See pages 5 and 6 of the instructions.)

Part I - Annualized Income Installment Method

			(a)	(b)	(c)	(d)
1	Annualization periods (see instructions).	1	First ____ months	First ____ months	First ____ months	First ____ months
2	Enter taxable income for each annualization period (see instructions).	2				
3	Annualization amounts (see instructions).	3				
4	Annualized taxable income. Multiply line 2 by line 3.	4				
5	Figure the tax on the amount in each column on line 4 by following the same steps used to figure the tax for line 14, page 1 of Form 1120-W.	5				
6	Enter other taxes for each annualization period (see instructions).	6				
7	Total tax. Add lines 5 and 6.	7				
8	For each annualization period, enter the same type of credits as allowed on lines 15 and 20, page 1 of Form 1120-W (see instructions).	8				
9	Total tax after credits. Subtract line 8 from line 7. If zero or less, enter -0-.	9				
10	Applicable percentage.	10	25%	50%	75%	100%
11	Multiply line 9 by line 10.	11				
12	Add the amounts in all preceding columns of line 41 (see instructions).	12	/////			
13	**Annualized income installments.** Subtract line 12 from line 11. If zero or less, enter -0-.	13				

Part II - Adjusted Seasonal Installment Method
(Use this method only if the base period percentage for any 6 consecutive months is at least 70%.)

			(a)	(b)	(c)	(d)
14	Enter taxable income for the following periods:		First 3 months	First 5 months	First 8 months	First 11 months
a	Tax year beginning in 1995	14a				
b	Tax year beginning in 1996	14b				
c	Tax year beginning in 1997	14c				
15	Enter taxable income for each period for the tax year beginning in 1998.	15				
16	Enter taxable income for the following periods:		First 4 months	First 6 months	First 9 months	Entire year
a	Tax year beginning in 1995	16a				
b	Tax year beginning in 1996	16b				
c	Tax year beginning in 1997	16c				
17	Divide the amount in each column on line 14a by the amount in column (d) on line 16a.	17				
18	Divide the amount in each column on line 14b by the amount in column (d) on line 16b.	18				
19	Divide the amount in each column on line 14c by the amount in column (d) on line 16c.	19				

JSA
7C1018 2.000

Form 1120-W (WORKSHEET) 1998 — Page 3

			(a) First 4 months	(b) First 6 months	(c) First 9 months	(d) Entire year
20	Add lines 17 through 19.	20				
21	Divide line 20 by 3.	21				
22	Divide line 15 by line 21.	22				
23	Figure the tax on the amount on line 22 by following the same steps used to figure the tax for line 14, page 1 of Form 1120-W.	23				
24	Divide the amount in columns (a) through (c) on line 16a by the amount in column (d) on line 16a.	24				
25	Divide the amount in columns (a) through (c) on line 16b by the amount in column (d) on line 16b.	25				
26	Divide the amount in columns (a) through (c) on line 16c by the amount in column (d) on line 16c.	26				
27	Add lines 24 through 26.	27				
28	Divide line 27 by 3.	28				
29	Multiply the amount in columns (a) through (c) of line 23 by the amount in the corresponding column of line 28. In column (d), enter the amount from line 23, column (d).	29				
30	Enter other taxes for each payment period (see instructions).	30				
31	Total tax. Add lines 29 and 30.	31				
32	For each period, enter the same type of credits as allowed on lines 15 and 20, page 1 of Form 1120-W (see instructions).	32				
33	Total tax after credits. Subtract line 32 from line 31. If zero or less, enter -0-.	33				
34	Add the amounts in all preceding columns of line 41 (see instructions).	34				
35	**Adjusted seasonal installments**. Subtract line 34 from line 33. If zero or less, enter -0-.	35				

Part III - Required Installments

			1st installment	2nd installment	3rd installment	4th installment
36	If only one of the above parts is completed, enter the amount in each column from line 13 or line 35. If both parts are completed, enter the **smaller** of the amounts in each column from line 13 or line 35.	36				
37	Divide line 22b, page 1 of Form 1120-W, by 4, and enter the result in each column. (**Note:** *"Large corporations," see the instructions for line 24 for the amount to enter.*)	37				
38	Enter the amount from line 40 for the preceding column.	38				
39	Add lines 37 and 38.	39				
40	If line 39 is more than line 36, subtract line 36 from line 39. Otherwise, enter -0-.	40				
41	**Required installments.** Enter the **smaller** of line 36 or line 39 here and on line 24, page 1 of Form 1120-W.	41				

JSA
7C1019 2.000

Form 1120-W (WORKSHEET) 1998 Page **4**

General Instructions

Section references are to the Internal Revenue Code unless otherwise noted.

Changes To Note

The Taxpayer Relief Act of 1997 (the "Act") made changes to the tax law for corporations. Some of the changes are discussed below.

- The research credit has been extended for amounts paid or incurred through June 30, 1998. For details, get **Form 6765**, Credit for Increasing Research Activities.
- The orphan drug credit has been permanently extended. For details, get **Form 8820**, Orphan Drug Credit.
- The work opportunity credit has been extended for wages paid to qualified individuals who begin work for the employer before July 1, 1998. For details, get **Form 5884**, Work Opportunity Credit.
- Employers that pay wages to qualified long-term family assistance (AFDC or its successor program) recipients who began work after December 31, 1997, may qualify to claim the welfare-to-work credit under new section 51A. The credit is figured on **Form 8861**, Welfare-to-Work Credit. See the 1997 instructions for Schedule J, line 4d, Form 1120 (Part I, line 2a, Form 1120-A).
- The penalty for failure to make electronic deposits of depository taxes using the Electronic Federal Tax Payment System (EFTPS) has been temporarily waived for filers who were required to first use EFTPS on or after July 1, 1997. For more information, see **Electronic deposit requirement** below.
- The alternative minimum tax (AMT) has been repealed for small corporations that meet certain gross receipts tests. See section 55(e) for more information. Other changes to the AMT rules include:

(1) The repeal of the depreciation adjustment for property (including pollution control facilities) placed in service after December 31, 1998. See section 56(a)(1) and 56(a)(5).

(2) The use by farmers of the installment method of accounting for tax years beginning after December 31, 1987. See section 56(a).

(3) The repeal of the special exception to the 90% foreign tax credit limitation for tax years beginning after August 5, 1997. See section 59(a)(2).

(4) The election by corporations to use a simplified foreign tax credit limitation for tax years beginning after December 31, 1997. See section 59(a)(3).

Who Must Make Estimated Tax Payments

- Corporations generally must make installment payments of estimated tax if they expect their estimated tax (income tax less credits) to be $500 or more.
- S corporations must also make estimated tax payments for certain taxes. S corporations should see the instructions for **Form 1120S**, U.S. Income Tax Return for an S Corporation, to figure the estimated tax payments of an S corporation.
- Tax-exempt organizations subject to the unrelated business income tax and private foundations use **Form 990-W**, Estimated Tax on Unrelated Business Taxable Income for Tax-Exempt Organizations, to figure the amount of their estimated tax payments.

When To Make Estimated Tax Payments

The installments are due by the 15th day of the **4th, 6th, 9th, and 12th** months of the tax year. If any date falls on a Saturday, Sunday, or legal holiday, the installment is due on the next regular business day.

Underpayment of Estimated Tax

A corporation that does not make estimated tax payments when due may be subject to an underpayment penalty for the period of underpayment (section 6655), using the underpayment rate determined under section 6621(a)(2).

Overpayment of Estimated Tax

A corporation that has overpaid its estimated tax may apply for a quick refund if the overpayment is at least 10% of its expected income tax liability **and** at least $500.

Quick refund.—To apply for a quick refund, file **Form 4466**, Corporation Application for Quick Refund of Overpayment of Estimated Tax, before the 16th day of the 3rd month after the end of the tax year, but before the corporation files its income tax return. Do not file Form 4466 before the end of the corporation's tax year.

Depository Method of Tax Payment

Some corporations (described below) are required to electronically deposit all depository taxes, including corporation income tax and estimated tax payments.

Electronic deposit requirement.—The corporation must make electronic deposits of all depository tax liabilities that occur after 1997 if:

- It was required to electronically deposit taxes in prior years,
- It deposited more than $50,000 in social security, Medicare, or withheld income taxes in 1996, or
- It **did not** deposit social security, Medicare, or withheld income taxes in 1995 or 1996, but deposited more than $50,000 in other taxes under section 6302 (such as the corporate income tax) in either year. (See Regulations section 31.6302-1(h) for more information.)

The Electronic Federal Tax Payment System (EFTPS) must be used to make electronic deposits. If the corporation is required to make electronic deposits and fails to do so, it may be subject to a 10% penalty. However, no penalty will be imposed prior to July 1, 1998, if the corporation was first required to use EFTPS on or after July 1, 1997. Corporations that are not required to make electronic deposits may voluntarily participate in EFTPS. To enroll in EFTPS, call 1-800-945-8400 or 1-800-555-4477. For general information about EFTPS, call 1-800-829-1040.

Deposits with Form 8109.—If the corporation does not use EFTPS, deposit corporation income tax payments (and estimated tax payments) with **Form 8109**, Federal Tax Deposit Coupon. Do not send deposits directly to an IRS office. Mail or deliver the completed Form 8109 with the payment to a qualified depositary for Federal taxes or to the Federal Reserve bank (FRB) servicing the corporation's geographic area. Make checks or money orders payable to that depositary or FRB. To help ensure proper crediting, write the corporation's EIN, the tax period to which the deposit applies, and "Form 1120" on the check or money order. Be sure to darken the "1120" box on the coupon. Records of these deposits will be sent to the IRS.

A penalty may be imposed if the deposits are mailed or delivered to an IRS office rather than to an authorized depositary or FRB. For more information on deposits, see the instructions in the coupon booklet (Form 8109) and **Pub. 583**, Starting a Business and Keeping Records.

Refiguring Estimated Tax

If after the corporation figures and deposits estimated tax, it finds that its tax liability for the year will be more or less than originally estimated, it may have to refigure its required installments. If earlier installments were underpaid, the corporation may owe a penalty for underpayment of estimated tax.

An immediate catchup payment should be made to reduce the amount of any penalty resulting from the underpayment of any earlier installments, whether caused by a change in estimate, failure to make a deposit, or a mistake.

Specific Instructions

Line 1—Qualified Personal Service Corporations

A qualified personal service corporation is taxed at a flat rate of 35% on taxable income. A corporation is a qualified personal service corporation only if it meets **both** of the following tests:

- Substantially all of the corporation's activities involve the performance of services in the fields of health, law, engineering, architecture, accounting, actuarial science, performing arts, or consulting, and
- At least 95% of the corporation's stock, by value, is owned, directly or indirectly, by **(1)** employees performing the services, **(2)** retired employees who had performed the services listed above, **(3)** any estate of an employee or retiree described above, or **(4)** any

Form 1120-W (WORKSHEET) 1998 — Page 5

person who acquired the stock of the corporation as a result of the death of an employee or retiree (but only for the 2-year period beginning on the date of the employee's or retiree's death). See Temporary Regulations section 1.448-1T(e) for details.

Lines 2, 4, and 6

Members of a controlled group.—Members of a controlled group enter on line 2 the smaller of the amount on line 1 or their share of the $50,000 amount. On line 4, enter the smaller of the amount on line 3 or their share of the $25,000 amount. On line 6, enter the smaller of the amount on line 5 or their share of the $9,925,000 amount.

Equal apportionment plan.—If no apportionment plan is adopted, members of a controlled group must divide the amount in each taxable income bracket equally among themselves. For example, Controlled Group AB consists of Corporation A and Corporation B. They do not elect an apportionment plan. Therefore, each corporation is entitled to:

- $25,000 (one-half of $50,000) on line 2,
- $12,500 (one-half of $25,000) on line 4, and
- $4,962,500 (one-half of $9,925,000) on line 6.

Unequal apportionment plan.—Members of a controlled group may elect an unequal apportionment plan and divide the taxable income brackets as they want. There is no need for consistency among taxable income brackets. Any member may be entitled to all, some, or none of the taxable income bracket. However, the total amount for all members cannot be more than the total amount in each taxable income bracket.

Line 12

Additional 5% tax.—Members of a controlled group are treated as one group to figure the applicability of the additional 5% tax and the additional 3% tax. If an additional tax applies, each member will pay that tax based on the part of the amount used in each taxable income bracket to reduce that member's tax. See section 1561(a). Each member of the group must enter on line 12 its share of the smaller of 5% of the taxable income in excess of $100,000, or $11,750.

Line 13

Additional 3% tax.—If the additional 3% tax applies, each member of the controlled group must enter on line 13 its share of the smaller of 3% of the taxable income in excess of $15 million, or $100,000. See Line 12 above.

Line 15

For information on **tax credits** the corporation may take, see the discussion of credits in the Instructions for Form 1120, lines 4a through 4e, Schedule J (Form 1120-A, lines 2a and 2b, Part I), or the instructions for the applicable line and schedule of other income tax returns. Also see **Changes To Note** on page 4.

Line 18

Alternative minimum tax (AMT) is generally the excess of tentative minimum tax for the tax year over the regular tax for the tax year. See section 55 for definitions of tentative minimum tax and regular tax. A limited amount of the foreign tax credit may be used to offset the minimum tax. See **Changes To Note** and sections 55 through 59 for more information on AMT.

Line 20

Complete **Form 4136,** Credit for Federal Tax Paid on Fuels, if the corporation qualifies to take this credit. Include on line 20 any credit the corporation is claiming under section 4682(g)(4) for tax on ozone-depleting chemicals.

Line 22a

Figure the corporation's 1997 tax in the same way that line 21 of this worksheet was figured, using the taxes and credits from the 1997 income tax return.

If a return was not filed for the 1997 tax year showing a liability for at least some amount of tax, **or** if the 1997 tax year was for less than 12 months, do not complete line 22a. Instead, skip line 22a and enter the amount from line 21 on line 22b. Large corporations, see the instructions for line 24 below.

Line 23

Calendar year taxpayers: Enter 4-15-98, 6-15-98, 9-15-98, and 12-15-98, respectively, in columns (a) through (d).

Fiscal year taxpayers: Enter the 15th day of the 4th, 6th, 9th, and 12th months of your tax year in columns (a) through (d). If the regular due date falls on a Saturday, Sunday, or legal holiday, enter the next business day.

Line 24

Payments of estimated tax should reflect any 1997 overpayment that the corporation chose to credit against its 1998 tax. The overpayment is credited against unpaid required installments in the order in which the installments are required to be paid.

Annualized income installment method and/or adjusted seasonal installment method.—If the corporation's income is expected to vary during the year because, for example, it operates its business on a seasonal basis, it may be able to lower the amount of one or more required installments by using the annualized income installment method and/or the adjusted seasonal installment method. For example, a ski shop, which receives most of its income during the winter months, may be able to benefit from using one or both of these methods in figuring one or more of its required installments.

To use one or both of these methods to figure one or more required installments, use Schedule A on pages 2 and 3. If Schedule A is used for any payment date, it must be used for all payment due dates. To arrive at the amount of each required installment, Schedule A automatically selects the smallest of (a) the annualized income installment, (b) the adjusted seasonal installment (if applicable), or (c) the regular installment under section 6655(d)(1) (increased by any recapture of a reduction in a required installment under section 6655(e)(1)(B)).

Large corporations.—A large corporation is a corporation that had, or its predecessor had, taxable income of $1 million or more for any of the 3 tax years immediately preceding the 1998 tax year. For this purpose, taxable income is modified to exclude net operating loss or capital loss carrybacks or carryovers. Members of a controlled group, as defined in section 1563, must divide the $1 million amount among themselves according to rules similar to those in section 1561.

If the annualized income installment method or adjusted seasonal installment method is not used, follow the instructions below to figure the amounts to enter on line 24. (If the annualized income installment method and/or the adjusted seasonal installment method are used, these instructions apply to line 37 of Schedule A.)

- **If line 21 is smaller than line 22a:** Enter 25% of line 21 in columns (a) through (d) of line 24.

- **If line 22a is smaller than line 21:** Enter 25% of line 22a in column (a) of line 24. In column (b), determine the amount to enter as follows:

    1. Subtract line 22a from line 21,
    2. Add the result to the amount on line 21, and
    3. Multiply the result in **2** above by 25% and enter the result in column (b).

    Enter 25% of line 21 in columns (c) and (d).

Schedule A

If only the annualized income installment method (Part I) is used, complete Parts I and III of Schedule A. If only the adjusted seasonal installment method (Part II) is used, complete Parts II and III. If both methods are used, complete all three parts. Enter in each column on line 24, page 1, the amounts from the corresponding column of line 41.

Caution: *Do not figure any required installment until after the end of the month preceding the due date for that installment.*

Part I—Annualized Income Installment Method

Line 1

Annualization periods.—Enter in the space on line 1, columns (a) through (d), respectively, the annualization periods that the corporation is using, based on the options listed below. For example, if the corporation elects Option 1, enter on line 1 the annualization periods 2, 4, 7, and 10, in columns (a) through (d), respectively.

Form 1120-W (WORKSHEET) 1998   Page **6**

Caution: *Use Option 1 or Option 2 only if the corporation elected to use one of these options by filing* **Form 8842**, *Election To Use Different Annualization Periods for Corporate Estimated Tax, on or before the due date of the first required installment payment. Once made, the election is irrevocable for the particular tax year.*

	1st Installment	2nd Installment	3rd Installment	4th Installment
Standard option	3	3	6	9
Option 1 . . .	2	4	7	10
Option 2 . . .	3	5	8	11

Line 2

If a corporation has income includible under section 936(h) (Puerto Rico and possessions tax credits) or section 951(a) (controlled foreign corporation income), special rules apply.

Amounts includible in income under section 936(h) or 951(a) (and allocable credits) generally must be taken into account in figuring the amount of any annualized income installment as the income is earned. The amounts are figured in a manner similar to the way in which partnership income inclusions (and allocable credits) are taken into account in figuring a partner's annualized income installments as provided in Regulations section 1.6654-2(d)(2).

Safe harbor election.—Corporations may be able to elect a prior year safe harbor election. Under the election, an eligible corporation is treated as having received ratably during the tax year items of income under sections 936(h) and 951(a) (and allocable credits) equal to a specified percentage of the amounts shown on the corporation's return for the first preceding tax year (the second preceding tax year for the first and second required installments).

For more information, see section 6655(e)(4) and Rev. Proc. 95-23, 1995-1 C.B. 693.

Line 3

Annualization amounts.—Enter the annualization amounts for the option used on line 1. For example, if the corporation elects Option 1, enter on line 3 the annualization amounts 6, 3, 1.71429, and 1.2, in columns (a) through (d), respectively.

	1st Installment	2nd Installment	3rd Installment	4th Installment
Standard option	4	4	2	1.33333
Option 1 . . .	6	3	1.71429	1.2
Option 2 . . .	4	2.4	1.5	1.09091

Line 6

Enter any **other taxes** the corporation owed for the months shown in the headings used to figure annualized taxable income. Include the same taxes used to figure lines 17 and 18 of Form 1120-W.

Alternative minimum tax.—Compute the AMT by figuring alternative minimum taxable income under section 55. Alternative minimum taxable income is based on the corporation's income and deductions for the annualization period entered in each column on line 1. Multiply alternative minimum taxable income by the annualization amounts (line 3) used to figure annualized taxable income. Subtract the exemption amount under section 55(d)(2). See **Changes To Note** for AMT tax law changes.

Line 8

Enter the credits to which the corporation is entitled for the months shown in each column on line 1. Do not annualize any credit. However, when figuring the credits, annualize any item of income or deduction used to figure the credit. For more details, see Rev. Rul. 79-179, 1979-1 C.B. 436. Also see **Changes To Note**.

Line 12

Before completing line 12 in columns (b) through (d), complete the following items in each of the preceding columns: line 13; Part II (if applicable); and Part III. For example, complete line 13, Part II (if using the adjusted seasonal installment method), and Part III, in column (a) before completing line 12 in column (b).

Part II—Adjusted Seasonal Installment Method

Complete this part only if the corporation's base period percentage for any 6 consecutive months of the tax year equals or exceeds 70%. The base period percentage for any period of 6 consecutive months is the average of the three percentages figured by dividing the taxable income for the corresponding 6-consecutive-month period in each of the 3 preceding tax years by the taxable income for each of their respective tax years.

Example. An amusement park with a calendar year tax year receives the largest part of its taxable income during a 6-month period, May through October. To compute its base period percentage for this 6-month period, the amusement park figures its taxable income for each May–October period in 1995, 1996, and 1997. It then divides the taxable income for each May–October period by the total taxable income for that particular tax year. The resulting percentages are 69% (.69) for May–October 1995, 74% (.74) for May–October 1996, and 67% (.67) for May–October 1997. Because the average of 69%, 74%, and 67% is 70%, the base period percentage for May through October 1998 is 70%. Therefore, the amusement park qualifies for the adjusted seasonal installment method.

Line 30

Enter any **other taxes** the corporation owed for the months shown in the column headings above line 14 of Part II. Include the same taxes used to figure lines 17 and 18 of Form 1120-W.

Alternative minimum tax.—Compute the AMT by figuring alternative minimum taxable income under section 55. Alternative minimum taxable income is based on the corporation's income and deductions for the months shown in the column headings above line 14 of Part II. Divide the alternative minimum taxable income by the amounts shown on line 21. Subtract the exemption amount under section 55(d)(2). For columns (a) through (c) only, multiply the alternative minimum tax by the amounts shown on line 28. See **Changes To Note** for AMT tax law changes.

Line 32

Enter the credits to which the corporation is entitled for the months shown in the column headings above line 14 of Part II. See **Changes To Note**.

Line 34

Before completing line 34 in columns (b) through (d), complete lines 35 through 41 in each of the preceding columns. For example, complete lines 35 through 41 in column (a) before completing line 34 in column (b).

Paperwork Reduction Act Notice.—Your use of this form is optional. It is provided to aid the corporation in determining its tax liability.

You are not required to provide the information requested on a form that is subject to the Paperwork Reduction Act unless the form displays a valid OMB control number. Books or records relating to a form or its instructions must be retained as long as their contents may become material in the administration of any Internal Revenue law. Generally, tax returns and return information are confidential, as required by section 6103.

The time needed to complete this form will vary depending on individual circumstances. The estimated average time is:

Form	Recordkeeping	Learning about the law or the form	Preparing the form
1120-W	7 hr., 25 min.	1 hr., 53 min.	2 hr., 5 min.
1120-W, Sch. A (Pt. I)	11 hr., 14 min.	12 min.	23 min.
1120-W, Sch. A (Pt. II)	23 hr., 26 min.	------------	23 min.
1120-W, Sch. A (Pt. III)	5 hr., 16 min.	------------	5 min.

If you have comments concerning the accuracy of these time estimates or suggestions for making this form simpler, we would be happy to hear from you. You can write to the Tax Forms Committee, Western Area Distribution Center, Rancho Cordova, CA 95743-0001. **DO NOT** send the tax form to this office. Instead, keep the form for your records.

☐ CORRECTED (if checked)			
PAYER'S name, street address, city, state, ZIP code, and telephone no.	1 Ordinary dividends $	OMB No. 1545-0110 **1998** Form **1099-DIV**	**Dividends and Distributions**
	2a Total capital gain distr. $		
PAYER'S Federal identification number | RECIPIENT'S identification number	2b 28% rate gain $	2c Unrecap. sec 1250 gain $	**Copy B For Recipient**
RECIPIENT'S name	2d Section 1202 gain $	3 Nontaxable distributions $	This is important tax information and is being furnished to the Internal Revenue Service. If you are required to file a return, a negligence penalty or other sanction may be imposed on you if this income is taxable and the IRS determines that it has not been reported.
Street address (including apt. no.)	4 Federal income tax withhled $	5 Investment expenses $	
City, state, and ZIP code	6 Foreign tax paid $	7 Foreign country or U.S. possession	
Account number (optional) | 2nd TIN Not. ☐	8 Cash liquidation distr. $	9 Noncash liquidation distr. $	

Form **1099-DIV** (Keep for your records.) Department of the Treasury - Internal Revenue Service

Do NOT Cut or Separate Forms on This Page

CHAPTER THIRTEEN

MAXIMIZING CORPORATE AND EXECUTIVE BENEFITS

There are a lot of reasons why you should go into business: to build something for the future; to leave a legacy that lasts beyond your lifetime; to create a better world. All are good reasons to start a business. However, in most cases, the main reason to start a business is the desire to increase your income. Consequently, understanding the various benefits that can be derived from having a business and incorporating it is important. You can organize the daily operations of your company in a way that produces the maximum benefits to you.

Michael Gerber, the author of *The E Myth*, talks about the frustration of entrepreneurs once they have started their businesses and actually begin to operate them. Soon they find themselves so involved in the day-to-day operations of the business that they forget why they went into business in the first place. The freedom that they sought in forming their business is now lost. In many cases, entrepreneurs simply become employees of their own business and are no better off than they were before. They are not only still unable to control their own lives, but also saddled with the responsibilities of a business owner.

The reason for starting a business in the first place is to make the business work for you. If that means that you want to make more money than you could working for someone else, then construct your organization in a manner that maximizes all the potential profit sources. If that can't be done, then perhaps you should reconsider your business plan. This chapter will outline some of the most profitable methods of maximizing the financial benefits of your corporate business.

Salary

Although you may be thinking that you didn't go into business simply to get a salary, the important thing to remember is that you do get one. Your salary should be structured to generate as much money as it can. If there are more shareholders in the company than you, but you are the one doing the work, then your salary should reflect your efforts. Don't fall into the trap of thinking that you'll receive money later out of profits of the company, because those profits may not ever come. Early on in my professional business career, a very good friend and mentor told me always to get money on the front end of the transaction and let the back end take care of itself. He knew that many times the profits never came as anticipated. I haven't always followed that advice, but every time I didn't, I have been sorry. It is one of those simple rules that can result in benefits that you may never receive otherwise. Consequently, I strongly encourage you to structure a salary that is commensurate with your work. Even if you do not receive the full salary in the beginning, you can defer it until a future date and make it up when the cash is there. If you don't do this, you will find that there always will be capital expense that can be purchased by the company to help it in the future. Pay your salary to yourself first, and you will be sure that you receive at least that.

In addition to your own salary, you should consider the opportunity of hiring other people in your family to do work that the corporation needs to have done, such as your spouse to keep the corporate books or run the warehouse operations of your business. In addition, you can hire your children and give them a salary equal to what you would have to pay someone outside your family. There is no age limit, but the children must be old enough to actually do the work performed. If your company is a family business, you won't have problems with state child labor laws. For comfort, however, you can check with your state employment commission.

There are a lot of benefits to hiring your children, including teaching them the value of work and the tax benefit of shifting dollars into the family unit at the child's income tax rate, which will be lower than your own. Once children begin to earn income, they can use that money to set up an IRA plan for themselves, sheltering at least $2,000 per year from tax. Because early contribution to a retirement plan compounds more over time, the child's IRA should grow into a substantial nest egg.

Free Insurance

A corporation can structure an insurance program for its employees. The corporation can deduct the premiums, and the benefit is not taxable to the employee. Without the corporate benefit, employees would have to purchase insurance with after-tax dollars. Even if you have a corporation and are the only employee, you can gain this tax benefit.

The insurance policies that employees (including yourself) are entitled to receive as a benefit include health insurance and life insurance. The life insurance is limited to one-year renewable term policies up to $50,000 per person. In addition, the corporation can purchase disability insurance. Although the premiums for the disability insurance are tax deductible to the corporation, the benefits that you receive from the insurance company should you become disabled are subject to income tax. On the other hand, if you pay the premiums yourself, then the benefits received are tax-free. You may be better off to have your company pay you any equal amount of money as additional salary and then pay the insurance premiums.

PROFIT STRATEGY:
Pay yourself first. Try to structure your benefits so that you profit from the beginning of your corporation.

One of the best benefits available to employees of C corporations is medical expense reimbursement. This reimbursement is in addition to medical insurance that covers most of the employee's medical costs. As most medical plans have both a deductible and specific medical treatments not covered under the plan, the medical reimbursement can step in and cover this cost. Using this benefit package, the corporation can pay for all of an employee's medicine and expenses.

To take advantage of a medical reimbursement program, your corporation should adopt a medical expense reimbursement plan as part of your corporate minutes. To assist you, I have included a sample form at the end of this chapter. It is worth consulting an attorney about the exact language you use for your company because you may want to exclude certain employees based on vesting rights.

Loans

One way to get money out of your corporation without currently paying income taxes is by borrowing the money. If you receive money as a loan, you will have to pay it back someday, unless the company decides to forgive the debt. If the company decides to forgive the debt, you will have to pay tax on the amount forgiven. In the meantime, however, you can use the money without having to pay income tax on it. An example of when you might authorize this benefit for employees would be for one-time major purchases, such as the down payment on your house. As an individual, you may not have adequate reserves for the down payment, but your company might. You can borrow money from your company by issuing a promissory note to the company with a stated interest rate, and those dollars can be used to complete your transaction.

If you do borrow money from your corporation, you need to make sure that you document the transaction by actually signing a promissory note and making payments on the note in conformity with the stated payment periods. If you don't document the loan and include corporate authority to enter into such transactions, the Internal Revenue Service may disallow the loan and treat it as an additional unreported income. If this occurs, you could be subject to additional fines and penalties for failing to report this income. A copy of a corporate promissory note as well as a corporate resolution are included at the end of this chapter. The corporate resolution should always be used to show approval by the board on a business transaction.

Paid Vacations

The corporation can pay you a salary when you are on vacation or sick. In addition, if

> **PROFIT STRATEGY:**
> Use money or assets in your corporation to borrow from if you need help with major purchases, such as a down payment on a house. You won't have to pay income tax on the borrowed money until it is forgiven by the company.

you arrange to conduct your business in places you would like to visit, the trip can also be deducted. The corporation can pay for the trip and deduct the portion of the trip that is applicable to the business purpose. For example, if you've always dreamed of going to New York City to see the Broadway productions and can schedule a business seminar in town, the trip to New York, as well as the cost of hotel and food, would be deductible. Your entertainment in the evening at the plays would not be. By using your corporate business structure, you would make your working vacation tax-deductible.

Day Care

Your overall benefits package that includes holidays,vacations, and medical and other insurance coverage can also reimburse corporate employees for day-care expenses. This additional benefit becomes deductible for the corporation as an employee benefit, but is not taxable to the employee receiving the benefit. These types of plans, normally referred to as cafeteria plans, must be carefully structured to make sure that they are in compliance with the laws governing them. I would recommend you consult with a CPA before designing such a plan.

PROFIT STRATEGY: Structure your business trips around places you want to see or go. Business trips are deductible even if they are enjoyable.

Educational Benefits

Educational benefits can be paid to employees, including family members who also are employees of the company. Any educational course required to maintain or improve the skills of the employee to do work-related duties can be deducted totally by the company and is not income to the employee. The key to this deduction is that the course is "required to maintain or improve." An entire college education would not fall under this rule. Included in the deduction would be the cost of any transportation, hotel room, and any other living expenses associated with completing the education. In conjunction with this same educational benefit a company also can develop a scholarship program for employees. This plan could benefit the children of the corporate owners at the same time as other employees. However, the scholarship program must benefit all children of the company's employees, not just those of senior-level management. Nevertheless, this is a strong benefit to employees and their families, and the tax savings for your own children's benefit may allow you to offer such a program for everyone at a neutral cost.

Deferred Compensation

Deferred compensation programs are ways in which you can defer collecting present income to a future date, at which time the corporation will receive a tax deduction for setting aside those dollars. Deferred compensation programs are excellent ways to subsidize income that you may need in the future. For the present time, the income is not taxable to you as the recipient, and consequently, you will benefit from tax deferral of those dollars to a time when you are more likely to be in a lower tax bracket. The disadvantage to using this program is that the money set aside is nevertheless subject to creditors' claims should any problems arise. If a creditor attacks the corporation, you would likely be considered only a general creditor of the corporation, and the money set aside would be at risk.

Travel and Entertainment

Any corporation can reimburse its employees for travel and entertainment expenses related to the job they are performing. Naturally, the IRS will insist that you save records and demonstrate that the expenses are directly related to your business. In addition, federal tax laws were tightened, so that only 50% of meal and entertainment expenses are deductible. You should keep records regarding the meetings and any business results that took place because of the meetings.

In addition to travel and entertainment, membership in country clubs and health clubs that are used primarily to conduct or develop business are tax deductible. However, as with the travel and entertainment expenses, great care should be taken to keep records of whom you talked to, what was discussed, the business relationship, and any business that derived therefrom. (See also Chapter 12.)

Automobiles

The business community and the Internal Revenue Service have had an ongoing battle about the deductibility of an automobile. As long as the automobile is used for business purposes and not simply commuting, the value of the automobile is deductible. There are two major ways to deduct the automobile. The first method is the actual cost of the automobile, keeping in mind the depreciation and expenses of operation. The second method is by deducting the actual mileage used in your work. Under the current laws, you may deduct 31.5¢ per mile traveled in business use. The IRS has designed a brochure that explains exactly how to do the computations and your rights under the law. You may order the IRS Publication 917 *Business Use of a Car* by calling (800) TAX-FORMS. (See also Chapter 12.)

Business Publications and Subscriptions

The cost for any subscription or business publication is deductible by the company if it is used by an employee. The publications need to be related to the business, but this limitation does not automatically exclude subscriptions to general-interest magazines and publications such as *Time* and *Newsweek*, which can give you ideas of trends regarding the overall economy that affect your current business.

Stock Options

Big business pays big salaries to officers and directors. Some of the major companies, such as Walt Disney, are paying salaries to presidents and board chairpersons in the range of those of sport superstars. However, most of the money that they receive is in the form not of salary, but of *stock options*. Options are a right to buy stock at a future date at a specified price today. For example, assume that your company gives you the right to purchase stock at the current value of $1 per share at any time in the future. If the stock increases to $5 per share and you exercise your stock option, the $4 difference is all profit to you. In addition, if you hold the stock for at least twelve months, you will qualify for capital gains treatment at the taxable rate of 28% as opposed to the maximum personal income rate, which now runs as high as 39%. Although stock options are not common in one-person corporations, they should still be considered if there are just a few shareholders in the company and one person is doing most of the work. Stock options can be used as a motivating factor to get that individual to work harder, and they are a way to compensate the person in the future without having to pay taxes at the present time. In addition, you help transform some of the employee's earnings from taxable income to capital gains with no loss to the company.

Retirement Plans

Perhaps the most common retirement plan in America today is the 401-K plan. Once a 401-K plan is adopted by a company, every employee may contribute money to the plan. These contributions are deductible by the individual and grow in the 401-K plan on a tax-deferred basis. In addition, the company may elect to match all or a portion of the employee's contribution to the plan. Even if they elect to match half of the employee's contribution, employees immediately benefit from a 50% return on their money. Consequently, 401-K plans are an exciting benefit that is attractive to employees.

As your company grows and is able to afford larger retirement plans, you may want to consider having a defined benefits plan for the company. Under this type of retirement program, each employee decides how much they would like to receive annually when they retire, then the company calculates how much money should be deducted from their salary between their present age and their anticipated age of retirement to achieve the retirement goal. For small companies, this program is difficult to establish, because you cannot vary your contributions based on your profitability. The result could create a great hardship for your company unless it has a strong cash flow.

PROFIT STRATEGIES: Retirement plans are the single most important tool for building personal wealth. Understand the rules, and maximize the savings of tax-deductible and tax-deferred dollars.

Selling Your Company's Stock

Ultimately there will come a time in the life of your company when it has reached a pinnacle of growth. You may decide that you either want to continue operating it yourself but take out some of its profits, or you may simply decide that it's time for you to move on to something else. In either case, the result will be to sell some or all of the interest in your company.

Taking your company public and selling a block of your stock to the general public may be the dream of a large number of entrepreneurs. Multimillionaires and billionaires have been made overnight by selling stock in an exciting growth company to the general public. In most cases, the sale results not only in a substantial profit by the owners, but also in continued control by those same owners once the company becomes public. It is the classic case of having your cake and eating it, too. Nevertheless, with the public sale come new regulations and restraints on how you operate your company. Increased reporting requirements and the exposure to the general public's knowledge of how you run your business are factors that some people consider unacceptable.

Another option is to sell some or all of your company to private investors. In this scenario, the company remains private, yet you are able to bring additional investors and dollars into the company by selling shares. This method also has its drawbacks because, although you are dealing with a smaller number of shareholders, they are nevertheless going to be concerned about the profits of the company and will want to make sure that the time you are spending is relative to the compensation you are receiving. Furthermore, when you are dealing with a handful of shareholders, you also are probably dealing with the situation in which those shareholders have invested more money per shareholder than if the corporation had been public. Therefore, the shareholders will likely be more concerned about the actual operation of the company and may even want to get more personally involved. This additional involvement by others is likely to cause problems for you as the chief operating officer of the company.

> **PROFIT STRATEGY:**
> Develop an exit strategy for your company. If done right, you can maintain income and defer some profits until retirement.

The third option is an outright sale of the entire business to another party. If the sale is for cash, much of the profit will be spent paying capital gains tax to the federal government. Owners should consider what their net profit will be after paying taxes before they decide to sell the business. You may be better off not selling the business but hiring expert management to run its day-to-day operations. Assuming you select a good manager, you may produce income for yourself for years to come. In addition, if the sale of your business is structured over several years, then you will have to be concerned with the future operation of the business, anyway. This may be unattractive as it will require continued involvement and you may find that you were better off owning the business and hiring more help.

Whichever method of sale you ultimately use, great care should be taken in spending time with a CPA to structure the sale to achieve maximum tax savings.

There are numerous methods of deferring sales proceeds, including tax-free exchanges of stock between the existing corporation and another corporation in which the shareholder may be willing to take a passive role. If the new corporation is a public entity, then the shareholders could either hold the stock for growth or sell off part for income as needed. Only when a sale is made would taxes be due.

Sample Forms

Name of Corporation

MEDICAL EXPENSE REIMBURSEMENT PLAN

This Medical Expense Reimbursement Plan (the "Plan") is adopted by _____, a <u>(state)</u> corporation (the "Company"), this _____ day of _____, _____.

SECTION 1. Reimbursement. Effective _____, _____, the Company shall reimburse any Eligible Employee (as defined in Section 3 hereof) for all reasonable uninsured expenses (as defined in Section 8 hereof) for medical care (as defined in Section 213(e) of the Internal Revenue Code of 1954, as amended) incurred by the Eligible Employee or the Eligible Employee's spouse or dependents, if applicable, subject to the limitation that the above benefits payable to or on behalf of an Eligible Employee in any taxable year of the Company shall not exceed the maximum allowed by law.

SECTION 2. Direct Payment Option. The Company may, in its discretion, reimburse expenses directly to the person or persons providing such medical care, in lieu of reimbursing the Eligible Employee after his or her payment thereof. In such event, the Company shall be relieved of all further responsibility with respect to that particular medical expense.

SECTION 3. Eligibility for Employee Coverage. Any employee of the Company shall become an Eligible Employee on the _____ day of _____ coinciding with or next following the later of (i) the employee's twenty-fifth birthday, or (ii) the date the employee completes his or her third year of continuous, full-time employment with the Company. An employee shall thereafter remain an Eligible Employee until the first of the following events occur:

 (a) The employee's status as a full-time employee terminates;

(b) The employee leaves the Company's employ for any reason.

For purposes of this Section, "full-time" employees are defined to include all common law employees of the Company who customarily work at least twenty-five hours per week and at least seven months per year.

SECTION 4. Spousal and Dependency Coverage. The medical expenses incurred by the spouse and dependents of an Eligible Employee (as defined in Section 152 of the Internal Revenue Code of 1954, as amended) shall also be covered by this plan, subject to the limitations described in Sections 1 and 8 hereof.

SECTION 5. Administration. The President of the Company shall appoint a Medical Expense Reimbursement Plan Administrator (the "Administrator") who may be an officer, employee or director of the Company, and who shall be responsible for administering the Plan. The Administrator's actions in connection with the Plan shall be binding on all persons.

SECTION 6. Reimbursement Claim Procedure. The Administrator, upon request, shall make claim forms available to all Eligible Employees that shall require the filing of such pertinent information, documentation or evidence of medical expenses as the Administrator deems necessary, which information, once submitted, shall remain in the files of the Company and shall remain confidential. The only grounds for disallowance by the Administrator of any claim made by an Eligible Employee hereunder shall be that the charges are insured (as defined in Section 8 hereof), that they are unreasonably high (in which case the reasonable part shall be allowed), or that the annual benefits limitation has been reached. Claims must be submitted to the Administrator no later than the end of the Company's taxable year following the calendar year in which the expenses were incurred. Expenses in excess of the annual benefits limitation may be carried forward for one taxable year of the Company beyond the year in which the limitation was reached, and shall be charged against the annual limitation for the year to which they are carried.

SECTION 7. Employee Contributions. No contributions are required of any Eligible Employee to ensure his or her coverage or that of his or her spouse and dependents hereunder. The Company shall pay the entire cost of all reimbursements allowed by the Administrator and all expenses arising in connection with the administration of the Plan. However, this Section shall in no way preclude the adoption by the Company of a program of insured accident and health benefits for its employees, and their spouses and dependents, to which the employees may be required to contribute.

SECTION 8. Reimbursement Only for Uninsured Expenses. Reimbursement will be made hereunder only to the extent that coverage for medical care expenses is not provided under any self-insured or insured plan of the Company or any other employer, or under Medicare or other federal or state law. In addition, an Eligible Employee shall seek to collect under any such other program first, if possible, before applying for reimbursement from the Company hereunder. To the extent of coverage under any such other program, the Company shall be relieved of all liability hereunder with respect to such expenses.

SECTION 9. Written Notice to Eligible Employees. The Company shall notify every Eligible Employee in writing of the date on which his or her coverage commences hereunder, and shall provide each such Eligible Employee with a copy of the Plan.

SECTION 10. Reimbursement after Death. Any amount payable hereunder to an Eligible Employee who dies prior to payment may be paid in any one or more of the following ways as the Administrator, in his or her sole discretion, elects:

(a) To such person's surviving spouse;
(b) To such person's duly appointed legal representative;
(c) To such person's heirs (pursuant to a statutory affidavit, if appropriate).

SECTION 11. Nonassignability of Benefits. Any amount payable to or on behalf of an Eligible Employee hereunder may be applied by the Company toward settlement of any debt of such individual to the Company, but shall not be subject to the claims of any other creditors of the Eligible Employee, and shall not be subject to assignment or encumbrance by the Eligible Employee.

SECTION 12. Qualification Intended. It is the Company's intention that benefits payable hereunder be eligible for exclusion from the gross income of the Eligible Employees on whose behalf they are paid, as provided in Section 105 of the Internal Revenue Code of 1954, as amended. In the event such an exclusion is disallowed by the Internal Revenue Service with respect to a particular Eligible Employee, the nonexcluded sums reimbursed on his or her behalf hereunder shall be considered to be additional compensation to such Eligible Employee.

SECTION 13. No Employment Guarantee. This Plan shall in no event be construed to constitute a contract of initial or continued employment with the Company or an assurance of any benefit not contained expressly in this Plan.

SECTION 14. Amendment and Termination. The Company reserves the right to amend and/or terminate this Plan at any time or times by resolution of its board of directors, provided, however, that any such amendment or termination shall not affect an Eligible Employee's right to reimbursement for expenses filed prior to such amendment or termination.

IN WITNESS WHEREOF, the Company has caused this Plan to be executed on this _____ day of _____, _____.

_____
Name of Corporation

By: _____
Authorized Officer

ATTEST:

_____
Its Secretary

(CORPORATE SEAL)

PROMISSORY DEMAND NOTE

_____ $_____
Date   Total Amount

     FOR VALUE RECEIVED, the undersigned promises to pay _____
_____, whose address is _____
city of _____, state of _____, the principal amount of _____ ($_____) plus interest at the annual rate of _____ percent (_____%) on any unpaid balance.

     THIS NOTE is immediately due and payable in full, including interest upon written demand of the noteholder to the borrower.

     THE NOTE is not assumable without the written consent of the borrower. The borrower waives presentment, demand, protest, and notice. In the event of any default, the borrower shall be responsible for all reasonable attorneys' fees and cost.

_____   _____
Witness   Borrower's Signature

_____   _____
Witness   Print Borrower's Name

                                  _____
                                  Address

                                  _____
                                  City, State, Zip

_____   _____
Witness   Co-Borrower (if any)

_____   _____
Witness   Print Co-Borrower's Name

                                  _____
                                  Address

                                  _____
                                  City, State, Zip

CORPORATE RESOLUTION OF

_____

A special meeting of the Board of Directors of _____ was held at the offices of the corporation on the _____ day of _____, _____. All of the Directors were present.

The meeting was called to Order.

The following Resolution was made and unanimously adopted by all of the Directors:

_____
_____
_____
_____
_____
_____
_____

There being no further business, upon motion duly made, seconded, and approved, the meeting was adjourned.

_____
Director

Approved:

_____
Director

CHAPTER FOURTEEN

THE ENTREPRENEUR'S BLACK BOOK OF RESOURCES

In many ways, this section is the most important of the book. This material is not just randomly selected. It is a special list from my own library and Rollodex of people, places, books, and materials that can help you and your corporation. I have spent thousands of dollars reading bad books just to find some of the good ones. The information is in no particular order so don't assume all the good stuff is up front; it is throughout. I listed the materials as I uncovered them in my library or in my notes. Research is half the fun, so happy hunting.

Advertising Brochure, U.S. Small Business Administration, SBA Publications, P.O. Box 30, Denver, CO 80201-0030, telephone: (800) 827-5722 or (202) 205-6665

This booklet costs $1.00 and presents basic pointers on how to advertise your products and services. However, don't stop with just this publication. You can get a lot of great information from the SBA, so make sure you ask them for their entire list of publications.

Guerilla Advertising, by J. Conrad Levinson, Houghton Mifflin Co., ISBN: 0-395-68718-7

This is one of the top-notch books from Guerilla Marketing Group. When you contact them, ask them for a complete list of their publications. Telephone: (800) 225-3362.

Living the Seven Habits, by Steven R. Covey, Nightingale Conant, 7300 North Lehigh Avenue, Niles, IL 60714, telephone: (800) 323-3938

This is a taped program that expands on the book *Seven Habits of Highly Effective People* by Steven Covey. If you don't want to spend $59.95 for tapes, at least get the book at any major bookstore.

Power Talk: Strategies for Life-Long Success, by Anthony Robbins, Nightingale Conant, 7300 North Lehigh Avenue, Niles, IL 60714, telephone: (800) 323-3938

This is a taped program with twelve different volumes of personal success and motivation. Each volume consists of one cassette with commentary given by Anthony Robbins and another tape with another interview by successful guests. Robbins also wrote two bestselling books, *Unlimited Wealth* and *The Giant Within*. Both of the books are very good and available at any major bookstore.

The Magic of Thinking Big, by David Joseph Schwartz, telephone: (800) 223-2336, ISBN: 0-671-64678-8

This is one of the classic books on motivation and how to control your thoughts to power your success.

Master Key to Success, by Napoleon Hill, Nightingale Conant, 7300 North Lehigh Avenue, Niles, IL 60714, telephone: (800) 323-3938

This program is an inspirational four-video set that demonstrates how to improve self-discipline and take control of yourself.

Seven Habits of Highly Effective People, by Steven R. Covey, Simon & Schuster, ISBN: 0-671-68796-4

A very successful book on personal management and business success.

Think and Grow Rich, by Napoleon Hill, Nightingale Conant, 7300 North Lehigh Avenue, Niles, IL 60714, telephone: (800) 323-3938

This is the tape version of the American classic written in 1937. It also is available in paperback at most bookstores. The book has been the centerpiece of many people's personal and professional success. I've read it numerous times and learn more each time. It is an essential book for entrepreneurs. If I recommended one book about going into business, this would be it.

Checklist for Going into Business, U.S. Small Business Administration, SBA Publications, P.O. Box 30, Denver, CO 80201, telephone: (800) 827-5722

This $1 book highlights the important factors you need to know before starting any business.

What Color Is Your Parachute?, by Richard Bolles, telephone: (800) 841-BOOK, ISBN: 0-891-5632-7

A classic on employment career changes. The book costs $14.95 and can be ordered by phone or be found in major bookstores. This is a classic book on career guidance.

How to Speak with Confidence, by Burt Decker, Nightingale Conant, 7300 North Lehigh Avenue, Niles, IL 60714, telephone: (800) 323-3938

This is a forty-five-minute video. Burt reveals his techniques for grabbing audiences' attention. He is an excellent speaker and has a wonderful ability to convey his thoughts. The cost is $69.95.

National Speakers Association, 1500 South Priest Drive, Tempe, AZ 85281, telephone: (602) 968-2552

This is a national organization that serves professional speakers and trainers by sponsoring national meetings and workshops to promote the profession.

CD-ROM Directory, telephone (800) 248-8466, ISBN: 1-870-88937-1

This program costs $139.00 and can be ordered by phone. This is a comprehensive directory of over 6,000 CD-ROM titles and of the company that produces them.

Hello, Direct, 5884 Eaton Park Place, San Jose, CA 95138-1859, telephone: (800) 444-3556

This company offers a full line of catalog telephone headsets and telecommunications equipment. If you talk on the phone a lot, headsets are really the way to go. They may look a little funny until you get used to them, but you'll be glad you got them.

Delivering Knock Your Socks Off Service, by Kristin Anderson and Ron Zemke, ISBN: 0-814-47777

This book costs $15.95. It is a practical, but creative book, on building excellent customer service. The author uses real examples and convinces you that this is the way to go.

Positively Outrageous Service, by T. Scott Gross, ISBN: 0-942-36182-2

The book costs $12.95. It is an excellent book on customer service that reveals ideas not frequently found in other publications. Good and well-written examples are provided. It is published by Mastermedia Limited.

Direct Marketing Association, 11 West 42nd St., New York, NY 10036-8096, telephone: (212) 768-7277

This is a national organization for people involved in marketing. If you would like to become involved in any of their conferences across the country, please contact them for additional information.

Guerilla Financing, by Jay Conrad Levinson, telephone: (800) 225-3362, ISBN: 0-395-52264-1

The book costs $10.95 and can be ordered by phone. This sourcebook presents different types of financing for small businesses. It's published by Houghton Mifflin Co.

The American Franchise Association, 53 West Jackson Boulevard, Suite 205, Chicago, IL 60604, telephone: (800) 334-4AFA, (312) 431-0545

This is a national trade association representing over 13,000 members. If you would like to have more information about financing, this is a good contact.

Entrepreneurs' Guide to Franchise and Business Opportunity, Entrepreneur Media, Inc., 2392 Morris Avenue, Irvine, CA 92714, telephone: (714) 261-2325

This is the annual publication put out by the Entrepreneur's Group regarding franchising and small business investment opportunities. This organization provides the entrepreneur with excellent information, and you should feel free to contact them about all of their products.

INC., 38 Commercial Wharf, Boston, MA 02110, telephone: (800) 234-0999

This is a magazine for small business and growing companies and an excellent publication for the business professional.

The Kiplinger Organization, 1729 H Street, N.W., Washington, DC 20006, telephone: (800) 726-0600

The Kiplinger Organization provides a wealth of information on both investments and small businesses. Contact them to learn about their entire product line.

The E Myth, by Michael E. Gerber, Harper Business, telephone: (800) 982-4377, ISBN: 0-887-30472-9

The book costs $14.95 and can be purchased by phone. The book discusses what Gerber refers to as the E myth of entrepreneurship, which explains why so many businesses fail. If you're not sure about going into business, this book will help you make the decision.

The US Small Business Administration, SBA Answer Desk, telephone: (800) YOU-ASK-SBA or (202) 205-6740

The toll-free number gives you access to a variety of prerecorded information about SBA programs. It also is a wonderful exercise in patience. You'll likely be on hold for a long time and learn why people hate voice mail. A good example how not to run a business.

Inc., Yourself, by Judith McQuown, HarperCollins, telephone: (800) 982-4377, ISBN: 0-887-30611-X

The book costs $12.00 and can be purchased by phone. The book provides guidelines for setting up your business and the reasons for choosing to operate as a corporation.

301 Great Management Ideas, by Sarah Notable, Inc. Publishing, telephone: (800) 468-0800 or (617) 248-8000, ISBN: 0-962-61464-5

A $12.95 publication, this book offers a collection of over three hundred creative management ideas.

American Management Association, 135 West 50th Street, New York, NY 10020, telephone: (800) 262-6969

The AMA is a professional association that offers a variety of publications and seminars on management throughout the country.

Board Room Reports, 330 West 42nd Street, New York, NY 10036, telephone: (800) 274-5611

This is part of the publications offered by Bottom Line Business. When contacting them, ask them for their complete line of publications.

Making It on Your Own, by Paul and Sarah Edwards, Putnam, telephone: (800) 631-8571, ISBN: 0-874-77636-8

This publication costs $11.95 and was written by the very successful and nationally known business management team. The book can be ordered by phone.

Getting to Yes, by Robert Fisher and William Ury, Penguin Books, telephone: (800) 253-6476, ISBN: 0-140-06534-2

A $5.95 classic negotiation book produced by the Harvard Negotiation Project that deals with strategies for successful negotiations.

Guerilla Marketing, by J. Conrad Levinson, Houghton Mifflin, telephone: (800) 225-3362, ISBN: 0-395-64496-8

I mention the Guerilla products so often you probably think I get a referral fee; I don't. They do have good books. An $11.95 publication, this book is part of the excellent Guerilla series on successful business strategies. You might want also to consider the *Guerilla Marketing Attack* (ISBN: 0-395-47693-3), *Guerilla Marketing Excellence*, (ISBN: 0-395-60844-9), and the *Guerilla Marketing Handbook* (ISBN: 0-395-70013-2). For further information about all of the Guerilla Publications, contact (800) 225-3362.

Getting Business to Come to You, by Paul and Sarah Edwards, Putnam, ISBN: 0-874-77629-5

This $11.95 publication is a good marketing book even though I would rate it more on a beginner's level.

Marketing without a Marketing Budget, by Craig Rice, Adams Media Corporation, telephone: (800) 872-5627, ISBN: 1-558-50-986-0

This $10.95 publication provides examples and strategies on how to compete in marketing.

Marketing on a Shoe String, by Jeff Davidson, Wiley, telephone: (800) CALL-WILEY or (212) 850-6000, ISBN: 0-471-31094-8

A $14.95 publication, this is an easy reading book with quick-start marketing ideas.

Positioning for the Battle of the Mind, by Al Ries and Jack Trout, Warner Books, telephone (800) 222-6747, ISBN: 0-446-34794-9

A $5.50 publication. Positioning your product or service is one of the most important elements to successful marketing. This book dedicates itself to helping you understand and master this concept.

Levenger, Inc., 420 Commerce Drive, Delray Beach, FL 33445-4696, telephone: (800) 544-0880

Contact them to receive their catalog of writing instruments and tools for the home office.

FAX, USA, Omni Graphics, telephone: (800) 234-1340 or (313) 961-1340, ISBN: 0-780-80030-3

A $58.00 directory of more than 85,000 fax numbers for businesses and organizations nationwide.

Sell Your Way to the Top, by Zig Ziglar, Nightingale Conant, 7300 North Lehigh Avenue, Niles, IL 60714, telephone: (800) 525-9000 or (800) 323-3938

A $59.95 six-audiotape set on the twelve keys of successful selling. By the way, Zig Ziglar is one of my favorite speakers. If you never heard him speak or read his work, you are missing out.

The Greatest Salesman in the World, by Og Mandino, Dannon Books, telephone: (800) 323-9872, ISBN: 0-553-27757-X

The $4.99 bestselling inspirational classic that teaches the principles of selling.

Entrepreneurs Magazine Group business start-up guides, telephone: (800) 333-3700

Offered by *Entrepreneur* magazine, each guide is on a particular business and tells you the A to Z of operating that business. The guides are available for $79.50 and can be ordered by phone.

Small Business Tax Forms, telephone: (800) TAX-FORM [(800) 829-3676]

The Internal Revenue Service has a complete list of tax forms to help the small-business person. You can obtain a list by calling. If you thought the SBA hotline was an exercise in patience, just wait for this.

How to Get Control of Your Time and Your Life, by Alan Lakein, Penguin Books, telephone: (800) 253-6476, ISBN: 0-451-16772-4

A $4.99 publication, this is the classic book on time management. There have been many imitators, but this is one of the first books on time management—and certainly one of the best. A different look at time management also is offered by Steven Covey (previously recommended) in his latest book *First Things First.*

The Popcorn Report, by Faith Popcorn, Harper Business, telephone: (800) 982-4377, ISBN: 0-887-30594-6

An $11.00 publication, this book forecasts trends for the future sharing Faith's insights and strategies for business. She has a new book out called *Clicking* that expands on the ideas she first developed in *The Popcorn Report.*

Trend Tracking, by Gerald Gelente, Wiley, telephone: (800) CALL-WILEY, ISBN: 0-446-39287-1

A $12.99 publication. I don't think you can ever get too much information on the future of your business. This author's track record is good.

Megatrends 2000: Ten New Directions for the '90s, by John Naisbitt and Patricia Aburdence, ISBN: 0-380-70437-4

This book is available in all bookstores. A good look into our future and helpful in thinking about new directions and opportunities for your business.

Working Solo Sourcebook, by Terry Lonier, telephone: (800) 222-7656, ISBN: 1-883-28250-0

Although this book includes some of my recommendations, it has a lot more of its own. Geared toward small companies, it is a good reference.

The Small Business Start Up Guide, by Hal Root and Steve Koenig, Source Books, Inc., telephone: (630) 961-3900, ISBN: 0-942-06167-5

A $9.95 publication. This is a basic start-up book, but it has some good ideas for new businesses.

Small Business Resource Guide, by Joseph R. Mancuso, Sourcebook, Inc., telephone: (630) 961-3900

Sourcebook, Inc., has quite a few excellent business publications. Ask them for a list. This author has been around for many years and has produced some excellent books. You'll find his sources for information very helpful.

U.S. Chamber of Commerce, Center for Small Business, 1615 H Street, N.W., Washington, DC 20062-2000, telephone: (202) 463-5503

A lot of people scoff at getting information from the U.S. Chamber of Commerce, but I believe they are an excellent source of not only free information, but also books specifically related to your area. I have listed here the U.S. Chamber of Commerce, but there are also regional offices throughout the United States as well as individual offices in all major cities and most small communities. I encourage you to visit and/or at least contact these offices prior to opening up your business.

The Open University, 24 South Orange Avenue, Orlando, FL 32801, telephone: (407) 649-8488

This is a private university founded by Lawrence J. Pino. It is a terrific source of information about entrepreneurial services and specific educational courses. In this case, I feel that I must disclose that, although I don't receive a referral fee from Larry and his organization, he has been my law partner for many years, and I have a high regard for the services he offers.

The Franchise Opportunity Handbook, Superintendent of Documents, U.S. Government Printing Office, telephone: (202) 512-1800, fax: (202) 512-2250

Mailing address: P.O. Box 371954, Pittsburgh, PA 15250-7954

This publication is offered through the U.S. Government and is one of the most inexpensive, but thorough, documents containing information about start-up businesses, such as the number of franchises and their start-up cost. This document costs $15.00. Ask for a list of business publications available.

Entrepreneur, 2392 Morris Avenue, Irvine, CA 92714, telephone: (714) 261-2325

The Entrepreneur Corporation is the publisher of *Entrepreneur* magazine and offers an unbelievable array of publications and magazines on small business, including their own annual franchise directory.

National Institute of Business Management, Inc., 1101 King Street, Alexandria, VA 22314, telephone: (800) 543-2051

This publication is a newsletter on ideas that businesses and businesspeople of all sizes can use. It frequently includes tax savings and marketing tips.

Consumer Information Catalog, Consumer Information Center -Y, P.O. Box 100, Pueblo, CO 81002

This book contains a listing of all informational booklets published by various agencies of the federal government, including those that apply to businesses.

INC., Inc., Special Reports, P.O. Box 54129, Boulder, CO 80322, telephone: (800) 234-0999

These reports are on a variety of business topics. Ask for a catalog.

The Kiplinger Tax Letter, 1729 H. Street, N.W., Washington, DC 20006, telephone: (800) 544-0155

The Kiglinger Group writes an excellent tax letter as well as several other business letters, including the *Washington Letter, Personal Finance Magazine,* the *Florida Letter,* and the *California Letter.*

Success, P.O. Box 3036, Harlan, IA 51593-2097, telephone: (800) 234-7324

An excellent monthly magazine that promotes and motivates entrepreneurs.

The Twelve Secrets to Cashing Out, by Robert L. Eergeth, Prentice-Hall, ISBN: 0-131-76462-4

A book that describes how to sell your company for maximum profit.

The Art of Negotiating, by Gerard I. Nierenberg, Barnes & Noble, ISBN: 1-566-19816-X

This book is one of the classics on negotiating.

The Negotiating Game, by Chester L. Krass, World Publishing, ISBN: 0-529-00862-9

This book was originally published in 1972 and also is considered one of the classics on negotiating. Mr. Nierenberg and Mr. Krrass form one of the most successful teaching teams on negotiation, and their ads have been in publications for years throughout the United States.

The One to One Future, by Don Peppers and Martha Rogers, a Currency Book, published by Doubleday Dell, ISBN: 0-385-42528-7

This book carefully explains the new approach to marketing one-on-one versus the traditional mass-marketing approach.

The One Minute Manager, by Kenneth Blanchard and Spenser Johnson, Berkeley Books

I would also recommend the entire *One Minute* series of books, which are available at all bookstores throughout the United States. These are simple, but effective, for specific business problems.

The Small Business Legal Kit, by J.W. Dicks, telephone: (800) 333-3700, ISBN: 1-558-50-699-3, and *The Small Business Legal Kit & Disk* by J.W. Dicks, ISBN: 1-55850-701-9

I do get a commission on these as I wrote them. They are a compilation of carefully selected business forms and contracts that can be used for a variety of purposes in solving problems in everyone's business. Using the software, you can conveniently customize and print each document. Both are available in all bookstores, or you can order toll-free through my office.

Swim with the Sharks without Being Eaten Alive, by Harvey McKay, ISBN: 0-804-10426-3

Creative business ideas from a man who built his business from scratch. The book is available in paperback form in most major bookstores and is published by Ivy Books.

Equifax Information Service Center, P.O. Box 40241, Atlanta, GA 30375-0241, telephone: (800) 685-1111

Exterian, formerly TRW, 505 City Parkway West, Orange, CA 92863, telephone: (714) 385-7000

These are major credit reporting services that will provide you with information regarding the credit on any potential customer. I encourage you to establish a relationship with these reporting entities prior to starting your business.

CHAPTER FIFTEEN

FLORIDA STATE COMPLIANCE

If you are reading this chapter, you've come a long way toward starting your own business and making your dream a reality. Now it is time to get serious; apply some of the things you've already learned; and put them into the context of Florida's laws, rules, and regulations.

One of the things you will discover early in your business career is that the entrepreneur is faced with many regulatory hurdles in starting his or her business. Although many business leaders have lobbied for less red tape, the inroads have been small. Unfortunately, if you want to be in business, you must realize the importance of dealing honestly with the government. Noncompliance with governmental regulation will mean that you have limited yourself and your company to the underground economy, never having a chance for the big time. If you ever become a large and successful company without adhering to government obligations, the regulators would eventually discover you and shut you down for not complying with their rules. It is hard enough to make money as it is; you don't need this headache on top of it.

Welcome back to reality. Now that we agree state laws must be mastered before you can successfully operate your business, the good news is that they are manageable.

In the following pages we have broken the process of Florida's state compliance into six essential steps. Although the steps can be accomplished out of order, we have selected this arrangement as being a logical way of accomplishing your goal.

The Six Steps to State Compliance:

1. Registering your business entity
2. Filing a fictitious name
3. Complying with security laws
4. Obtaining your business license and permits
5. Complying with tax laws
6. Understanding employee and labor laws

STEP 1: REGISTERING YOUR BUSINESS ENTITY

Sole Proprietorship

If you have read Chapter 1 on selecting your business entity and have decided to operate as a sole proprietorship, we have good news for you: the state of Florida does not require you to register. You can now proceed to step 2. However, there are very specific reasons you may want to choose one of the other forms of business entities. If you have not read Chapter 1 regarding the selection of a business entity, we encourage you to do so. This is not the time for speed reading or taking short cuts.

General Partnerships

If two or more individuals or even other business entities have decided to go into business together, the general partnership is a viable option. Like the sole proprietor, you can skip to step 2 of our compliance process because Florida does not require registration of a general partnership. We will likewise caution prospective general partners that selecting this method of operation should be done with careful thought because you may be exposing yourself and others to potential liabilities that might be avoided using other business entities.

Limited Liability Partnerships

The state of Florida has adopted a new business entity called the limited liability partnership. This business entity became effective on July 1, 1995. The limited liability partnership is different from both a general partnership and a limited partnership. Its purpose is to act as a blend between the two entities, allowing partners who wish to be in business together with equal management control to continue to have some form of limitation to their liability.

This new form of partnership is an excellent compromise between the general and limited partnerships. It allows business owners to form business ventures without the concern that they may be accountable for the actions of their other partner. Previously, the only way to escape this was to form a limited partnership, which had the negative aspect of creating two tiers of partners, general and limited, while also being classified as a security. The limited liability partnership overcomes both of these disadvantages.

The primary use of this new entity may very well be with professional entities. Previously, when professionals formed partnerships, not only could they be liable for malpractice claims for the actions of their partners, but also all other types of torts. The use of the limited liability partnership will certainly limit the liabilities related to all other types of claims and may very well limit liability in malpractice cases to the individual partner that committed the act. This is clearly the intent of the act as stated in Section 620.782 (1), where it states that

...a partner in a registered limited liability partnership is not individually liable for obligations, or liabilities, of the partnership whether in tort, contract, or otherwise, arising from errors, omissions, negligence, malpractice, or wrongful acts committed by another partner or by an employee, agent, or representative of the partnership while the partnership is a registered limited liability partnership.

This new structure offers a tremendous advantage over all currently existing general partnerships, and you may need to consider changing over to the limited liability partnership. The only real disadvantage of being a limited liability partnership is the cost of registration and the annual renewal. However, this additional expense, compared to the safeguard of limiting one's liability, is extremely small. The current fee for registration is $100 for each partner in the partnership, and a renewal fee of $100 each year for each partner. The bottom line is that for $100 a year, a partner in the state of Florida can now get the equivalent of total liability protection for another partner's acts. To investigate further all the requirements of filing the limited liability partnership, contact the Florida Division of Corporations at (904) 488-9000. Ask them to send you their booklet, *Partnerships in*

Florida, which describes all the costs and contains the actual forms used for filing.

Limited Partnership

The limited partnership is a creature of state law. Florida, like most states, has adopted the Uniform Limited Partnership Act. The Act specifically requires registration, filing fees, and annual reports. For small businesses in Florida, it may be one of the most expensive business entities to form because of the way the fees are structured. On the other hand, many benefits to the limited partnership may make the cost worthwhile. For a review, refer to Chapter 1, which covers the advantages and disadvantages of limited partnerships.

An extra word of caution. Limited partnerships have gotten a bad reputation over the years because of the large number of public and private partnerships that failed in the late 1980s with the collapse of the real estate market and, to a lesser degree, oil and gas prices. Consequently, if your business has a problem and it is a limited partnership, you will have a strike against you if you are facing any regulator or judicial body. This is neither fair nor just, but it is the way it is. Thus, even though the limited partnership has some very positive aspects for a business, the black mark it carries may be a reason for you to consider another entity.

To obtain specific information regarding the cost and requirements of forming a Florida limited partnership, call the Florida Division of Corporations at (904) 488-9000. Ask them for the their booklet *Partnerships in Florida.* This book contains all the forms needed for registration in the state of Florida, but it does not contain an actual limited partnership agreement or any of the requirements that might be needed to comply with the Florida Division of Securities.

Corporations

The Florida corporation is created by statute. To form a corporation, you must follow the requirements of the statute. Once you have created this new entity, you must continue to maintain it as an entity by complying with those same laws. Failure to continue with annual compliance will result in the demise of your corporation. This can be a big problem because officers, directors, and even shareholders of the former corporation can become personally liable for its acts. What's more, severe tax consequences can result.

The first step in the actual formation of your corporation would be to contact the Division of Corporations of the Florida Department of State:

> Division of Corporations
> Florida Department of State
> P.O. Box 6327
> Tallahassee, FL 32314
> Tel.: (904) 488-9000

Request that they send you their booklet, *Florida Business Corporations Act*, which outlines all the requirements for operating your corporation and includes forms and a description of filing fees. You won't have to wait for the book to file your incorporation because we have included the necessary forms here; you may, however, find it helpful.

For tax questions about your corporation, contact:

> Division of Taxpayer Assistance
> Florida Department of Revenue
> P.O. Box 7443
> Tallahassee, FL 32314-7443
> Tel.: (904) 488-6800
> (800) 352-3671

Note: Sometimes you will find that getting through on 800 numbers can be difficult. For that reason, we list toll as well as toll-free numbers when possible. Toll numbers frequently mean time savers.

Domestic Corporation Versus Foreign Corporations

All corporations that are formed within the state are called domestic. Corporations that are formed in another state but desire to do business in Florida are called foreign corporations. They do not have to be formed outside the United States to be a foreign corporation although non-U.S. corporations are also foreign corporations.

If your corporation is a foreign corporation and you want to do business in Florida, you must register in Florida as a foreign corporation. You will also need to have a registered agent to accept service of process for official papers that may be filed on your corporation.

Because foreign corporate registration is mandatory, there is little reason to form your corporation outside Florida if you live there. At one time, people promoted Delaware, and more recently, Nevada as preferred states to form a corporation in because of their particular state laws. This is no longer true if indeed there ever were any advantages. Florida has very favorable corporate laws, and the requirement of foreign registration eliminates any advantage of filing elsewhere.

The C Corporation

The C corporation is the regular corporation in Florida. Normally, you will not see the letter C used, but when it is, the reason is to distinguish it from the S corporation. When you complete the paperwork to form a corporation, you will have formed a C corporation unless you take the extra step to file for Sub Chapter S status with the Internal Revenue Service.

The S Corporation

The Florida S corporation stands for the Sub Chapter S corporation as described in the Internal Revenue Code. Unlike a C corporation, the S corporation pays no income tax itself, and all income is taxed at the shareholder level. Consequently, all profits and losses flow through directly to the individual shareholder. For a complete discussion of the S corporation including the recent changes in the law, see Chapter 2. Although the S corporation pays no income tax in Florida, it must file a corporate income tax return on Form F-1120 the first year it elects to be taxed as a Sub S Corporation. For a copy of the form, call the Division of Taxpayer Assistance at (904) 488-6800 or (800) 352-3671. To qualify for Sub Chapter S status, you must file Form 2553, Election by a Small Business Corporation. For a copy of the form, call (800) 829-1040. You should also request publication 589, Tax Information on S Corporations.

The Professional Corporation

The designation professional corporation (PC or PA) does not mean that the other types of corporations are not used by professionals or that you aren't professional if you use them. Instead, it is simply a type of corporation that authorizes only members of the designated profession to be shareholders. Doctors, lawyers, and CPAs are three examples of professionals who frequently use professional corporations. Generally, if you are not a licensed professional, you cannot own shares in a professional corporation.

Thus, an unlicensed individual could not own part of a doctor's practice by simply becoming a shareholder. The individual would first have to become a doctor. Professional corporations are taxed like regular corporations. However, unlike a regular corporation, which insulates shareholders from liability, a professional corporation does not protect the shareholders from malpractice claims against the professional or, in some cases, others in the corporation. The professional corporation does provide liability protection for shareholders from other actions such as personal injury.

The Limited Liability Company

The limited liability company (LLC) is the new corporate kid on the block. It was created to combine the best points of a partnership and a corporation without the shareholders having to meet some of the strict requirements of S corporate status.

One of the big advantages of the LLC is the ability to pass through tax profits and losses similar to a partnership. Simply put, the LLC is treated like a partnership for all tax purposes, and all income is passed to the shareholder's individual return. Florida adopted the provision for federal tax pass through but not corporate tax.

Limited liability is the major attraction to this type of corporation. Even though you are taxed as a partnership, you don't have the very dangerous personal liability that comes with a general partnership.

LLCs were created to overcome some of the restrictions on Sub S corporations such as the former limitation on the number of shareholders to thirty-five. Recently, however, many of these limitations have been lifted through new federal legislation and the use of LLCs may not expand as fast as once expected. (For example, Sub S Corporations can now have seventy-five shareholders).

If your corporation will do business in other states, how they treat LLCs is also important since they may not recognize these corporations the same way Florida does. You might discover that another state does not recognize the limited liability for shareholders or the corporate tax is greater than planned. Until more case law is developed in this area, it is better to remain cautious if you venture out of Florida.

If you know the operations of your company will remain in Florida, the LLC's advantages would likely outweigh these other concerns. For more information about forming the LLC, contact the Division of Corporations of the Florida Department of State at the address and phone number previously mentioned.

How to File Your Corporation in Florida

The actual process of filing a corporation is not difficult in Florida. It truly is fill in the blank. After looking at the form, everyone always questions how an attorney could charge $500 to $1,000 for something so easy. Remember, it isn't for filling out the form that you should pay such a fee. It is for understanding and explaining the ramifications of what you are doing. Don't ever pay for filling out forms, pay for the advice and planning. Good advice is cheap.

To form your Florida corporation, complete the following forms, and include the appropriate fees listed.

Explanation of Forms

Form 1 — Instructions for a Profit Corporation. The State of Florida has generously provided a set of sample instructions for filing your corporation. The instructions are helpful and worthwhile.

Form 2 — The Transmittal letter is a simple form that tells the state what you want to do. There is no need to type up a lengthy wordy letter when they provide you with such an easy form.

Form 3 — The Articles of Incorporation form provides you the essential elements you need to incorporate in Florida. Take out Form 1 and go over it as you complete the blanks in Form 3. When you are done, you have a corporation.

Form 4 — The Certificate of Designation of Registered Agent/Registered Office is used to tell the state the name and address of the person your company has chosen to receive any "official" correspondence. When lawyers held exclusive providence for incorporation, they always listed themselves so they had a reason to call the client and send a bill. If it's your corporation, put yourself down as registered agent.

Florida Department of State
Sandra B. Mortham
Secretary of State
Division of Corporations
P.O. Box 6327
Tallahassee, FL 32314

Instructions for a Profit Corporation

The following are instructions, a sample transmittal letter, and sample articles of incorporation pursuant to Chapter 607, Florida Statutes. The sample copy may be used by typing or printing *all* information. All information included in the articles must be in English. Pursuant to Section 607.0120, Florida Statutes, a document must be typewritten or printed legibly, and if this requirement is not met, the document will be returned to the person submitting it for correction. The Division of Corporations suggests using the sample merely as a guideline rather than an application. Pursuant to section 607.0202, Florida Statutes, additional information may be contained in the articles, which may be set forth on additional sheets.

This office does not provide you with corporate seals, minute books, or stock certificates. It is the responsibility of the corporation to secure these items once the incorporation process has been completed.

This form is not applicable when filing a professional association pursuant to Chapter 621, Florida Statutes. Forms for a professional association are not available.

Questions concerning S Corporations should be directed to the Internal Revenue Service by telephoning (800) 329-1040. This is a federal regulation and is not determined by this office.

NOTE: THIS FORM FOR FILING ARTICLES OF INCORPORATION IS BASIC. EACH CORPORATION IS A SEPARATE ENTITY AND AS SUCH HAS SPECIFIC GOALS, NEEDS, AND REQUIREMENTS. THE DIVISION OF CORPORATIONS RECOMMENDS THAT CORPORATE DOCUMENTS BE REVIEWED BY YOUR LEGAL COUNSEL. THE DIVISION IS A FILING AGENCY AND AS SUCH DOES NOT RENDER ANY LEGAL, ACCOUNTING, OR TAX ADVICE. THE PROFESSIONAL ADVICE OF YOUR LEGAL COUNSEL TO ASCERTAIN EXACT COMPLIANCE WITH ALL STATUTORY REQUIREMENTS IS STRONGLY RECOMMENDED.

Pursuant to section 607.0202, Florida Statutes, the articles of incorporation must set forth the following:

ARTICLE I

The name of the corporation must include a corporate suffix such as Corporation, Corp., Incorporated, Inc., Company, or Co. A preliminary search for name availability may be obtained by calling (904) 488-9000.

ARTICLE II

The address of the principal office, if known, and the mailing address of the corporation.

ARTICLE III

The number of shares the corporation is authorized to issue. (Additional stock structure information may need to be included in this article.)

ARTICLE IV

The street address of the corporation's initial registered office and the name of its initial registered agent at this office. Pursuant to sections 607.0501 and 607.0505, Florida Statutes, every corporation is required to have and continuously maintain in this state a registered office and registered agent upon whom process may be served. The registered office must have a Florida street address and may be, but need not be, the same as the corporation's address. The registered agent must sign in the space provided accepting the designation as registered agent. The information listed in this article must be the same as what is contained in the "registered agent certificate of designation."

ARTICLE V

The name(s) and addresses of the incorporator(s). Only one of the incorporators needs to sign the document as set forth in section 607.0120 (6)(b), Florida Statutes. NOTE: Affixing an officer title after a signature of an incorporator does not constitute the designation of officers. (Notarization of signature(s) is not required)

Pursuant to section 607.0202, Florida Statutes, the following information is not required but may be set forth in your articles of incorporation:

- The name(s) and street address(es) of the initial officer(s)/director(s). (Post Office Box address is NOT sufficient.)
- The purpose or purposes.
- Provisions concerning management and regulations of the affairs of the corporation.
- Powers of the corporation, board of directors, and shareholders.
- Par value or classes of shares.
- Provisions for personal liability of shareholders.
- Any provision required or permitted to be set forth in the bylaws.

Pursuant to section 607.0123, Florida Statutes, a delayed effective date may be specified but may not be later than the 90th day after the date on which it is filed. Pursuant to section 607.0203, Florida Statutes, an effective date may also be within five (5) business days prior to the date of filing. An effective date must be specified in the articles or the date of receipt will be the file date.

The fee for filing a profit corporation is:

$35.00 Filing Fee
$35.00 Designation of Registered Agent
$52.50 Certified Copy (optional)
$8.75 Certificate of Status (optional)

(Make checks payable to Department of State)

Please send completed articles to:

Department of State
Division of Corporations
Post Office Box 6327
Tallahassee, FL 32314
(904) 487-6052

For Courier Service ONLY send to:

Department of State
Division of Corporations
409 E. Gaines St.
Tallahassee, FL 32399
(904) 487-6052

Please Note: Documents received by Courier Service will have a filing date the same as the date received. *This does not guarantee same day return.*

Transmittal Letter

Department of State
Division of Corporations
P.O. Box 6327
Tallahassee, FL 32314

SUBJECT: _____
(Proposed corporate name - must include suffix)

Enclosed is an original and one (1) copy of the articles of incorporation and a check for:

❑ $70.00
Filing Fee

❑ $78.75
Filing Fee
& Certificate

❑ $122.50
Filing fee
& Certified Copy

❑ $131.25
Filing fee,
Certified Copy,
& Certificate

Additional Copy Required

FROM: _____
Name (printed or typed)

_____
Address

_____
City, State & Zip

_____
Daytime Telephone Number

Note: Please provide the original and *one copy* of the articles.

Articles of Incorporation

The undersigned incorporator(s), for the purpose of forming a corporation under the Florida Business Corporation Act, hereby adopt(s) the following Articles of Incorporation.

ARTICLE I: NAME

The name of the corporation shall be:

_____

ARTICLE II: PRINCIPAL OFFICE

The principal place of business and mailing address of this corporation shall be:

_____

_____

_____

ARTICLE III: SHARES

The number of shares of stock that this corporation is authorized to have outstanding at any one time is: _____

ARTICLE IV: INITIAL REGISTERED AGENT AND STREET ADDRESS

The name and address of the initial registered agent is:

_____

_____

_____

ARTICLE V: INCORPORATOR(S)

See instructions for officers/directors.

The name(s) and street addresses of the incorporator(s) to these Articles of Incorporation is (are):

_____

_____

_____

The undersigned incorporator(s) has(have) executed these Articles of Incorporation this _____ day of _____, 19_____.

(An additional article must be added if an effective date is requested.)

_____
Signature

_____
Signature

_____
Signature

Notarization is not required.

Note: Affixing an officer title after a signature of an incorporator does not constitute the designation of officers.

Filing Fee $70.00

Certificate of Designation of
Registered Agent/Registered Office

_____

PURSUANT TO THE PROVISIONS OF SECTION 607.0501, FLORIDA STATUTES, THE UNDERSIGNED CORPORATION, ORGANIZED UNDER THE LAWS OF THE STATE OF FLORIDA, SUBMITS THE FOLLOWING STATEMENT IN DESIGNATING THE REGISTERED OFFICE/REGISTERED AGENT, IN THE STATE OF FLORIDA.

1. The name of the corporation is:

   _____

2. The name and address of the registered agent and office is:

   _____
   (Name)

   _____
   (P.O. Box or Mail Drop Box NOT Acceptable)

   _____
   (City/State/Zip)

Having been named as registered agent and to accept service of process for the above stated corporation at the place designated in this certificate, I hereby accept the appointment as registered agent and agree to act in this capacity. I further agree to comply with the provisions of all statutes relating to the proper and complete performance of my duties, and I am familiar with and accept the obligations of my position as registered agent.

_____   _____
(Signature)   (Date)

DIVISION OF CORPORATIONS, P.O. BOX 6327, TALLAHASSEE, FL 32314

Florida Department of State
Division of Corporations

DIRECTOR'S OFFICE 487-6000

BUREAU OF COMMERCIAL RECORDING (Chief) 487-6900
    Amendment Section 487-6050
        Function: All amendments and mergers to domestic & foreign corporations and limited liability companies; amendments and cancellations of limited partnerships; dissolutions and withdrawals; resignations of officers, directors and registered agents; and registered agent changes.
    New Filing Section 487-6052
        Function: All domestic profit and not for profit business entities.
    Registration Section 487-6051
        Function: All new limited partnership filings, trademarks and all corporation and limited partnership reinstatements.
    Tax Lien and Foreign Qualification Section 487-6091
        Function: Tax lien registrations and qualification of all foreign corporations.
    UCC Filing Section 487-6055
        Function: All UCC1 and UCC3 filings for secured transactions and liens.

BUREAU OF COMMERCIAL INFORMATION SERVICES (Chief) 487-6890
    Certification Section 487-6053
        Function: Certified copies of all division records, certificates of status and service of process pursuant to Chapter 48, Florida Statutes.
    Public Inquiry Section 488-9000
        Function: 100 incoming trunk lines for general corporate & fictitious name information, name availability, name reservations and corporate printouts. Phone lines open from 7:30 a.m. to 5:30 p.m.

Records Search Section 487-6063
    Function: Secured transaction searches.
Public Assistance Section 487-6963
    Function: Walk-in filings and information requests.

BUREAU OF DATA SYSTEMS (Chief) 487-6802
    Public Access Section 487-6866
        Function: Information for on-line access to records maintained by the Division of Corporations' data base.

BUREAU OF COMMERCIAL RECORDS MANAGEMENT (Chief) 487-6883
    Annual Reports Section 487-6056
        Function: Corporation Annual Reports and Limited Partnership Annual Reports.
    Fictitious Names Section (DBAs) 487-6058
        Function: Fictitious name applications, reregistrations and cancellations.

Division of Corporations, P.O. Box 6327, Tallahassee, FL 32314

Corporation Fees

Profit and Not for Profit Florida and Foreign Corporations

Filing Fees	$35.00
Registered Agent Designation	$35.00
Certified Copy (optional)	($52.50)
	$122.50

Amendment of any record	$35.00	Foreign Name Renewal	$87.50
Annual Report	$200.00	Merger (per party)	$35.00
(& Supplemental Fee)		Name Reservation	$35.00
Annual Report fee	$225.00	(120 day non-renewable)	
after May 1		Reinstatement	$175.00
Articles of Correction	$35.00	Resignation of Registered Agent	
Certificate of Status	$8.75	(active corporation)	$87.50
Certified Copy of any record	$52.50	(inactive corporation)	$35.00
Change of Registered Agent	$35.00	Revocation of Dissolution	$35.00
Dissolution & withdrawal	$35.00	Substitute service of	$8.75
Foreign Name Registration	$87.50	process (Chapter 48, F.S.)	

Requirements for Filing an S Corporation with the Internal Revenue Service

The following is only an excerpt from IRS publication 589, Tax Information on S Corporations. Individuals interested in obtaining S corporation status should contact the Internal Revenue Service for additional information before filing with the Division of Corporations.

A corporation is taxed on its income under corporate tax rules. When it distributes dividends to its shareholders, the shareholders include these already taxed amounts in their income. In effect, corporate income is taxed twice, once to the corporation and again to the shareholders.

However, an eligible domestic corporation can avoid double taxation by electing to be treated as an S corporation under the rules of Subchapter S of the Internal Revenue Code. In this way, the S corporation passes its items of income, loss, deduction and credits through to its shareholders to be included on their separate returns. Individual shareholders may benefit from a reduction in their taxable income during the first years of the corporation's existence when it may be operating at a loss.

Only qualifying corporations may elect S corporation status.

A corporation may become an S corporation if:

1. It meets the requirements of S corporation status.
2. All its shareholders consent to S corporation status.
3. It uses a permitted tax year, or elects to use a tax year other than a permitted tax year.
4. It files Form 2553, Election by a Small Business Corporation, to indicate it chooses S corporation status.

To qualify for S corporation status, a corporation must meet all the following requirements:

1. It must be a domestic corporation. It must be a corporation that is either organized in the United States or organized under federal or state law. The term "corporation" includes a joint-stock company, certain insurance companies, or an association that has the characteristics of a corporation.
2. It must have only one class of stock.
3. It must have no more than 35 shareholders.
4. It must have as shareholders only individuals, estates (including estates of individuals in bankruptcy), and certain trusts. Partnerships and corporations cannot be shareholders in an S corporation.
5. It must have shareholders who are citizens or residents of the United States. Nonresident aliens cannot be shareholders.

To receive forms, or for additional information concerning IRS S corporation filing requirements, contact the Internal Revenue Service at 800 TAX-FORM (800 829-3676).

CORPORATE KIT

In addition to the Articles of Incorporation or Articles of Organization, we have included all the forms needed to actually complete your corporate formation and start your business. The forms should be kept in a file along with all other records of the corporation to show that it was properly started and operated.[1]

The first form is the Stock Subscription Agreement. This is the contract that shareholders have with the company to actually buy the stock. It is very straightforward and simply names the parties, the amount of stock, and what the parties will pay for the stock.

You will note that the column headed "Cash or Property" implies that a person may pay something other than cash for his or her stock. In addition to property, you could list services since it is sometimes the case that individuals are given stock in exchange for services they perform in establishing the company or coming up with the business idea. Anyone who receives stock in this fashion will be liable to pay income tax on the value of the stock received.

The second form is the Bylaws of the corporation. The Bylaws are more extensive than the Articles of Incorporation. It is

---

[1] These forms have been taken from the *Small Business Legal Kit*, which is available in all bookstores or can be ordered by calling (800) 333-3700. This book includes more than 434 pages of forms that can be used by all small businesses on topics ranging from contracts, employment documents, powers of attorney, loan agreements and guarantees, credit collections, bills of sale, partnerships and joint ventures, corporations, real estate, and special forms.

the Bylaws that provide specific detail regarding the actual operation of your company. The Articles of Incorporation are publicly filed, but the Bylaws are not.

The third form is the Minutes of the First Meeting of the Incorporators. Minutes of meetings are extremely important because they demonstrate in concrete fashion that you are operating as a corporation and not as an individual or a partnership. If an issue of liability ever develops, good records of meetings will be necessary for you to show that you have a valid corporation. Without these minutes, lawyers will attempt to "pierce the corporate veil" and have you treated as a sole proprietorship or partnership for liability purposes.

The fourth form is the Waiver of Notice of the First Meeting of Incorporators. The notice must be given for all meetings of the corporation. The number of days notice required will be in the Bylaws. If a meeting is needed quickly, and everyone waives notice, the meeting can go on, and anything adopted will be valid.

The fifth form is the Waiver of Notice of the Organizational Meeting of Directors. Now that the Board has been elected, it needs to have a meeting. The meeting can be noticed, or everyone can agree to waive notice.

The last form included in your corporate kit is the Minutes of the Organizational Meeting of the Board of Directors. Using this form, the Board of Directors notes the proceedings of its meetings. The Board runs the corporation through the officers it appoints. Consequently, the Board is what really decides what a company can or cannot do. The president and other officers simply follow the Board's instructions.

Stock Subscription Agreement

FOR VALUE RECEIVED, the undersigned parties hereby agree to subscribe to the capital stock of a corporation to be formed in the state of _____ for the purpose of _____ and to be named _____. The corporation will have an initial capital of $_____, with _____ shares of Common Stock with a par value of $_____ per share. We agree to subscribe to the number of shares designated as follows and to pay cash or property as stipulated:

Name	Number of Shares	Cash or Property
_____	_____	_____
_____	_____	_____
_____	_____	_____

The payment for said shares shall be made within ___ days of the commencement of existence of the corporation.

This agreement shall be considered among the parties and shall additionally be enforceable by the corporation when formed.

IN WITNESS WHEREOF, the parties hereto have affixed their hands and seals on this the _____ day of _____, 19 ___.

_____(Seal)

_____(Seal)

_____(Seal)

_____(Seal)

Bylaws of

_____
Name of Corporation

ARTICLE I. OFFICES
The principal office of the corporation shall be located in the city of _____, county of _____, state of _____. The corporation may have such other offices, either within or without the state of _____, as the Board of Directors may designate or as the business of the corporation may require from time to time.

ARTICLE II. SHAREHOLDERS
    Section 1. Annual Meeting. The shareholders of the corporation shall hold a meeting at least annually each year for the purpose of electing directors and for the transaction of such other business as may come before the meeting.

    Section 2. Special Meetings. Special meetings of the shareholders may be called by the president or by the Board of Directors, and shall be called by the president at the request of the holders of not less than _____ of all outstanding shares of the corporation entitled to vote at the meeting.

    Section 3. Place of Meeting. The Board of Directors may designate any place, either within or without the state of _____, as the place of meeting called by the Board of Directors.

    Section 4. Notice of Meeting. Written notice stating the place, day, and hour of the meeting and, in case of a special meeting, the purpose or purposes for which the meeting is called shall be delivered not less than ten nor more than sixty days before the date of the meeting, either personally or by first class mail, by or at the direction of the president, or the secretary, or the officer or other persons calling the meeting, to each shareholder of record entitled to vote at such meeting. If mailed, such notice shall be deemed to be delivered when deposited in the United States mail, addressed to the shareholder at his address as it appears on the stock transfer books of the corporation, with postage thereon prepaid.

    Section 5. Closing of Transfer Books or Fixing of Record Date. For the purpose of determining shareholders entitled to notice of or to vote at any meeting of shareholders or entitled to receive payment of any dividend, or in order to make a determination of shareholders for any other proper purpose, the Board of Directors of the corporation may provide that the stock transfer books shall be closed for a stated period but not to exceed, in any case, sixty days. If the stock transfer books shall be closed for the purpose of determining shareholders entitled to notice of or to vote at a meeting of shareholders, such books shall be closed for at least ten days immediately preceding such meeting. In lieu of closing the stock transfer books, the Board of Directors may fix in advance a date as the record date for any such determination of shareholders, such date in any case to be not more than sixty days and, in case of a meeting of shareholders, not less than ten days prior to the date on which the particular action requiring such determination of shareholders is to be taken.

Section 6. Voting Record. The officer or agent having charge of the stock transfer books for shares of the corporation shall make, at least ten days before each meeting of shareholders, a complete list of the shareholders entitled to vote at such meeting of shareholders. Such list shall be kept on file at the registered office of the corporation. The list shall be available for inspection of any shareholder during the meeting.

Section 7. Quorum. A majority of the outstanding shares of the corporation entitled to vote, represented in person or by proxy, shall constitute a quorum at a meeting of shareholders. If less than a majority of the outstanding shares are represented at a meeting, a majority of the shares so represented may adjourn the meeting without further notice.

Section 8. Proxies. At all meetings of shareholders, a shareholder may vote in person or by proxy. Such proxy shall be filed with the secretary of the corporation before or at the time of the meeting.

Section 9. Informal Action by Shareholders. Any action required or permitted to be taken at a meeting of the shareholders may be taken without a meeting if a consent in writing, setting forth the action so taken, shall be signed by the holders of outstanding stock having not less than the minimum number of votes that would be necessary to authorize or take such action at a meeting at which all shares entitled to vote thereon were present and voted.

Section 10. Cumulative Voting. At each election for directors every shareholder entitled to vote at such election shall have the right to vote, in person or by proxy, the number of shares owned by him for as many persons as there are directors to be elected and for whose election he has a right to vote, or to cumulate his votes by giving one candidate as many votes as the number of such directors multiplied by the number of shares shall equal, or by distributing such votes on the same principle among any number of such candidates.

ARTICLE III. BOARD OF DIRECTORS

Section 1. General Powers. The business and affairs of the corporation shall be managed by its Board of Directors.

Section 2. Number, Tenure and Qualifications. The number of directors of the corporation shall be ____. Each director shall hold office until the next annual meeting of shareholders and until his successor shall have been elected and qualified.

Section 3. Regular Meetings. An annual meeting of the Board of Directors shall be held without notice immediately after the annual meeting of shareholders. Additional meetings may be held at the option of the directors with two days written notice. Any director may waive notice, and attendance at the meeting shall constitute waiver unless an objection is made.

Section 4. Quorum. A majority of the number of directors shall constitute a quorum for the transaction of business at any meeting of the Board of Directors.

Section 5. Action without a Meeting. Any action required or permitted to be taken by the Board of Directors at a meeting may be taken without a meeting if a consent in writing, setting for the action so taken, shall be signed by all of the directors.

Section 6. Vacancies. A vacancy occurring in the Board of Directors may be filled by the affirmative vote of a majority of the remaining directors. A director elected to fill a vacancy shall be elected for the unexpired term of his predecessor in office.

Section 7. Compensation. By resolution of the Board of Directors, each director may be paid his expenses, if any, of attendance at each meeting of the Board of Directors, and may be paid a stated salary as director or a fixed sum for attendance at each meeting of the Board of Directors or both. No such payment shall preclude any director from serving the corporation in any other capacity and receiving compensation therefor. Directors may set their own compensation for service as officers as well as for service as directors.

ARTICLE IV. OFFICERS

Section 1. The officers of the corporation shall be a president, one or more vice presidents, a secretary, and a treasurer, each of whom shall be elected by the Board of Directors. Such other officers and assistant officers as may be deemed necessary may be elected or appointed by the Board of Directors. Any two or more offices may be held by the same person.

Section 2. Election and Term of Office. The officers of the corporation to be elected by the Board of Directors shall be elected annually by the Board of Directors. Each officer shall hold office until his successor shall have been duly elected and shall have qualified or until his death or until he shall resign or shall have been removed from office.

Section 3. Removal. Any officer or agent may be removed by the Board of Directors whenever in its judgment the best interest of the corporation will be served thereby.

Section 4. Vacancies. A vacancy in any office because of death, resignation, removal, disqualification, or otherwise, may be filled by the Board of Directors for the unexpired portion of the term.

Section 5. President. The president shall be the principal executive officer of the corporation and, subject to the control of the Board of Directors, shall in general supervise and control all of the business and affairs of the corporation. He shall, when present, preside at all meetings of the shareholders and of the Board of Directors. He may sign, with the secretary or any other proper officer of the corporation, certificates for shares of the corporation and deeds, mortgages, bonds, contracts or other instruments that the Board of Directors has authorized to be executed.

Section 6. The Vice Presidents. In the absence of the president or in the event of his death, inability, or refusal to act, the vice president designated the "senior vice president" shall perform the duties of the president, and when so acting, shall have all the powers of and be subject to all the restrictions upon the president. Any vice president may sign, with the secretary or an assisting secretary, certificates for shares of the corporation, and shall perform such other duties as from time to time may be assigned to him by the president or by the Board of Directors.

Section 7. The Secretary. The secretary shall: (a) keep the minutes of the proceedings of the shareholders and of the Board of Directors in one or more books provided for that purpose; (b) see that all notices are duly given in accordance with the provisions of these Bylaws or as required by law; (c) be custodian of the corporate records and of the seal of the corporation and see that the seal of the corporation is affixed to all documents the execution of which on behalf of the corporation under its seal is duly authorized; (d) keep a register of the post office address of each shareholder, which shall be furnished to the secretary by such shareholder; (e) sign with the president, or a vice president, certificates for shares of the corporation, the issuance of which shall have been authorized by resolution of the Board of Directors; (f) have general charge of the stock transfer books of the corporation; and (g) in general perform all duties as from time to time may be assigned to him by the president or by the Board of Directors.

Section 8. The Treasurer. The treasurer shall: (a) have charge and custody of and be responsible for all funds and securities of the corporation; (b) receive and give receipts for moneys due and payable to the corporation from any source whatsoever, and deposit all such moneys in the name of the corporation in such banks, trust companies, or the depositaries as shall be selected in accordance with the provisions of Article V of these Bylaws; and (c) in general perform all duties as from time to time may be assigned to him by the president or by the Board of Directors.

ARTICLE V. CONTRACTS, LOANS, CHECKS, AND DEPOSITS

Section 1. Contracts. The Board of Directors may authorize any officer or agent to enter into any contract on behalf of the corporation. The authority may be general or confined to specific instances.

Section 2. Loans. All loans taken on behalf of the corporation must be authorized by a specific resolution of the Board of Directors.

Section 3. Checks, Drafts, etc. All checks, drafts, or other orders for the payment of money, notes or other evidences of indebtedness issued in the name of the corporation shall be signed by such officer or agent of the corporation as shall from time to time be determined by resolution of the Board of Directors.

Section 4. Deposits. All funds of the corporation not otherwise employed shall be deposited to the credit of the corporation in such banks, money markets, or other depositaries as the Board of Directors may select.

ARTICLE VI. CERTIFICATES FOR SHARES AND THEIR TRANSFER

Section 1. Certificates for Shares. Certificates representing shares of the corporation shall be in such form as shall be determined by the Board of Directors. Such certificates shall be signed by the president and by the secretary and sealed with the corporate seal. The name and address of the person to whom the shares represented thereby are issued, with the number of share and date of issue, shall be entered on the stock transfer books of the corporation. All certificates surrendered to the corporation for transfer shall be cancelled and no new certificate shall be issued until the former certificate for a like number of shares shall have been surrendered and cancelled, except that in case of a lost, destroyed, or mutilated certificate, a new one may be issued therefor upon such terms and indemnity to the corporation as the Board of Directors may prescribe.

Section 2. Transfer of Shares. Transfer of shares of the corporation shall be made only on the stock transfer books of the corporation by the holder of record thereof or by his legal representative, who shall furnish proper evidence of authority to transfer such shares. The person in whose name shares appear on the books of the corporation shall be deemed by the corporation to be the owner thereof for all purposes.

ARTICLE VII. FISCAL YEAR

The fiscal year of the corporation shall begin on the first day of January and end on the thirty-first day of December each year.

ARTICLE VIII. DIVIDENDS

The Board of Directors may, from time to time, declare and the corporation may pay dividends on its outstanding shares in the manner and upon the terms and conditions provided by law and the Articles of Incorporation.

ARTICLE IX. CORPORATE SEAL

The Board of Directors shall provide a corporate seal, which shall be circular in form and shall have inscribed thereon the name of its corporation and the state of its incorporation and the words "Corporate Seal."

ARTICLE X. WAIVER OF NOTICE

Whenever any notice is required to be given to any shareholder or director of the corporation under the provisions of these Bylaws or under the provisions of the Articles of Incorporation or under the provisions of the state, a waiver thereof in writing signed by the person or persons entitled to such notice, whether before or after the time stated therein, shall be deemed equivalent to the giving of such notice.

ARTICLE XI. AMENDMENTS

These Bylaws may be altered, amended, or repealed and new Bylaws may be adopted by the Board of Directors or by the shareholders at any regular or special meeting.

    Adopted the _____ day of _____, 19____.

_____
Director

_____
Director

_____
Director

Minutes of the First Meeting of the Incorporators

_____
Name of Corporation

The first meeting of the incorporators was held at ____ o'clock a.m. on the ____ day of _____, 19____, at _____, city of _____, state of _____.

The following incorporators were present in person at the meeting:

Name	Address	Number of Shares
_____	_____	_____
_____	_____	_____
_____	_____	_____

The above persons constitute all of the incorporators of the corporation.
_____ was elected as Chairman, and _____ as Secretary of the meeting.

The Secretary presented a written Waiver of Notice of the First Meeting of Incorporators, signed by all the incorporators. The Secretary was directed to include said waiver in the minute book.

The Secretary next presented and read a copy of the Articles of Incorporation of the corporation, which was filed with the state on _____, 19_____. The Secretary was directed to include a copy of the Articles of Incorporation in the minute book as the first document appearing therein.

The Secretary next presented and read the proposed bylaws for the corporation.

The bylaws were unanimously approved, with the directors granted the power to adopt new and amend existing bylaws without the approval of the shareholders, unless inconsistent with provisions of the corporate laws of the state of _____, and the Secretary was directed to include a copy of the bylaws in the minute book.

The corporate seal was presented to the incorporators and approved, and the Secretary was directed to place an imprint of the corporate seal at the bottom of these minutes.

The proposed stock certificate form was presented to the incorporators and approved, and the Secretary was directed to include a copy of the stock certificate in the minute book.

The following were nominated for directors of the corporation:

Name	Address
_____	_____
_____	_____
_____	_____

to serve from the date of election until their respective successors shall be elected and qualified. No further nominations were made. The incorporators then unanimously elected the nominees as directors.

The incorporators next unanimously voted to authorize the Board of Directors to issue the share of capital stock as authorized by the Articles of Incorporation in such amounts and for such consideration in cash, property, or services as from time to time the Board of Directors may determine and as may be allowed by laws.

Upon motion duly made, seconded and unanimously approved, the meeting was adjourned.

_____
Secretary of the Meeting

Approval of minutes

_____

_____

_____
Signatures of all present

Waiver of Notice of the First Meeting of Incorporators

_____
Name of Corporation

    THE UNDERSIGNED, being all of the incorporators of _____, waive notice of the first meeting of the incorporators of the said corporation, and do hereby consent that the time and place for holding said meeting shall be _____ o'clock (a.m.) (p.m.) on the _____ day of _____, 19___, at _____ in the city of _____, state of _____, and do hereby further consent to the transaction of such business as may lawfully come before said meeting, including the election of directors and the adoption of bylaws.
    Date _____, 19___.

_____
Incorporator

_____
Incorporator

_____
Incorporator

Waiver of Notice of the Organizational Meeting of Directors

_____
Name of Corporation

THE UNDERSIGNED, being all of the directors of the corporation, severally waive notice of the organizational meeting of the directors of the said corporation, and do hereby consent that the time and place for holding said meeting shall be _____ o'clock (a.m.) (p.m.) on the _____ day of _____, 19____, at _____, in the city of _____, state of _____, and do hereby further consent to the transaction of such business as may lawfully come before said meeting.

Dated_____, 19___.

_____

_____

_____
Signatures

Minutes of the Organizational Meeting of the Board of Directors

_____
Name of Corporation

The organizational meeting of the Board of Directors of _____ was held at _____ o'clock a.m. on the _____ day of _____, 19____, at _____ in the city of _____, state of _____.

The following directors were present in person at the meeting:

Name	Address	Number of Shares
_____	_____	_____
_____	_____	_____
_____	_____	_____

The above persons constitute all of the incorporators of the corporation.

By majority vote, _____ was elected Chairman of the Board, and _____ was elected Secretary of the meeting. The Secretary presented the written Waiver of Notice of the First Meeting of the Board of Directors signed by all of the directors.

The Secretary next presented and read to the meeting the Minutes of the First Meeting of the Incorporators, which were then, upon motion duly made, seconded and unanimously approved and ratified.

The Secretary next presented and read to the meeting the bylaws, which were then, upon motion duly made, seconded and unanimously approved and ratified.

The Chairman then accepted as nominations for the appointment of officers the following persons, said officers to serve until their respective successors should be appointed and qualify.

President _____

Vice President _____

Secretary _____

Treasurer _____

No other nominations were made, and the Secretary polled the vote, which unanimously elected to the offices indicated above those persons so nominated, to serve until their respective successors shall be elected and qualify.

Upon motion duly made, seconded and approved, the annual salaries of the officer, payable in 12 equal monthly installments in arrears, were individually approved, unanimously.

President	$ _____
Vice President	$ _____
Secretary/Treasurer	$ _____

Upon motion duly made, seconded, and approved, the directors approved the form of stock certificate and corporate seal as adopted by the subscribers and directed the Secretary to include an imprint of the corporate seal at the end of these minutes.

Upon motion duly made, seconded and approved, it was

RESOLVED, that the Board of Directors be and it hereby is authorized in its discretion to issue the capital stock of this corporation to the full amount or number of shares authorized by the Articles of Incorporation, in such amounts and for such considerations in cash, property, or services as may from time to time be determined by the Board of Directors and as may be permitted by law.

Upon motion duly made, seconded, and approved, it was

RESOLVED, that the president be authorized and directed to open an account with the _____ bank.

Upon motion duly made, seconded and approved, the meeting was adjourned.

_____
Secretary of the Meeting

Approval of minutes

_____

_____

_____
Signatures of all present

STEP 2: FILING A FICTITIOUS NAME

A fictitious name is any name other than your real name or the addition of a word such as "Associates" or "Group" to imply that others are involved in your business. For example, if your name is John Smith and you call your business John Smith Consultant, you wouldn't have a fictitious name that required registration. On the other hand, John Smith and Associates Consultants would likely be considered fictitious because it implies others are in the business.

The previous example would similarly hold for a general partnership made up of Jones and Smith. The name Jones and Smith Consultants would not likely require registration, but the name Jones, Smith, and Associates Consultants would.

For corporations, the key is to operate exactly as you are incorporated since that is the official name. Even if the corporation doesn't have the name of an individual, the name used for incorporation is the official name. Thus, Best Care Products, Inc. is not a fictitious name if incorporated that way. If Best Care Products, Inc. also did business as Second Best Products, Inc., that name would be fictitious and require registration.

Until recently, fictitious names did not need to be registered anywhere except the county in which you operated. Now you must also register all fictitious names on the state level.

The first step to registering a fictitious name is to determine its availability for use. To do this, contact the name availability section of the Division of Corporations (904) 488-9000. Once you've determined the name is available, you can ask for the registration form by calling (904) 487-6058.

To complete the requirements for registration of your fictitious name, you must publish the fictitious names notice in a newspaper in the county where your business is located. Proof of that publication must then be filed with your affidavit to the Florida Department of State at the following address:

Fictitious Names Registration Office
P.O. Box 1300
Tallahassee, FL 32300-1300

Don't take fictitious name filing lightly. There are potential criminal fines for failure to register although they are rarely enforced. If you fail to register properly, you would be prevented from conducting a lawsuit in your name or answering one if you were named.

Currently, fictitious name filings are good for five years and can be renewed for another five years for $50.

Note: The Fictitious Names Act has nothing to do with protecting your name under copyright, trademark, or service mark laws. Florida does have separate trademark laws offering protection for ten years. However, readers should also be cautioned to consider the impact of trade across state lines and whether national protection may be necessary. For more information about federal copyright and trademark protection, see Chapter 12. For information on Florida laws specifically, contact:

> Trademark Section
> Division of Corporations
> P.O. Box 6327
> Tallahassee, FL 32314
> Tel.: (904) 487-6051

STEP 3: COMPLYING WITH SECURITY LAWS

If you are forming a corporation, you will by definition be selling a security since the owners of the corporation will receive stock certificates, and all stock certificates in every state in the United States are considered a security. Consequently, any sale that is made comes under the regulation of either the federal government through the SEC, the state government through its Division of Securities, or both. As a general rule, if you are selling to shareholders within the same state, you will not need to concern yourself with the federal securities laws since you will be involved in what is referred to as an intrastate transaction. If any of your shareholders are out of state, then, having crossed state lines, you come under federal jurisdiction and would have to also comply with federal laws.

For most start-up corporations, the securities laws, as cumbersome as they are, create no real problems since, generally speaking, we are dealing with a few initial organizers who are collectively putting the corporation together. If, on the other hand, you are the organizer and you have solicited shareholders who are not actively involved in putting together the corporation but are simply passive investors, then you will have to consider the applications of the various securities laws. Although we will list the laws as they apply to the state of Florida, it is important to provide a caveat to anyone who is forming a corporation and seeking outside investors: seek the advice of an attorney as it relates to the securities laws. Outside investors who do not have a great deal of say about the organization and operation of the company tend to become unhappy investors if the company goes broke. Once these investors become unhappy, they may contact the regulators, who will investigate to determine whether or not you have complied with the securities laws. Failure to comply will not only cause you personal anguish, it could result in substantial fines and penalties. These penalties could certainly include the return of all the investors' money, as well as potential damages. Consequently, the securities laws should not be taken lightly.

Having said all that, we will discuss the securities laws as they relate specifically to Florida. As a general rule, if you are a part of several investors putting together your own corporation, you will not need to worry about the securities laws because there are exemptions from registering your corporation's securities. Naturally, you must meet these exemptions, so it is important to know what they are. The Florida Securities Act is found in Chapter 517 of the Florida Statutes. It is referred to as the Florida Securities and Investor Protection Act as amended. In particular, as it relates to start-up corporations, you need to determine if there is a specific exemption from registration. If there isn't, you would need to go through the lengthy, time-consuming, and expensive process of registering your securities with the state. Obviously, most companies don't do that, and they rely on the exemption from registration. Florida's exemption is found in section 517.061, titled "Exempt Transactions." Within that section, you will find the following language:

§517.061 Exempt Transactions. The exemption for each transaction listed below is self executing and does not require any filing with the Department prior to claiming such exemption. Any person who claims entitlements to any of the exemptions bears the burden of proving that such entitlement in any proceedings brought under this Chapter. The registration provisions of § 517.07 do not apply to any of the following transactions; however, such transactions are subject provisions of §§ 517.301, 517.311, and 517.312:

(11)(a) The offer or sale, by or on behalf of an issuer, of its own securities, which offer or sale as part of an offering in accordance with all of the following conditions:

1. There are no more than 35 purchasers, or the issuer reasonably believes that there are no more than 35 purchasers, of the securities of the issuer in this state during an offering made in reliance upon

this sub-section or, if such offering continues for a period in excess of 12 months, in any consecutive 12 month period.
2. Neither the issuer nor any person acting on behalf of the issuer offers or sells securities pursuant to this subsection by means of any form of general solicitation or general advertising in this state.
3. Prior to the sale, each purchaser or his representative, if any, is provided with, or given reasonable access to full and fair disclosure of all material information.
4. No person defined as a "dealer" in this chapter is paid a commission or compensation for the sale of the issuer's securities, unless such person is registered as a dealer under this chapter.
5. When sales are made to five or more persons in this state, any sale in this state made pursuant to this subsection is voidable by the purchaser in such sale either within three days after the first tender of consideration is made by such purchaser to the issuer, and an agent of the issuer, or an escrow agent, more than three days after the availability of that privilege is communicated to such purchaser, whichever occurs later.

In the preceding extract from the Florida Statute, you will note that there is an exemption for thirty-five or fewer people to invest in a corporation providing they meet certain criteria. In further sub-sections of that statute, you will find that there are also exceptions to the number thirty-five, allowing for additional investors who meet certain criteria. In sum, if you are dealing with outside investors, you should seek the opinion of an attorney regarding the compliance of the securities laws. Additionally, if you are selling stock to thirty-five or so investors, you should seek the advice of an attorney to make sure you are in compliance.

STEP 4: OBTAINING YOUR BUSINESS LICENSE AND PERMITS

The next step in starting your small business is to secure any business license or permits that may be required to operate. Generally speaking, professionals will be required to obtain a state license to operate, and all other businesses will, at a minimum, have to get an operating license from the local municipality where their office is located.

In order to accurately determine the specific license that you might need and whether or not there are any special bonding or educational requirements, we suggest that you contact the Florida Department of Business and Professional

Regulation. This department sets up all the qualifications and requirements for any profession to do business in the state.

>Florida Department of Business and
>   Professional Regulation
>1940 North Monroe Street
>Tallahassee, FL 32309-7570

If you would like to contact them by telephone to ask them specific questions, you may call the Bureau of Business Assistance at (800) 342-0771.

In addition to the state business license, you may have to obtain a local license from the city, county, or other municipality in which your business operates. To find out those proper procedures and costs, contact your local municipal courthouse and ask for the department for business license and permits; they will send you the required applications.

STEP 5: COMPLYING WITH TAX LAWS

The state of Florida has good news and bad news when it comes to taxes. The good news is that there is no personal income tax, and that law has been established by constitutional amendment so it is not likely to be changed. The bad news is that a good many other taxes are assessed against businesses to make up for the missing personal income tax. Florida does have a corporate income tax. To receive specific information about the corporate tax and the proper forms you need to use in order to meet state compliance, we recommend that you contact the Division of Taxpayer Assistance at the following address.

>Division of Taxpayer Assistance
>Florida Department of Revenue
>P.O. Box 7443
>Tallahassee, FL 32314-7443
>Tel.: (800) 352-3671

Many of you will decide, after reading this book, to use one of the forms of corporate structure that does not require a corporate tax, but instead allows all income to flow directly to the benefit of the shareholders. Even if you do follow this tax preferential route, we encourage you to contact the Florida Department of Revenue to make sure that you qualify under any state guidelines that they may have.

Sales Tax and Use Tax

Florida does have a statewide sales tax. In addition, various counties and municipalities within the state have their own sales tax on top of the amount required by the state. If your business is involved in the sale of any goods, you will be required to pay a sales or use tax. Today, even if your business involves services, most of them fall under the sales tax requirements. It is important for you to check with the state to determine the appropriate amount of tax you should collect.

The first step in this process is to contact the Florida Department of Revenue, which will grant you authority to collect sales tax on goods that you sell. This requires a separate registration for each facility where you operate.

To obtain a permit, you will need to secure the application for sales and use tax registration and submit a $5 fee to the state for this registration. There are some rather harsh penalties for failure to file and collect sales tax, including a $100 penalty for simply failing to register. Consequently, we encourage you to contact the Florida Department of Revenue before you begin to operate your business:

Division of Taxpayer Assistance
Florida Department of Revenue
P.O. Box 7443
Tallahassee, FL 32314-7443
Tel.: (800) 352-3671

Intangible Personal Property Tax

Florida imposes a tax on all intangible personal property belonging to individuals, corporations, partnerships, or trusts. The tax is assessed as of January 1 of each year against the person holding the intangible property.

Intangible property includes stocks, bonds, notes, accounts receivable loans, loans, limited partnership interest, beneficial interest in trust, and other stated obligations. There are numerous exemptions, including a specific dollar amount exemption of $20,000 per year for an individual and $40,000 for joint returns. The tax is calculated at the rate of $2 per $1,000 of value.

In order to comply with this law, the intangible tax must be filed by June 30 of each year with the Department of Revenue. The appropriate form for filing the intangible tax can be secured at the Department of Revenue.

Property Taxes

If you operate your business at a location on property that you own, you will be subject to property taxes. These taxes are collected by the local county in which your property is located and are assessed annually. For specific information regarding these taxes, contact the local county tax assessor. This office can be found in your county courthouse and will be listed in your telephone directory under local government.

Other Types of Taxes

There are two additional major taxes that you need to remember to pay. One is workers' compensation insurance, which is mandated for most companies with employees. This insurance provides wage loss and medical benefits to employees who are injured on the job. Workers' compensation insurance is especially important for a start-up company because it will also protect you from legal action for damages that are incurred for injuries suffered by your employees. For further information regarding workers' compensation, contact:

> The Bureau of Workers' Compensation Compliance
> Florida Department of Labor and Employment Security
> Forest Bldg., Suite 100
> 2728 Center View Drive
> Tallahassee, FL 32399-0680
> Tel.: (904) 488-2713

The other tax is the state unemployment tax for workers who are dismissed. As an employer, you are required to pay the unemployment tax on all employees other than yourself, and you are required to submit various information directly to your employees. To get the latest information regarding these requirements, contact the following:

> Division of Unemployment Compensation
> Florida Department of Labor and Employment Security
> Caldwell Bldg., Suite 201
> 107 E. Madison
> Tallahassee, FL 32399-0206

STEP 6: UNDERSTANDING EMPLOYEE AND LABOR LAWS

A one-man operation has it easy compared to the new responsibilities you gain once you hire employees. That is why many small companies do everything in their power not to have employees. If they need workers and can't get them from a leasing company, employers sometimes try to get around the law by calling the employee an independent contractor. The reason is that independent contractors are not subject to all the employee-related mandates.

The problem with this strategy of avoidance is that neither Florida nor the federal government likes employers calling their employees independent contractors. The government likes the employer–employee relationship because they can force the employer to collect social security payments and other taxes. The government knows that using employers as collection agencies is the best method it has of collecting taxes. Consequently, unless you really have an independent contractor relationship, calling a person independent doesn't make it so. In other words, if it looks like a duck, quacks like a duck, and swims like a duck, you have a duck even if you call it a chicken.

Similarly, if you set hours for your workers, control how they perform their work, and generally treat them as employees, the state of Florida and the federal government will regard them as employees no matter what name you give them. Skirting the law will subject your company to fines for not complying with their viewpoint. In some cases, you could be held liable for all unpaid taxes that the employee failed to pay. It isn't worth it. Unless you can truly prove independent contractor status, treat your workers as employees.

Now that you have faced the fact that you must pay attention to your employees' status, what does Florida require you to do for your employees? The good news is that it is not much more than what the federal government requires. The bad news is that it is a lot.

Florida is a right-to-work state, which means that anyone has a right to work without joining a union. The result of that position is that unions are not as strong as they may be in other states, and that is why there are fewer state laws protecting employees. For example, Florida has no state minimum wage requirement. That doesn't mean employers are free to do what they want, but it does mean that they must follow federal law as it applies to minimum wage. Currently, the federal minimum wage is $4.75 per hour unless the employee meets a stated exception. The federal minimum wage will increase to $5.15 per hour on September 1, 1997.

Child labor, on the other hand, is different. Like most states, Florida has a child labor law because it is particularly concerned about the welfare of children. The state wants to encourage children to stay in school, so the laws are structured to encourage school but allow for children who must work to do so. Florida law prohibits the employment of minors under the age of 14 with limited exceptions. One such exception, for children above the age of 11, is for operating paper routes. Children ages 14 and 15 are allowed to work under certain circumstances but are prohibited in the following areas: they may not work during school hours, they may work only three hours on school days or when school is scheduled the following day, they may work only fifteen hours per week when school is in session, they may work a daily maximum of eight hours and a weekly maximum of forty hours during holidays and summer vacations, they may work only between 7:00 a.m. and 7:00 p.m. when school is scheduled the following day, and they may work only until 9:00 p.m. during holidays and summer vacations. Children 16 and 17 years of age may work only thirty hours per week when school is in session, but no more than eight hours per day. They may work between 6:30 p.m. and 11:00 p.m. when school is scheduled the next day, and they may not work during school hours with certain exceptions. One of the major exceptions to this rule is children who have graduated from high school, or have GED equivalency. Additionally, children enrolled in cooperative educational programs or who receive waivers on the restriction from the school superintendent will be allowed to work. For additional information regarding Florida's child labor laws, contact the Child Labor Section, Florida Department of Labor and Employment, at (904) 488-2713.

Discrimination between employees is a concern in Florida as you would expect in all states. Generally, the law follows federal law that prohibits discrimination based on race, color, religion, national origin, sex, age, disability, or marital status. Like the federal law, Florida makes certain allowances in qualification to perform certain types of jobs. However, we caution employers to thoroughly understand the exemption and its application because discrimination laws can be costly to violate. A judgment against an employer for violating these laws could allow for civil penalties, damages for the individual, and the recovery of attorneys fees. For answers to specific questions about discrimination in employment and for additional information, contact the Florida Department of Labor at (904) 488-2713.

For information on safety and health compliance that may be related to your company, contact the Bureau of Workers' Compensation Compliance at (904) 488-2713.

Many disputes between employers and employees are governed by the award of cost of litigation to the prevailing party. These costs include such items as copy charges, witness fees, and disposition transcripts. In addition, many federal and Florida laws allow by statute prevailing employees to recover attorneys fees. This can be potentially devastating to small-business owners and should be carefully considered when any disputes arise with an employee. Early settlement could mean the difference between staying in business and not.

Florida Department of State
Jim Smith, Secretary of State

Affidavit of Resignation of Officer and/or Director

STATE OF _____
COUNTY OF _____

I, _____, after being duly sworn, state that to the best of my knowledge, information and belief, and under the penalties of perjury, the following is true and correct:

I, _____, hereby resign as _____
                                                                                               (Title)
of _____, a Florida Corporation;
          (Name of Corporation)

That the corporation has been notified in writing of the resignation.

_____
Signature of resigning officer/director

Sworn to and subscribed before me this _____ day of _____.

_____
NOTARY PUBLIC

My Commission Expires: _____

FILING FEE IS $35.00

DIVISION OF CORPORATIONS, P.O. BOX 6327, TALLAHASSEE, FL 32314

Florida Department of State
Jim Smith
Secretary of State

This will acknowledge receipt of your request for information regarding amending the articles of incorporation of a Florida profit corporation.

A corporation can amend its articles of incorporation by filing Articles of Amendment with the Division of Corporations. The articles of amendment must be prepared in compliance with section 607.1006, Florida Statutes.

For your convenience attached is a sample form for articles of amendment. Additional sheets may be attached if necessary. Section 607.0120, Florida Statutes, requires that the document be typed or printed and must be legible.

Pursuant to section 607.0123, Florida Statutes, a delayed effective date may be specified but may not be later than the 90th day after the date on which the document is filed.

If the registered agent is changed by amendment, the new agent must sign accepting the appointment, and must state that he or she is familiar with and accepts the obligations of the position.

The filing fee for the articles of amendment is $35. Certified copies of the amendment are $52.50 each. A certificate of status is $8.75. Submit one check for the correct amount made payable to the Department of State. Please include a cover letter containing your telephone number and return address.

Any further inquiries on this matter should be directed to the Amendment Section by calling (904) 487-6050, or by writing: Division of Corporations, P.O. Box 6327, Tallahassee, FL, 32314.

NOTE: This form for filing articles of amendment is basic. Each corporation is a separate entity and as such has specific goals, needs and requirements. Additional sheets may be attached as required. The Division of Corporations recommends that corporate documents be reviewed by your legal counsel. The Division is a filing agency and as such does not render any legal, accounting, or tax advice. The professional advice of your legal counsel to ascertain exact compliance with all statutory requirements is strongly recommended.

Articles of Amendment
to
Articles of Incorporation of

_____

_____
(present name)

Pursuant to the provisions of section 607.1006, Florida Statutes, this corporation adopts the following articles of amendment to its articles of incorporation:

FIRST: Amendment(s) adopted: _____
(indicate article number(s) being amended, added or deleted)

SECOND: If an amendment provides for an exchange, reclassification or cancellation of issued shares, provisions for implementing the amendment, if not contained in the amendment itself, are as follows: _____

THIRD: The date of each amendment's adoption: _____.

FOURTH: Adoption of Amendment(s) (check one)

❑ The amendment(s) was/were approved by the shareholders. The number of votes cast for the amendment(s) was/were sufficient for approval.

❑ The amendment(s) was/were approved by the shareholders through voting groups.

_____
The following statement must be separately provided for each voting group entitled to vote separately on the amendment(s):

"The number of votes cast for the amendment(s) was/were sufficient for approval by _____."
(voting group)

❑ The amendment(s) was/were adopted by the board of directors without shareholder action and shareholder action was not required.

❑ The amendment(s) was/were adopted by the incorporators without shareholder action and shareholder action was not required.

Signed this _____ day of _____, 19_____.

Signature_____
               (By the Chairman or Vice Chairman of the
               Board of Directors, President or other officer
               if adopted by the shareholders)

OR
(By a director if adopted by the directors)

OR
(By an incorporator if adopted by the incorporators)

_____
Typed or printed name

_____
Title

Florida Department of State
Jim Smith, Secretary of State

Statement of Change of Registered Office
or Registered Agent
or Both for Corporations

_____

Pursuant to the provisions of sections 607.0502, 617.0502, or 617.1508, Florida Statutes, the undersigned corporation organized under the laws of the State of Florida submits the following statement in order to change its registered office or registered agent, or both, in the State of Florida.

   Ia. The name of the corporation is: _____
   _____.

   Ib. The mailing address of the corporation is: _____
   _____.

   Ic. Date of incorporation: _____
       Document Number: _____

   2. The name and address of the current registered agent and office:
   _____
   _____
   _____

   3. The name and address of the new registered agent and office (P.O. Box Not Acceptable):
   _____
   _____
   _____

The street address of its registered office and the street address of the business office of its registered agent, as changed, will be identical.

Such change was authorized by resolution duly adopted by its board of directors or by an officer so authorized by the board.

_____   _____
(Signature of an officer, chairman or   (Date)
vice chairman of the board)

_____
(Printed or typed name and title)

Having been named as registered agent and to accept service of process for the above stated corporation, I hereby accept the appointment as registered agent and agree to act in this capacity. I further agree to comply with the provisions of all statutes relative to the proper and complete performance of my duties, and I am familiar with and accept the obligation of my position as registered agent.

_____   _____
(Signature of Registered Agent)   (Date)

FILING FEE: $35.00

DIVISION OF CORPORATIONS, P.O. BOX 6327, TALLAHASSEE, FL 32314

FLORIDA DEPARTMENT OF STATE
Jim Smith
Secretary of State

Thank you for your recent request for information concerning a change of name, duration, jurisdiction, or purpose for a foreign profit or nonprofit corporation qualified to do business or conduct its affairs in Florida as required by section 607.1504 or 617.1504, Florida Statutes. The following requirements must be met within 30 days after the occurrence of such a change:

1. Complete the appropriate application for amendment attached to this letter.
2. An original certificate from the state of incorporation evidencing the amendment must be submitted with the application. The certificate must be issued within the last 90 days.
3. The document must be signed by the chairman or vice chairman of the board of directors or any officer or fiduciary if appropriate (see section 607.0120 or 617.01201, Florida Statutes).
4. Fees for the amendment are:

    $35.00 Filing Fee
    $52.50 Certified Copy (optional)
    $8.75 Certificate of Status (optional)

5. Send one check in the total amount made payable to the Department of State.
6. Please include a cover letter containing your telephone number and return address.

Please send application to:

Amendment Section
Divisions of Corporations
P.O. Box 6327
Tallahassee, FL 32314

For further information, you may call (904) 487-6050.

DIVISION OF CORPORATIONS, P.O. BOX 6327, TALLAHASSEE, FL 32314

Profit Corporation
Application by Foreign Profit Corporation to File
Amendment to Application for Authorization to Transact Business in Florida

(Pursuant to s. 607.1504, F.S.)

SECTION I
(1-3 must be completed)

1. _____
   Name of corporation as it appears on the records of the Department of State.
2. _____
   Incorporated under laws of
3. _____
   Date authorized to do business in Florida.

SECTION II
(4-7 complete only the applicable changes)

4. If the amendment changes the name of the corporation, when was the change effected under the laws of its jurisdiction of incorporation? _____
5. _____
   Name of corporation after the amendment, adding suffix "corporation," "company," or "incorporated," or appropriate abbreviation, if not contained in new name of the corporation.
6. If the amendment changes the period of duration, indicate new period of duration.
   _____
7. If the amendment changes the jurisdiction of incorporation, indicate new jurisdiction.
   _____

_____   _____
Signature   Date

_____   _____
Typed or printed name   Title

Articles of Amendment
to
Articles of Incorporation of

_____

_____
(present name)

Pursuant to the provisions of section 617.1006, Florida Statutes, the undersigned corporation adopts the following articles of amendment to its articles of incorporation.

FIRST: Amendment(s) adopted: _____

SECOND: The date of adoption of the amendment(s) was: _____

THIRD: Adoption of Amendment *(check one)*

❑ The amendment(s) was (were) adopted by the members and the number of votes cast for the amendment was sufficient for approval.

❑ There are no members or members entitled to vote on the amendment. The amendment(s) was (were) adopted by the board of directors.

_____
Corporation Name

_____
Signature of Chairman, Vice Chairman, President or other officer

_____
Typed or printed name

_____   _____
Title   Date

Florida Incorporation Checklist

- ❏ Check the availability of the corporate name with the Secretary of State, Division of Corporations, and request information concerning where to mail your Articles of Incorporation, filing fees, and fees for certifying a copy of the Articles of Incorporation. This information can usually be obtained over the phone.
- ❏ Prepare the Articles of Incorporation.
- ❏ Mail the original Articles of Incorporation, together with a copy for certification and the appropriate fees, to the Secretary of State, Division of Corporations.
- ❏ Upon receipt of a returned certified copy of the Articles of Incorporation, order a corporate book containing preprinted forms from an appropriate supplier. Check with a local office supply store.
- ❏ Prepare the Bylaws and a Notice or Waiver of Notice and Minutes of Organizational Meeting or Consent to Action Taken in Lieu of Organizational Meeting of Incorporators. Preprinted forms are usually supplied with your corporate book if requested.
- ❏ Comply with all applicable state laws concerning any fictitious name under which the corporation will conduct its activities.
- ❏ If S corporation status is desired, file an Election by a Small Business Corporation, IRS Form No. 2553, with the Internal Revenue Service. This form can be obtained from the IRS.
- ❏ Apply for and obtain a federal identification number. Use IRS Form No. 9-82 for this purpose. This form can be obtained from the IRS.
- ❏ Apply for a state sales tax number if the corporation will be responsible for collecting state sales tax.
- ❏ Prepare a Stockholders' Agreement if desired.
- ❏ Issue stock certificates to the stockholders of the corporation.
- ❏ Prepare a Waiver of Notice or Notice and Minutes of Annual Meeting of Stockholders and Directors.
- ❏ Comply with all state statutes concerning annual meetings of stockholders and directors, filing of annual reports, and payment of annual fees by the corporation. This should be done routinely by March 1 of each calendar year.
- ❏ File annually with the Internal Revenue Service a Form 1120 and related schedules or a Form 1120S and related schedules by the fifteenth day of the third month following the end of the corporation's tax year.

Florida Start-Up Business Checklist

The following checklist will remind you of everything you need to do to get your business going.

- ❏ Select your operating entity (corporation, partnership, and the like).
- ❏ File your Articles of Incorporation with the secretary of state or corporate commission. (If you chose a limited partnership, file your Certificate of Limited Partnership; if you chose a general partnership, prepare your Partnership Agreement.)
- ❏ If you are electing Sub S corporate status, file your declaration with the IRS.
- ❏ If you are using a fictitious name, qualify the name.
- ❏ Prepare your Bylaws.
- ❏ Hold your shareholders meeting.
- ❏ Hold your directors meeting.
- ❏ Issue your stock, and make sure you collect appropriate money.
- ❏ Determine whether a professional license is needed in your state.
- ❏ Secure your local occupational license.
- ❏ Secure tax returns for quarterly filings.
- ❏ Register to pay sales tax with the state of Florida.
- ❏ Call your local county tax office about personal property taxes.
- ❏ Check on workers' compensation payments.
- ❏ Order the IRS publications and SBA publications recommended in this book.
- ❏ Apply for a federal ID number and file Form SS-4.
- ❏ Secure all required federal and state posters, and hang them on your office wall in the appropriate space.
    - ❏ Federal Equal Employment Opportunity
    - ❏ Federal Age Discrimination
    - ❏ Employee Polygraph Protection
    - ❏ Family and Medical Leave Act (employers with fifty or more employees)
    - ❏ Minimum Wage
    - ❏ OSHA
- ❏ Have annual meeting; file minutes in corporate book.
    - ❏ Shareholders
    - ❏ Directors
- ❏ Pay annual corporate fee

INDEX

A
Accounting periods and methods, 168-170
Accounts receivable, as collateral, 52
Accounts receivable financing, 40
Age Discrimination and Employment Act (ADEA), 101-102
Alternative dispute resolution, 70-71
American Arbitration Association, 72
Americans with Disabilities Act (ADA), 102-103
and lease negotiation, 81
Arbitration, as alternative to lawsuits, 71-72
Articles of incorporation, 8
preparation of, 19-25, 26-27
Asset lenders, 40

B
Balance sheet methods of valuation, of existing businesses, 111-112
Benefits
available within corporation, 11, 195-210
and Sub Chapter S corporations, 13
Board of directors
of corporation, 29
first meeting of. *See* Organizational meeting
Business interruption insurance, 146
Bylaws, of corporations, 28-32

C
Capital gains tax, 11
Capital, raising, 35-64
Car expenses, 180-183
Certificates of shares, 30-31, 33-34
Chattel mortgages, 52
Child labor laws, 99-100
Collateral
for bank loans, 50-53
for purchase of existing businesses, 124
Comakers, and loans, 51
Common area maintenance (CAM) expenses, and lease negotiation, 80-81
Contracts
arbitration/mediation clauses in, 71
basics of, 75-76
strategy for, 76-77

Convertible debenture, 37
Convertible preferred stock, 37
Copyrights, 150-151, 160-161
Corporate benefits, 195-210
Corporate partnerships, 37-38
Corporate stock. *See* Shares
Corporations
basics of, 8-11
bylaws of, 28-32
purpose of, and articles of incorporation, 24-25
as separate entity, from tax standpoint 9-10
Covenants, and loan restrictions, 54
Creative financing, 40-41
Credit card fraud, 137-138
Credit law, 132-139
Credit, offered by corporations, 131-139
Credit reporting services, 139
Cumulative shares, 23-24, 36

D
Debt instruments, corporate issuance of, 37
Discounted future cash flow method of valuation, of existing businesses, 112-115, 113-114
Discrimination, in workplace, 100-101
Dividends, 31, 164, 193
Documentation, importance of, 32-33
Double taxation, 10-11, 14

E
Election by a Small Business Corporation, Form 225, 12
Electronic Communications Privacy Act (ECPA) of 1986, 105-106
Electronic funds transfer funds, 137-138
Employee leasing, 86-87
Employee Polygraph Protection Act (EPPA) of 1988, 105
Employees
hiring of, 88-94
planning for, 85-88
training of, 94-95
Employer ID number (EID), 8, 166

Employment agencies, 86
Employment applications, 91-92, 93
Employment interviews, 88-94
Employment laws, 97-106
Employment taxes, 164-165
Endorsers, and loans, 50-51
Entertainment expenses, 175-177
Environmental Protection Agency (EPA), and lease negotiation, 81-82
Equal Credit Opportunity Act (ECOA), 135
Equipment financing, 40
Estimated tax returns, 163-164, 187-193
Executive benefits, 195-210
Existing businesses
purchase of, 107-130
valuation of, 109-122, 113-114

F
Factoring, 40-41
Fair Credit Billing Act, 134
Fair Credit Reporting Act, 135-137
Fair Debt Collection Practices Act (FDCPA), 138-139
Fair Labor Standards Act (FLSA), 97-99
Family and Medical Leave Act (FMLA), 106
Family limited partnerships, 9
Federal securities regulations, 42-47
Fictitious corporate names, 18-19
Financial planning, formal, importance of, 62-63
Financing. *See also* Raising capital of purchase of existing businesses, 124-126
Form K-1, and limited partnerships, 7
Form TX, and copyright registration, 150, 160-161
Franchises, purchase of, 122

G
General partnerships, 4-6
Gift expenses, 177-178
Guarantors, and loans, 51

I
Income
and general partnerships, 5
and sole proprietorships, 2

Income statement methods of valuation, of existing businesses, 112-116
Incorporators, 8, 24
Informal Partnership Tax Return, Form 1065, 5
Insurance
    within corporation, 197-198
    for corporations, 141-147
    types of policies, 143-147
Intellectual property, protection of, 149-160
Interviews. *See* Employment interviews
Inventory financing, 40
Investors, and small corporations, 11

J

Joint ventures. *See* General partnerships

L

Lawsuits, 72-73
    alternatives to, 69-71
Lawyers
    fees for, 68-69
    selection of, 65-68
Leases
    cautions regarding, 80-83
    negotiation of, 77-80
Legal disputes, 69-73
Leveraged buyouts, 125
Liability insurance, 144-145
Licenses, 155-159
Life insurance policies, as collateral, 52-53
Limited liability companies (LLCs), 13-15
Limited liability partnerships (LLPs), 15-16
Limited offering exemptions, and limited partnerships, 7
Limited partnerships, 6-8
    family, 9
Loans
    limitations and restrictions on, 53-55
    made from corporations, 198
    made to corporations, 47-55
Local transportation expenses, 178-180
Long-term loans, made to corporations, 50

M

Mediation, as alternative to lawsuits, 70-71

N

Name of corporation, selection of, 17-20
Negotiation, as alternative to lawsuits, 70

O

Occupational Safety and Health Act (OSHA), 103-104
Officers, of corporation, 29-30
    salaries paid to, 33
Operating entity, selection of, 1-16
Organizational meeting, 32-33

P

Par/no-par value, of stocks, 24
Partnerships, 3-8
Patents, 154-155
"Perpetual existence," of corporations, 25
Personal property insurance, 144
Preferred stock, 23, 36-37
Private offering, 41-42
Private offering memorandum, 46-47
Professional liability insurance, 145-146
Publications, for entrepreneurs, 211-221
Purchase agreement, for existing businesses, 123-124

R

Raising capital, 35-64
Real estate, as collateral, 52
Recordkeeping requirements
    for corporations, 166-168
    for tax deductions, 183-186
Registered agents, and articles of incorporation, 24
Rent. *See* Leases
Resources, for entrepreneurs, 211-221
Retirement benefits, and sole proprietorships, 3

S

Salaries
    paid to officers, 33
    paid to owner of corporation, 196-197
    paid to shareholders, 10-11
Savings accounts, as collateral, 52
Schedule of taxation, 163, 164
S corporations. *See* Sub Chapter S corporations
Securities laws, 41-47
Securities laws, and limited partnerships, 6-7
Service marks. *See* Trademarks
Sexual harassment, in workplace, 100-101

Shareholders
    and corporations, 8, 28-29
    first meeting of. *See* Organizational meeting
    salaries paid to, 10-11
    in Sub Chapter S corporations, 12
Shares
    and articles of incorporation, 20-24
    certificates of, 30-31, 33-34
    classes of, 22-24
    sale of, for raising capital, 36-37
Short-term loans, made to corporations, 49-50
Sign ordinances, and lease negotiation, 82
Small business investment companies (SBICs), 39
Small claims court, 73
Sole proprietorships, 1-3
Stock. *See* Shares
Sub chapter S corporations, 12-13
    versus limited liability companies, 14
    tax treatment of, 12-13, 163

T

Taxation
    and corporations, 9-10, 163-193
    double, 10-11, 14
    and limited liability companies, 15
    and Sub Chapter S corporations, 12-13, 163
Tax deductions, and sole proprietorships, 2-3
Taxpayer identification number, and corporations, 8, 166
Temporary employees, 87-88
Trademarks, 17, 151-154
Transportation expenses, local, 178-180
Travel expenses, 170-175, 171
Trust receipts/floor planning, as collateral, 51
Truth in Lending Act, 133-134

V

Venture capital, 38-40, 55-62
    cautions regarding, 39-40
    forums for, 53
    types of firms, 61-62

W

Warehouse receipts, as collateral, 51
Workers' Compensation Law, 104-105
Written contracts, importance of, 75-76

Appendix of Florida State Forms and Checklists

The following forms and checklists specific to Florida appear on pages listed below.

- Affidavit of Resignation of Officer and/or Director, 268
- Application by Foreign Profit Corporation to File Amendment to Application for Authorization to Transact Business in Florida, 275
- Articles of Amendment to Articles of Incorporation, 270
- Articles of Incorporation, 236
- Articles of Incorporation Transmittal Letter, 235
- Bylaws, 246
- Certificate of Designation of Registered Agent/Registered Office, 238
- Florida Incorporation Checklist, 277
- Florida Start-Up Business Checklist, 278
- Minutes of the First Meeting of the Incorporators, 252
- Minutes of the Organizational Meeting of the Board of Directors, 256
- Statement of Change of Registered Office or Registered Agent or Both for Corporations, 272
- Stock Subscription Agreement, 245
- Waiver of Notice of the First Meeting of Incorporators, 254
- Waiver of Notice of the Organizational Meeting of Directors, 255

Find more on this topic by visiting BusinessTown.com

Developed by Adams Media, **BusinessTown.com** is a free informational site for entrepreneurs, small business owners, and operators. It provides a comprehensive guide for planning, starting, growing, and managing a small business.

Visitors may access hundreds of articles addressing dozens of business topics, participate in forums, as well as connect to additional resources around the Web. **BusinessTown.com** is easily navigated and provides assistance to small businesses and start-ups. The material covers beginning basic issues as well as the more advanced topics.

- ✓ **Accounting**
  Basic, Credit & Collections, Projections, Purchasing/Cost Control
- ✓ **Advertising**
  Magazine, Newspaper, Radio, Television, Yellow Pages
- ✓ **Business Opportunities**
  Ideas for New Businesses, Business for Sale, Franchises
- ✓ **Business Plans**
  Creating Plans & Business Strategies
- ✓ **Finance**
  Getting Money, Money Problem Solutions
- ✓ **Letters & Forms**
  Looking Professional, Sample Letters & Forms
- ✓ **Getting Started**
  Incorporating, Choosing a Legal Structure
- ✓ **Hiring & Firing**
  Finding the Right People, Legal Issues
- ✓ **Home Business**
  Home Business Ideas, Getting Started
- ✓ **Internet**
  Getting Online, Put Your Catalog on the Web
- ✓ **Legal Issues**
  Contracts, Copyrights, Patents, Trademarks
- ✓ **Managing a Small Business**
  Growth, Boosting Profits, Mistakes to Avoid, Competing with the Giants
- ✓ **Managing People**
  Communications, Compensation, Motivation, Reviews, Problem Employees
- ✓ **Marketing**
  Direct Mail, Marketing Plans, Strategies, Publicity, Trade Shows
- ✓ **Office Setup**
  Leasing, Equipment, Supplies
- ✓ **Presentations**
  Know Your Audience, Good Impression
- ✓ **Sales**
  Face to Face, Independent Reps, Telemarketing
- ✓ **Selling a Business**
  Finding Buyers, Setting a Price, Legal Issues
- ✓ **Taxes**
  Employee, Income, Sales, Property, Use
- ✓ **Time Management**
  Can You Really Manage Time?
- ✓ **Travel & Maps**
  Making Business Travel Fun
- ✓ **Valuing a Business**
  Simple Valuation Guidelines

http://www.businesstown.com

Adams Streetwise® books

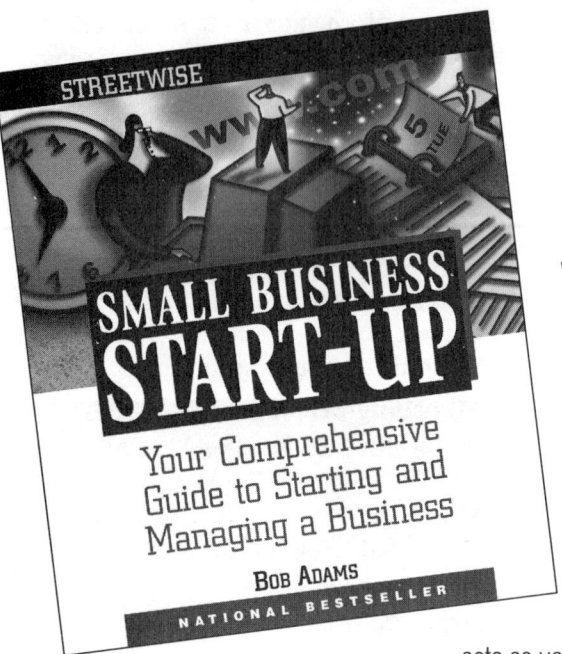

Adams Streetwise® Small Business Start-Up

When you start a small business you soon discover that things just don't happen in the real world the way they tell you in business textbooks: invoices don't get paid by their due dates, ads don't consistently bring in customers, sales don't continually rise, and profits aren't always there. In this book, small business maverick Bob Adams shows you how things *really* get done and acts as your mentor by providing instant access to Streetwise advice on every small business topic.

NATIONAL BESTSELLER
by Bob Adams
8" x 9 1/4", 416 pages,
two-color, illustrated, $17.95
ISBN 1-55850-581-4

- Develop a strategy to beat the competition
- Position products and services success
- Get big results from low-budget advertising
- Tap the power of direct mail
- Find and keep customers
- Get free publicity
- Create a dynamic business plan

- Boost sales with cheap marketing tricks
- Get all the financing you need
- Manage cash
- Develop a winning team
- Master accounting in minutes
- Stay out of legal trouble
- And more!

"...great graphics...easy-to-read...lots of do's and don'ts."
— *The Wall Street Journal*

for growing your business

Complete Business Plan
$17.95
ISBN 1-55850-845-7

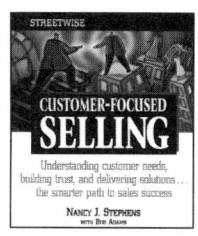

Customer-Focused Selling
$17.95
ISBN 1-55850-725-6

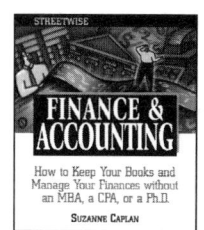

Finance & Accounting
$17.95
ISBN 1-58062-196-1

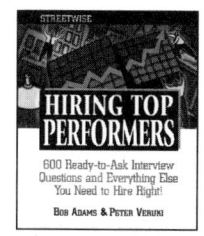

Hiring Top Performers
$17.95
ISBN 1-58062-684-5

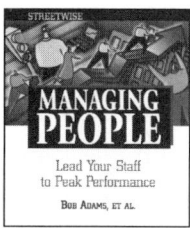

Managing People
$17.95
ISBN 1-55850-726-4

Business Forms w/CD-ROM
$24.95
ISBN 1-58062-132-5

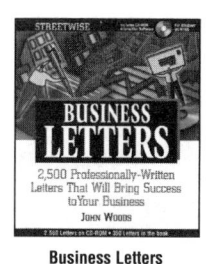

Business Letters w/CD-ROM
$24.95
ISBN 1-58062-133-3

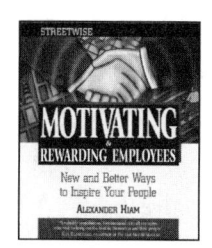

Motivating & Rewarding Employees
$17.95
ISBN 1-58062-130-9

Time Management
$17.95
ISBN 1-58062-131-7

Do-It-Yourself Advertising
$17.95
ISBN 1-55850-727-2

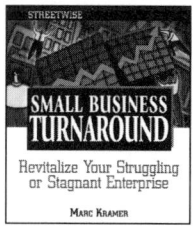

Small Business Turnaround
$17.95
ISBN 1-58062-195-3

Business Tips
$17.95
ISBN 1-58062-778-7

Available wherever books are sold.

How to order: If you cannot find this book at your favorite retail outlet, you may order it directly from the publisher. BY PHONE: Call 1-800-872-5627. We accept Visa, Mastercard, and American Express. $4.95 will be added to your total order for shipping and handling. BY MAIL: Write out the full title of the book you'd like to order and send payment, including $4.95 for shipping and handling to: Adams Media Corporation, 260 Center Street, Holbrook, MA 02343. 30-day money-back guarantee.

Visit our exciting business site at http://www.businesstown.com

About the Author

J.W. Dicks is an attorney by profession and an entrepreneur by choice. In addition to his law practice, Pino & Dicks, he owns numerous corporations and advises small business owners in all aspects of developing their companies, from strategic planning to public offerings.

As a leading seminar instructor on financial topics, J.W. Dicks has traveled the country, speaking to over 150,000 people on small business, stocks, mutual funds, law, and real estate. In addition to his lectures, he has written numerous articles, manuals, and newsletters on the same topics.

Mr. Dicks has authored several business and legal books, including: *The American Dream, Financial C.P.R., The Florida Investor, The Small Business Legal Kit, The 100 Best Investments for Your Retirement, Mutual Fund Investing Strategies,* and *How to Incorporate and Start a Business.*

For information about availability for speaking engagements, legal business consulting services or for a complimentary copy of his newsletter, *Small Business Advisor,* phone (800) 593-4257.